Curses!
Broiled Again!

Other books by Jan Harold Brunvand

THE MEXICAN PET

THE CHOKING DOBERMAN

THE VANISHING HITCHHIKER

THE STUDY OF AMERICAN FOLKLORE

READINGS IN AMERICAN FOLKLORE

Curses!
Broiled Again!

The Hottest Urban Legends Going

JAN HAROLD BRUNVAND
UNIVERSITY OF UTAH

W · W · NORTON & COMPANY
New York · London

The text of this book is composed in 11/13 Baskerville,
with display type set in Isbell Medium Italic.
Composition and manufacturing by The Haddon Craftsmen, Inc.

Library of Congress Cataloging-in-Publication Data
Brunvand, Jan Harold.
Curses! broiled again! : the hottest urban legends going / Jan
Harold Brunvand.—1st ed.
p.   cm.
Includes index.
1. Urban folklore—United States. 2. Legends—United States.
3. United States—Social life and customs. I. Title.
GR105.B688 1989
398.2'09173'2—dc19   89-2883

W. W. Norton & Company, Inc., 500 Fifth Avenue, New York, N.Y. 10110
W. W. Norton & Company Ltd., 37 Great Russell Street, London WC1B 3NU

The modern legend constitutes one of the most, may indeed even constitute the most widespread, popular, and vital folklore form of the present day; and what strikes me as perhaps its most outstanding feature is the creativity, imagination, and virtuosity brought to its performance by all kinds of people, old and young, well read and barely literate, educationally privileged and educationally deprived.

—from "The Modern Urban Legend," Katharine Briggs Lecture No. 1, delivered November 3, 1981, to the Folklore Society at University College London, by Stewart F. Sanderson, director of the Institute of Dialect and Folk Life Studies in the University of Leeds

CONTENTS

7

PREFACE

Once upon a time, folklorists were interested only in what one would think of as "folksy" subjects, like ancient ballads or fairy tales. Nowadays, however, we examine things like college customs, drug lore, and office traditions. Even those photocopied fake memos you see posted on the company bulletin board qualify as folklore, and some pieces of such "Xeroxlore" are included in this book.

But my speciality is modern urban legends—those bizarre but believable stories about batter-fried rats, spiders in hairdos, Cabbage Patch dolls that get funerals, and the like that pass by word of mouth as being the gospel truth. Except that they aren't true—they are contemporary folklore. There is no fixed text of such stories, and the more variations you collect, the more you can deduce about an urban legend.

For years I have collected, classified, compared, and even computer-catalogued urban legends, trying to figure out where they come from, what changes they undergo, and why people continue to tell them to each other, despite the power of the mass media, which so much shape our views of the world. In 1986, having published my third book of urban legends—*The Mexican Pet*—and having appeared on countless radio talk shows, been four times on "Late Night with David Letterman," and several times on other local and national television programs, I came to realize how many more stories I was collecting by mail via letters and clippings than by just talking to the people with whom I have personal contact. Readers of my books* and the audiences for my media appearances had become wonderful sources of urban legends, and I joked that I should start a syndicated newspaper column and reach even more people with my collecting and writing.

That summer, to my surprise, David Hendin, editorial director of United Media Enterprises and United Feature Syndicate invited me to write a twice-weekly column for national circulation. Here was my chance to join my heroes like Jack Anderson and Miss Manners, reaching a gigantic audience of daily newspaper readers with my own scoops divulging the real sources and meanings of urban legends and my own replies to readers' questions about which stories to trust and which to bust.

A Swedish folklorist I know, who also writes about urban legends in the popular media, has the wonderful name Bengt af Klintberg. Bengt tells me that newspapers in Sweden now label urban legends "Klintbergers." That has a nice ring to it that I'm afraid "Brunvanders" lacks, though I liked the idea.

My column did not match the circulation of Jack Anderson's, but it was a thrill to see my picture in the United Media catalogue right across the page from J.A.'s portrait and next to Miss Manners's. Her hair was pictured there in perfect control, and her "humor and common sense" were listed as her "weapons against sav-

---

*The first two were *The Vanishing Hitchhiker* (1981) and *The Choking Doberman* (1984).

agery." My hair in the catalogue picture seemed fetchingly rumpled, and my mission was stated as to "uncover the truth behind the legends." Thus began my career as a columnist.

At first, I wrote lots of the "600 to 700 word columns" I needed that ran instead to 1,000 words or more (not counting footnotes). Then I received a crash refresher course in journalistic writing (Rule No. 1: Don't use footnotes), first from David Hendin's scrawled comments on both sides of my pages, and later from the expert editorial work of Kevin Krajik and Paul Elie of United Feature Syndicate. Thanks, guys, one more time.

On January 26, 1987, my column—"Urban Legends"—was launched in thirty-five papers. This book contains revised and expanded columns from the first year and a half, using only stories that are not discussed at length in my previous books. I chose columns about the stories that were most often submitted by readers, thus selecting the hottest urban legends going.

Column No. 1 carried the ambitious headline "Modern Folklorist Tracks Our Subconscious." I began by quoting another folklore scholar who had said: "Being a folklorist means you have to explain yourself a lot." I agreed with her, because, despite public belief to the contrary, folklorists seldom tell stories professionally but instead collect and study them. We are researchers, not raconteurs.

The purpose of the column is to reveal my findings about weird but credible stories—urban legends—that everyone tells as if they are true, though mostly they are fiction. From the start, I urged readers to submit rumors and stories circulating in their own communities.

Things worked out fine in that department. I receive scores of legends from readers every week, probably learning as much from their comments as they do from my essays. Often I see new trends emerging, such as leg-

ends about AIDS or about the dangers of tanning salons.
I can also track the re-emergence of older legends, which
means that a "hot" new legend may actually be a re-
heated leftover story to a folklorist—still interesting,
though not as fresh as the public may think.

Rarely, my queries about stories unearth the apparent
origin of a plot. Thus, with readers' help, I tracked
through *Reader's Digest* and other publications and then
back to its Midwestern source, a hilarious anecdote
about a woman's high heel caught in a grate. Later, a
student of mine spotted the same incident dramatized in
an old Doris Day film. The whole history of this legend is
revealed under the title "The Heel in the Grate" in
Chapter 4.

Sometimes actual events like this generate urban legends, but legends about real incidents get so localized
and stylized that they soon exist independently as oral
stories, detached from their origins. For example, a few
cars really have been filled with concrete, and perhaps
one such case started the legend. But the events described did not occur in all the times and places where
"The Solid Concrete Cadillac" is told.

Most urban legends are pure fantasies from someone's
imagination. These fictional stories change as they
spread but are always told as true—which is really the
definition of "legend."

Sometimes readers challenge me that stories I have
labeled apocryphal really happened. These people usually either remember an event that slightly resembled a
legend, or they repeat a story that they assume (incor-
rectly) was told by a firsthand witness. Neither "proof" is
airtight.

For example, a reader assured me that "The Runaway
Grandmother" is "not a myth," because in 1976 she saw
a car in Tennessee with what looked like a wrapped
corpse tied on top. Having heard the stolen grand-

mother legend, she figured the body she thought she saw might have gotten lost in a similar manner.

She had observed, as she wrote, "a small older-model car with a strange object on the roof." The package she described was long, well padded, and rounded on one end.

Without even speaking to the couple driving, she decided that their child had died on a trip and that they were transporting the body home for burial on their own because of lack of funds.

The letter concluded, "It is easy to imagine that some prankster stole the bundle at some stop along the route and disposed of it."

You may imagine what you wish, dear reader, but remember that Americans have been telling this "Runaway Grandmother" legend about a supposed vacation mishap in Mexico since the early 1960s. The basic plot goes back to a European legend of the post–World War II days.

Another reader sent this "proof" of "The Nude Housewife" legend: "I happen to know a woman who was doing the laundry in the basement and she took off all of her clothes and put them in the machine. The meter man came, and she covered her head and ran up the stairs! I'm beginning to wonder how thorough you are?"

Gee, I am sorry I wasn't on the scene to interview that woman!

The legend this reader remembered was one in which a woman is caught in the nude except for a football helmet. The scene prompts the gas man to remark, "I don't know what game you're playing, lady, but I hope your team wins."

I have dozens of versions of "The Nude Housewife," many told as true, coming from oral tradition and print over a twenty-five-year period. But I have never spoken to a first-person participant in the supposed event, though I've met plenty of secondhand true believers.

Eugene W. Dillenburg of Chicago raised a pertinent point in a letter. He suggested that the average Joe hears several versions of an urban legend from different sources and thinks, "Hey, they can't all be wrong, so there must be some truth to it."

For a folklorist, however, multiple versions from different places betray a story's oral circulation and variation. Even if we find the source of a legend, as I stated before, the story may have a life of its own.

"The Attempted Abduction" was the latest urban legend a reader wrote me about, saying that "somewhere along the way these stories did happen. But in the retelling the location was changed because someone couldn't remember exactly where it happened."

She mentioned the case of a child abducted from a theater restroom a few years ago in her city, the presumed origin of this urban legend. But "The Attempted Abduction" legend has a detailed plot involving cutting and coloring the child's hair, sedating her, changing her clothes except for shoes, the mother's recognition because of the shoes, and suppression by authorities of the crime report.

Numerous shopping malls and stores have had this story told about them, but none ever had exactly that crime committed. Police and journalists have debunked "The Attempted Abduction," and folklorists have found centuries-old antecedents for it.

So the similar crimes in real life must be simply part of the climate in which the old legend still flourishes.

With my story files steadily growing as the column continues, so is my level of journalistic accuracy, since readers quickly catch my errors. A recent solid example is a letter from California commenting on my discussion of

"The Solid Cement Car." (A man suspects his wife has taken on a lover and fills the competitor's car with cement.) It turns out, as the man wrote, that *cement* is only "the grey powder stuff that you buy in bags"; when mixed with sand, aggregate, and water, he explained, it becomes *concrete, mortar,* or *grout,* depending on the mix.

I should have known that, my father being a retired highway engineer who uses words like "aggregate" when talking of his work. I retitled the story, "The Concrete Car," risking a letter pointing out that the car is merely *filled with* concrete, not made of it.

People wonder why I don't plant invented legends to see how they grow. I do not believe it's my business to make up folklore; nor do I think contrived stories would catch on. But a family in Colorado wrote once saying they had just invented a nifty new legend and were setting it in motion toward me via oral tradition. So far—many months later—no further word of it has arrived, but maybe it got stuck on the grapevine around Grand Junction.

When a reader, in Yellowknife, Northwest Territories, wrote offering to be my listening post for urban legends up there, I thought, "Sure, ha ha; urban and suburban folklore can't possibly get that far into the wilds." A week later, he sent me notes on a couple of good ones he had just heard in Yellowknife. When I got a similar call from White Horse up in the Yukon, I listened.

A misconception about writers in general gravitates to me more often nowadays. Some people think that writers personally print, bind, and sell their own books; so they sometimes write to me complaining that the binding in their copy of a book I wrote is loose, or asking for book prices and ordering information, or even wondering if I have extra copies to give away.

Please note, as I wrote in one column, that the book

business doesn't work that way. My books are listed in the reference *Books in Print,* whence they may be ordered by any bookseller. Soon after I wrote that, though, I heard from an irritated writer who does, in fact, publish and sell his own books and who thought that my comments would cost him business.

Then there's "My alabi for misspelling 'alibi,' " as another column was headed. Some readers assume that journalists write the headlines that appear over their stories. I got an angry, unsigned, typewritten letter from this guy in—well, I won't mention the city. He enclosed a photocopy of my column with the big fat misspelled word "Alabi" circled in the headline, and he commented: "I am wondering where you studied journalism and what school you learned to spell, or maybe I should say tried to learn to spell."

"Hey, mister," I responded, "no writers for your paper, whether local or national, compose their own headlines. Besides, the word 'alibi' didn't even appear in the column, only in the headline; but the hard words 'occurred' and 'gullible' did appear, and they were spelled right too."

But to answer his question seriously, I majored in journalism for my bachelor's degree at Michigan State University, but that was before I saw the light and went into folklore.

At any rate, the folklore of journalism is merging with the folklore of folklorists in my case. But, then, it's all grist for the mill. (I do hope it's "grist" and not "grain" or "grits" that I mean here.)

Please keep those cards and letters coming, I asked my readers, and they certainly did keep writing. In one column, I demonstrated what piles of interesting mail I was getting by summarizing only one day's intake—a dozen letters—from readers of just one newspaper, the *San Jose*

(California) *Mercury-News*. In that single stack of correspondence, I found queries about individual urban legends, several new texts, some corrections and additions to my earlier columns, and one complaint from a reader who found my debunking of a sexy legend to be offensive. (She ought to see the ones I have to leave out!) There was even a note from *Mercury-News* feature writer Caroline Grannon, who was forwarding the mail; she couldn't resist adding a question of her own regarding an apocryphal story about Walt Disney.

The sentence "Altered substances are being passed around" headlined another column in which I tried to show by analogy how stories—like other things—may change as they are circulated.

The process of creating variations is like that old parlor game called "Telephone" or "Gossip." The players stand in a circle, and one person whispers a phrase to the person to his or her left, who whispers it to the next person, and so on. When the last player recites the phrase that he or she heard, it's sometimes barely recognizable as a variation of the original.

Perhaps reflecting this process, there are a couple of common legends about objects that are passed around until they return in a new form. The two items passed on in these stories are either a joint of marijuana or a lottery ticket. It's the pot or the lot, so to speak.

I've collected the legend about the joint from people who remember hearing it as long ago as 1968. These particular people heard it in Alaska, California, North Carolina, and Pennsylvania, so I assume that it's known nationwide.

A police officer is giving a lecture about the dangers of drugs to students in a high school. At one point, he puts a real joint of marijuana on a dish and passes it around for the students to see and smell. "When that dish gets back to me, the Cannabis exhibit had better be on it," he warns them. "And if it isn't, there will be an inspection, because I borrowed it from the evidence room at head-quarters."

When the exhibit comes back to him, not only is the joint still on the dish, there are three others as well.

In some versions, the policeman's threat has been ignored, and the joint has been exchanged for an ordinary cigarette.

I first came across the lottery-ticket variation of this legend in Michigan. The state began to operate a lottery in 1972, and by the end of the year this story was going around.

A man is in a bar where the lottery numbers are being shown on TV, and he sees that he is a big winner. Thrilled by his good luck, he passes his winning ticket around the bar for everyone to see. When it comes back to him, though, it's not the same ticket.

A reader from New Orleans tells me that he heard virtually the same story in 1969. The only difference is that a winning horse-racing ticket, not a lottery ticket, is passed around.

That such things do sometimes occur in real life is illustrated by a reader's personal experience described in another letter. I'm suppressing the place and name here to avoid embarrassing anyone.

The reader wrote to tell me about the time she had attended the broadcast of a national TV interview program. Among the guests was a celebrity author. Afterward, at a large city bookstore, this reader was able to buy an autographed copy of that author's latest book.

She later told her co-workers about her visit to the show, and several of them asked to borrow the book. She consented, and the book made its way around the office. When it was finally returned to her, after several co-workers had read it, it bore the price sticker of a local bookstore. And the space where the autograph had been was blank.

The lesson of these stories, I suppose, is that you can't trust people when they are in groups. Whether they are passing around contraband or tickets or books—or *folklore*—someone is bound to pull a switcheroo.

Reading a profile in *The New Yorker* ("Boy Wonder" by Lawrence Weschler, November 17 and 24, 1986) about musical lexicographer Nicolas Slonimsky, I discovered that both of us are bedeviled by falsehoods in our fields that seem impossible to eradicate from the popular mind. Slonimsky repeatedly has to debunk fallacies about music history, while I have to deal with fantasies about things like exploding toilets, stolen cat corpses, and the Procter & Gamble company trademark.

As Lawrence Weschler wrote in his essay on Slonimsky: "The horror of horrors [he said] was the inadvertent factual errors that, once born into print, refused to die, and, indeed spread exponentially from one sourcebook to another, eternally. They haunted his sleep like vengeful wraiths."

I know the feeling, Nick! I'm also reminded of a line in Joe Adamson's book *Groucho, Harpo, Chico and Sometimes Zeppo* (New York: Simon & Schuster, 1973) that a column reader pointed out to me: "We have a fascination," Adamson wrote, "for utter transcendent unlikelihoods that we are not likely to shake, so long as we are human." Sounds just like urban legends to me.

With everyday life offering so many chances to be misunderstood, it's not surprising that lots of urban legends— and some true anecdotes—illustrate the difference between what people say and what they mean.

The most common legend of this sort is one I call "The Elevator Incident." At a hotel in New York City, a large man, leading a fierce-looking dog by a leash, boards an elevator occupied by three women tourists. When the man, who happens to be black, commands "Sit, Lady!" the women, apparently believing he is a mugger, sit down on the elevator floor. But it turns out that "Lady" is merely the dog's name, and the man is a celebrity—Reggie Jackson, say, or Lionel Richie. He apologizes profusely and tries to make up for their embarrassment by paying their dinner or hotel bill.

To my knowledge, no such incident has ever occurred to Jackson, Richie, or any other celebrity.

After reading my account of this legend in one of my earlier columns, Dr. K.H. of Syracuse, New York, recalled a similar misunderstanding involving the "teams" of interns and residents in a hospital where he once worked.

At one time, the teams were called red, white, and blue. But one day a female patient who was black asked an intern whether her husband had visited.

Without thinking, the intern replied, "I don't know him. I'm on the white team."

K.H. changed the team names not long afterward.

S.H., also of Syracuse, recalls one from his days as a fighter pilot in the air force. This story sounds awfully legendary, although S.H. says that it really happened.

While training to be a gunner, he was practicing firing at a target pulled by another plane. "SAVE YOUR BRASS," the instructor, sitting behind him in the cockpit, yelled above the noise of the engine—meaning "Save the shell casings." But S.H. thought the instructor said something else: "Save your ass." He pressed the release on his ejection seat and parachuted out of the plane, landing in a Florida swamp.

Not every misunderstanding story is so dramatic. Take the anecdote told among librarians, for instance. A library patron searching for cross references in the card catalogue comes to a card printed with the instruction

"Go to Main Entry." So the patron goes to the front door and looks for references there.

That one's drier than a musty old book.

There's the classic story about a new member of Weight Watchers who is trying trying to follow the diet exactly. But one instruction is just too demanding. "I followed the diet as faithfully as possible," the dieter explains at the second week's meeting. "But for the life of me I just could not eat forty-six eggs."

The instructions, of course, were to eat "four to six" eggs per week.

And then there's the story about an amateur cook who was carefully following a recipe for homemade cookies. "Spoon dough on cookie sheet," the recipe instructed. "Leave room to rise."

The cook spooned out the dough and then went into the next room, peeking into the kitchen now and then to see if the cookies were rising.

And every elementary-school teacher has probably heard the story about the teacher who, while on a bus, thinks she recognizes the man sitting a few seats in front of her.

"Hello there, Mr. Johnson," she says, but the man doesn't respond.

She keeps calling out until—with everyone on the bus now looking at her—he finally turns around. And then she sees that she doesn't know him after all. "Sorry," she says, "I thought you were the father of one of my children."

Here's one more story, only faintly related to the theme of misunderstood words, but I happen to like it. It was told to me twice recently with assurances that it had actually happened at an international conference that my source had attended. But only to a friend of a friend* of

---

*A FOAF.

my source, and alleged to have happened on two different continents.

Supposedly, there is a translator provided at the conference who is rendering a talk being given by a German
delegate for an English-speaking member of the audience. The speaker proceeds *auf Deutsch,* and the translator whispers each equivalent sentence in English.

It's all going along quite smoothly until at one point in
the presentation the speaker has been going on for several minutes without the translator saying anything.

Finally the English speaker whispers, "What's going
on?" and the translator hisses, "Shhh! I'm waiting for
the verb."

If it didn't happen, it should have.

In revising my columns for book publication, I have left
some of them largely in their original form, while others
were considerably expanded to reflect material that was
left out for lack of space or new variations and further
information I have gathered. I have incorporated as
much reader response as possible, without excessively
repeating similar versions of legends.

The stories are organized using the same rough subject headings used in my earlier books, even though such
categories inevitably overlap. I have stretched the definition of "legend" a bit in order to include sections on
some popular traditions that are more like rumors,
pranks, or customs than genuine narratives. But these
are all manifestations of modern folkloric behavior,
whatever their genre. I have also felt free to include some
examples—like "The Welfare Letter," "Going by the
Old-fashioned Rules," and "Grandma's Washday"—
that are transmitted in written or printed form rather
than orally.

From January through May 1988, I visited New Zealand—writing my column and working on this book all

the while. That explains the several discussions in this book of urban legends and other folklore from the wonderful land of the Kiwis. For invaluable assistance while I was in New Zealand, I wish to thank especially Colin and Chris Fitzpatrick, Phil Twyford, Chris Alpe, Karen Ferns, and Karen Thompson.

My address, for those who wish to send me legends or queries, is as follows:

Professor Jan Harold Brunvand
Department of English
University of Utah
Salt Lake City, UT 84112

Curses!
Broiled Again!

1

Horrors

"Curses! Broiled Again!"

I like to designate the most popular urban legend of the time as "the hottest story going," and this one was certainly hot during the summer of 1987. In fact, it's *still* hot (would I give you old news?). Read on.

The basis of the story is that a young woman wants a quick tan and somehow contrives to schedule extra sessions at a tanning salon. The result of her indiscreet vanity is that she cooks her insides.

First credit for telling me this shocker goes to my University of Utah colleague, Professor Robert Steensma. When he came back to town in mid-August 1987 from a summer-school teaching stint at Augustana College in Sioux Falls, South Dakota, Steensma told me two versions he had heard there.

In one, a girl wanting to look nice and tan repeatedly visited the same salon at different times of day. Soon she began feeling ill, and she consulted a doctor. He told her that she had cooked her insides. Version 2 from South Dakota claimed that she fried a muscle in an arm and that the limb had to be amputated.

Later the same day, a student from my summer folklore class reported a story she had heard the night before. This supposedly happened, she said, to the wife of the cousin of the man who had told it to a woman friend of hers who then told her. Something like that.

This time the tanning salon had a rule to protect customers from overexposure: a thirty-minutes-per-day limit. But this girl—friend of a friend of a friend—circumvented that by signing up at four different salons, thus getting four times the recommended dosage.

Her husband began to notice that she "smelled funny," and her doctor gave her the bad news. Cooked insides and certain death. "It's funny," I commented, "that such a dramatic event never made the Salt Lake City papers."

My student had discussed the story with another friend, who claimed that the tanning-salon roasting had really happened to a girl who was tanning herself into shape to be a swell-looking bridesmaid for her best pal.

So I'm sitting in my office in the second stage of folkloristic research (first, collection; second, classification; third, analysis). I'm labeling a file folder "Cooked Alive: New Legend?" when the telephone rings. The caller, a local person, reads my column in the *Deseret News,* and she had just heard this awful story from someone at work and was delegated to call and ask whether I thought it was an urban legend.

In her version, a young lady from the small northern Utah town of Tremonton needed a good tan to take to summer cheerleader camp at Utah State University over in Logan. So she signed up at several different tanning salons and went in four or five times per day.

Again, the bad smell developed, and she showered, then showered again. The smell didn't go away, and when her mother noticed it, she rushed her daughter to the doctor. The diagnosis was "microwaved insides." Another cooked goose, just for wanting a fast tan.

At that point, I wrote one of my newspaper columns

on the story of the girl who was sizzled to medium rare in the tanning salon. When the Salt Lake City *Deseret News* ran the column on Friday, September 18, they assigned it the wonderful headline that provides the title to this book: "Curses! Broiled Again!" Then the following Tuesday, September 22, in publishing the regular "Dear Abby" column for that day, the *DN* added the note, "Other variations on the following tanning salon story appeared in last Friday's 'Urban Legends' column by Jan Harold Brunvand."

Oddly enough, the cooked-goose legend came to Abby from the city of Provo in the state of Utah, via Springfield, Oregon. A concerned mother of a Brigham Young University student had written to ask Abby to warn her readers about the fate of a seventeen-year-old girl that her daughter had described in a letter. The teenager had supposedly fried herself under the tanning lamps and was said to be lying "totally blind" in the Utah Valley Regional Medical Center in Provo with an estimated twenty-six days to live.

Abby was suspicious about that precise figure of "twenty-six days" and called the medical center. She learned that there was no such patient being treated, though the story was known to the center spokesperson. In fact, Joann Cox, the secretary who answered the telephone, told Abby's staff that she had also heard the same story told recently in Pocatello, Idaho.

Dozens of my readers clipped Dear Abby's column for that day and forwarded it to me along with the versions they had heard in Pennsylvania, New York, Ohio, and even Florida. (Why do they need tanning salons in Florida?) Noting the emphasis on Utah in the two column versions, one folklorist sent me the "Dear Abby" clipping with the scribbled note, "Is Utah now the center of new urban legends?"

Actually, I had wondered the same thing at first. Practically everyone I spoke to in Utah for the next few months tried to tell me a new variation on the legend. My favorite was from a caller in the city of West Jordan who said the doctor had told the victim, "To cure this condition would be like frying a steak and then trying to bring it back to life." Huh? You couldn't bring a *raw* steak back to life, could you?

Anyway, there are at least two interesting questions here. First, did the story just develop out of the blue in the middle of the summer of '87? Second, had it, perhaps, actually happened somewhere, possibly in the West or Midwest, where many of the versions I collected came from?

But coming "out of the blue" seemed too simple, and I soon found that the story was older and more widespread than I suspected. The first publication of it that I have uncovered, however, was still from the Midwest. A news story on July 16, 1987, bylined Ross Bielema, in the *Dubuque* (Iowa) *Telegraph Herald,* described and debunked several local versions of the story. The young woman was said to be seventeen, worked at Hartig Drug store, was a student at Loras College, needed the tan for a wedding; she had a bad smell, got the bad news, etc.— the works. Bielema did a nice job on the story, incidentally, and (I must admit it) he scooped both Abby and me by a month.

Meanwhile, I learned that just about the same time that I was beginning to hear the story told in Utah, the same legend had been posted to the nationwide computer hookup "ARPANET" on August 10 by a subscriber at Stanford University. (Why do they need tanning salons in California?)

"Curses! Broiled Again!" was obviously an appealing story that summer more because of its horror content and warning function than because of any actual gruesome medical case that any of the informants knew about firsthand. In other words, the cardinal rule of urban legends definitely applies here: The truth never stands in the way of a good story. But where does a story like this come from?

I would trace one theme in the legend to an earlier rumor about home tanning lamps, which always carry important safety warnings and require certain precautions. Last summer, a man in Ohio wrote me this: "About six years ago when I was shopping for a sun lamp, the appliance salesman emphasized the reliable timer on one model. Then he recounted as a fact that a woman using a lesser product fell asleep and had her contact lenses fused to her eyeballs."

The fused-cornea-and-contact story, you may remember, is an urban legend usually associated with an imaginary welding accident that somehow generates microwaves that allegedly dry up the fluids in the eye.

Another connection here is the specialized horror stories about microwaved pets and babies, which are part of the lore warning against modern technology and product misuse. While accidents with appliances do happen, these horror stories floating around in different versions in oral tradition almost certainly did *not* happen. In some of them, as in the tanning-salon story, it sounds like people are confusing ultraviolet tanning rays with the microwaves used in cooking.

What could follow from overuse of a home sunlamp or extra tanning sessions is serious burns to the skin. That's just good old-fashioned sunburn, which doesn't smell bad, unless you count the ointments used to soothe the ache.

There's another growing fear expressed in this story: the mounting evidence that too much tanning will increase your risk of skin cancer. Nearly everyone knows by now of the danger from too much sun, but nearly everyone seems willing to catch a few extra rays anyway.

"It can't happen to me" is the assumption, though it might happen to some silly young thing like this girl in the story. So far I have heard only of females suffering this particular fate, but it may be that male versions of the cooked-insides story just have not yet made their way to me.

The tanning-salon-accident story has not died out; in fact, it seems to have held on through the winter and revived strongly the following summer. In January 1988, for example, I got the story again from Bill Kestell of New Holstein, Wisconsin, who says his secretary heard it from a girlfriend who was told it by a friend at work who was supposed to have been in the same wedding party as the victim. In March, a graduate student in English at Iowa State University, Ames, reported the legend being told by her roommate who heard it from a friend who thought she may have read it in *Glamour* magazine. Could be, I suppose, though I have not found it there.

The following month I got a report from Pacifica, California. This victim was a bride, not a bridesmaid, and the storyteller asserted that the lamps at tanning salons really do emit microwaves, as this story proves. I thought it was the other way around, that the lack of microwaves in tanning lamps proves that the story is false.

The latest versions of "Curses! Broiled Again!" came in the mail during the summer of 1988, about a year after I first heard it from Bob Steensma. Here's a report from Christine A. Lehman, writing from Santa Ana, California, whose letter demonstrates one way that the story may be inserted into conversations: "I was looking at a newspaper ad for a tanning parlor and mentioned to one of my co-workers that I might go check it out. She got a very serious look on her face. 'Oh, you better be real careful. I just heard the most awful story about those places from my cousin. Her best friend was about to get married, and she decided she wanted to have a real dark tan . . . ."

Need I continue this sad story? The moral it teaches, of course, is "Curses! Broiled Again!"

Most recently, I have been hearing what might be called "The General Health and Fitness Version" of the legend. For example, Lynda M. Sholly of Granger, Indiana, wrote me in July 1988 about the story as she heard it, concerning "a young woman who was physically active in exercise . . . always very careful regarding her appearance and bodily habits. She strove to always look and smell her best."

There is nothing whatever in this version about brides or bridesmaids, cheerleaders, trips to Hawaii, or even deliberate overuse of tanning salons. But when the inevitable bad smell develops, the fitness freak's doctor asks whether she has been going to a tanning salon. When she replies in the affirmative, he warns her, "There's really nothing I can do. You wanted this artificial tan, and now you are paying for it, but you are rotting away from the inside, and eventually you'll die from the rotting." (In a similar version of the story sent from Illinois, the doctor explains that his patient's body is unable to clear itself of dead cells caused internally by excessive exposure to the tanning lamps and that his patient will be dead in six months.)

It would seem, in the final analysis, that "Curses! Broiled Again!" is partly a warning against overdoing a health routine in general, rather than merely against tanning salons in particular.

Postscript: In October 1988, I received a letter from a woman in Orem, Utah, who had just heard at her hairdressers about a girl, "probably a BYU coed," who had cooked her insides by visiting several tanning salons in one day. The woman commented, "This sounds too bizarre to be true. Do you know if it is fact or legend?" I sent a one-word answer to her question—the L-word, if you know what I mean.

This is where I came in with this particular urban legend.

"Death in the Funhouse"

Every year as summer begins and amusement parks open, it becomes the season for the re-emergence of the annual legends about deadly dangers in funhouses, tunnels of love, and carnival rides. True, accidents do happen, and occasionally some pretty bizarre ones. But amusement-park mishaps couldn't possibly occur at the rate that folklore suggests, or else no insurance companies would issue liability coverage, and very few parks would survive.

Another clue that we are dealing with legends is that so many alleged accidents at such a large number of parks all supposedly stem from the same few hazards—electrocution, razor blades, and, especially, snakes.

I'll pass over the stories describing the fatal last step onto the electrified rail of a ride, as well as those stories about razor blades said to be stuck with chewing gum on the water slides by vandals, because these stories—as common as they are—seldom show much imagination or variation in their details.

The snake stories are much juicier. These tales are told about almost every amusement park in the country, old run-down places and classy new ones alike. I will not mention names, since I don't care to give even the slightest credence to the stories nor to be sued. I regard the vast bulk of the stories as being merely traditional expressions of people's fears concerning these popular, but always slightly suspect, places. Maybe we suffer some guilt for having fun, and that leads us to project stories about accidents onto the amusement parks.

The story usually goes that a small child on a popular ride complains about stings or bites. At first, the parents laugh, but eventually they investigate. The cause proves to be an infestation of poisonous snakes. First aid is provided too late to save the child.

Here's a typical example from the Midwest: A man took his little girl to a carnival and put her on the merry-go-round. She soon began to complain that the horse was biting her, and she begged to be taken off. The father kept saying, "Don't be silly. The horse can't be biting you." Soon the little girl slumped over and died, and it was discovered that the old wooden horses, which were full of cracks, were also full of snakes.

It seems that when the horses had been stored for the winter in Florida, they became a haven for the creatures. This is a nice touch to the story—legendary venomous serpents and other nasty things often originate somewhere in the South, possibly revealing northerners' suspicions of that region. Sometimes, the infested horses are imported from India as replacements for old, worn-out ones. Frankly, I doubt that new merry-go-round horses are imported very often nowadays from anywhere.

I've also heard a story in which a car for a roller coaster is brought out of the warehouse in which it had been stored for a long time. A large crowd shows up on the first day of the park's season. On the first trip with the extra car attached, a child suddenly stands up in the car and screams. It turns out that a den of rattlesnakes had taken up winter quarters there and were stirred up by the ride's motion.

In another form of the story, told of many different parks, some kind of ride employing little boats—like a tunnel of love or a log flume ride—has poisonous water snakes living in the stream. They bite passengers who are unlucky enough to dangle their hands over the side of the boat. Or, in a more dramatic snake attack, the snakes drop from above, where they have been lurking. It begins to sound like an old Tarzan film at this point.

Further along the trail, some of the stories begin sounding like updated versions of the serpent in the Garden of Eden. The *Montreal Gazette* reported in July 1983 that local brides were scared to pose for traditional wedding photos in the Montreal Botanical Garden. The reason? According to a completely unverified story going around at the time, a June bride was killed by a poisonous snake that had crept out of a flower bed.

The details of the alleged tragedy were vivid. She was but twenty-three years old, and the viper crept up under her gown and stung her. She complained of a sharp pain but was not heeded. By the time help was provided she was too far gone to be saved. The gory details of the effects of the bite went through many imaginative reworkings in Montreal that summer. At times the snake was said to be a python, a rattlesnake, or even a tarantula.

No hard facts were uncovered to substantiate the great Montreal snake scare of '83. And, as a Botanical Garden spokesman sensibly asked, "In downtown Montreal where is this venomous snake supposed to come from?"

Where, indeed? Why from traditional early-summer amusement-park horror folklore, that's where.

"A Bug in the Ear"

The proverbial expression "to put a bug in your ear," meaning to implant an idea in your mind, originates from the belief that insects called "earwigs" frequently creep into people's ears. There is, indeed, an insect called an earwig, which the *Encyclopaedia Britannica* describes as a "nocturnal insect . . . usually herbivorous." The encyclopedia also notes "a widespread, but unfounded, superstition that earwigs crawl into the ears of sleeping people."

But just as the name "woodchuck" misleads people to speak of "woodchucks chucking wood," the name "earwig" has perpetuated a fear of insects crawling around in the auditory canals. And this belief has been encouraged further by a common urban legend.

The *Oxford English Dictionary (OED)*—the Bible of every word watcher—traces the word "earwig," meaning "ear-insect," to Old English and Middle English prototypes that look like the modern word as it might be spelled by someone with an insect buzzing in his ear: *earwicgan, eorwicga,* and so forth. The *OED* dates "the notion that it penetrates into the head through the ear" to as early as the year 1000.

In the most common modern version of the story, a woman is lying on a beach, when a tiny earwig slips into her ear and crawls straight ahead as far as possible. The woman leaves the beach unawares. But several days later, she suffers an intense earache, and goes to a doctor for an examination.

"Hmmm. He's too far in to grab," the doctor says. "We'll just have to wait. He'll work his way through and come out the other side."

But the doctor has made a big mistake. Weeks later, when the insect emerges from the woman's other ear, the "he" bug turns out to be a "she." So the doctor offers a revised opinion. "I'm afraid this female earwig may have laid eggs in your head. If so, they'll hatch and eventually eat out your brain."

The doctor's lack of regard for the woman's initial problem and his grim diagnosis later on give this away as an urban legend. Besides, how can an herbivorous insect get from the ear canal into the brain and then back to the ear canal on the other side of the head? The other thing I've always wondered about is whether medical students take entomology courses in college just so they will be able to distinguish male from female earwigs when the need arises.

To return to the metaphorical "bug in your ear," the *OED* also records the verb "to earwig," meaning to pester, influence, or bias a person by insinuating yourself (like an earwig) into his confidence.

Which brings me to a recent manifestation of the legend in popular culture. In *Star Trek II: The Wrath of Kahn,* a big film hit a few years back, the villainous Kahn insinuates space creatures into the ears of two Starship *Reliant* (sister ship of the *Enterprise*) officers in order to make the officers obey his commands.

In the summer of 1982, when the film was first released, a newspaper editor in Boise, Idaho, remembered an eleven-year-old local news item about an earwig. The editor revived the item, which he found in the paper's back file, and it was sent out by Associated Press as a sort of footnote to the *Star Trek* film. The story was that in 1971, when the Boise area was infested with earwigs, a woman in Boise consulted her doctor about an intense earache. Using forceps, the doctor extracted what the news story reports as an earwig from her ear.

In the years that I have been collecting versions of the

earwig story, I have also heard from four other people who claim a firsthand knowledge of a family member who had an earwig in his or her ear. Considering the earwig's exaggerated reputation for ear crawling, this doesn't really seem to be a problem of epidemic proportions.

Such rare and random occurrences of earwigs getting into people's ears have little connection to the bug-in-the-ear legend, apart from making it seem more plausible to those few who know about the experiences. An earwig is really no more likely to crawl into a person's ear than an ant or a spider. The fact that the Associated Press regarded the Boise event as national news testifies to its unlikelihood.

So while an earwig can indeed crawl into a person's ear, it seems that a place has to be pretty darn earwiggy for such a thing to happen by chance. And one has to be positively smothering in fear of earwigginess to flee the beach for fear of earwigs.

I found those wacky, wonderful words, *earwiggy* and *earwigginess,* in the *OED* too, but they have not been used in English since the 1870s. Let me put this bug in your ear: How about introducing both words back into current usage?

But don't believe the story about female earwigs laying eggs in the middle of someone's brain. That's just another urban legend.

Footnote: After my earwig column appeared, a number of people wrote to describe their recollections of an old television thriller apparently based on the earwig legend. Most people agreed that Laurence Harvey played a role in which he tried to kill a man by having an earwig placed into his ear. But the plan went awry, and the Harvey character himself received the earwig implant. It turned out to be a female insect that crawled through the head and left eggs in the brain.

What my correspondents were not so sure about was when the show was aired or on what series the episode appeared. Their guesses ranged from ten to twenty years ago and either in "Night Gallery," "Alfred Hitchcock Presents," "Thriller," or "The Twilight Zone." I looked it up (the envelope please), and the correct answer is: "Night Gallery" episode entitled "The Caterpillar," broadcast March 1, 1972.

Final footnote (I hope): A high-school class in Elkton, Maryland, wrote to send me the lyrics of a song called "Earwig" by a punk-rock group called the Dead Milkmen. Its most memorable, much-repeated line is "You got an earwig, crawling towards your brain."

Thanks, class.

"The Plant's Revenge"

Michael Bell, a folklorist at the University of Colorado, knew as soon as he heard it that "Saguaro," a song by a group called the Austin Lounge Lizards, was linked to a legend.

In case you, like me, are not up on the music of this little-known group, I'll summarize the lyrics of the song, which appears on their 1984 album "Creatures from the Black Saloon." Bell hosts a weekly folk-music radio program in Boulder, and when I was in town recently he spun the disk for me.

In "Saguaro," a parody of a Western "hero ballad," a "noxious little twerp," who is target-shooting in the desert, fantasizes that giant saguaro cacti are gunmen and begins to fire randomly at them. But there is another rifleman on a nearby ridge also shooting at cacti. The second gunman finally hits one, and the huge plant falls on the twerp, crushing him to death.

This plot seems like a songwriter's fantasy, and it bears a marked resemblance to stories that I call "animal's revenge" legends.

But the song is based on a real incident. Although the Lizards embroidered the plot, the name of the victim— David Grundman—and the size of the saguaro— "twenty-seven feet of succulent"—given in the song echo news reports about the event from which the group drew their inspiration. (Succulents are plants, such as cacti, whose tissues are adapted to conserve moisture.)

In the original incident, reported in the *Phoenix Gazette* and the *Arizona Republic* on February 5, 1982, and subsequently picked up by the Associated Press, Grundman did indeed shoot at a giant saguaro cactus, which then toppled over and killed him.

When I first heard reports of the incident without seeing the news articles, I regarded them as legends. They reminded me of the stories in which a person tortures a wild animal by tying explosives to the poor thing. The animal then turns on the tormentor or his property and inflicts considerable damage.

In variations of "The Animal's Revenge" legends, dynamite is tied to coyotes or jackrabbits, grenades are tossed to sharks, and foxes' tails are set on fire. The explosive goes off as the animal moves under the person's camper or boat, blowing it to smithereens.

In one variation of "The Animal's Revenge," a Vermont hunter shoots a porcupine out of a tree, but the porcupine falls directly on him. The animal's quills puncture the hunter so badly that the man dies.

The saga of David Grundman's death caused by a cactus toppling on him seems like a further variation of "The Animal's Revenge," especially the porcupine-in-the-tree version. But so many people insisted that they had read it in a newspaper that I asked *Arizona Republic* Food Editor Judy Hille if she could track the story down. She owed me one for the help I gave her in debunking Phoenix versions of the legend about Mrs. Fields' secret recipe (see Chapter 6).

Hille dug up the aforementioned news stories, as well as a follow-up piece that appeared in the *Republic* on February 9. Although the details of people's retold versions of "The Plant's Revenge" all differed from the news items, the basic facts of the story were verified. Grundman and his roommate, Joseph Suchochi, were sharpshooting in the desert two miles north of Arizona 74, just west of Lake Pleasant, when the incident occurred.

There were a few differences between the two newspapers' accounts of Grundman's death. The *Republic* reported that he was twenty-seven years old, while the *Ga-*

zette said he was twenty-four. The *Republic* described the plant as a "26- to 27-foot" saguaro, while the *Gazette* reported that it was twenty-four feet tall. And the *Republic* cited provisions of state law that declared the destruction or mutilation of protected native plants to be a misdemeanor.

Both newspapers provided the odd detail that Grundman had yelled "tim" just as the plant fell, adding that it was believed that he had meant to say "timber," but the giant cactus got him first.

In its follow-up story, the *Republic* modified Grundman's age to twenty-four, held the cactus's size to an even twenty-six feet, and reported that Grundman had actually yelled not "tim," but "Jim," the first name of his roommate, whose name was now given in full as James Joseph Suchochi.

It appears that the variations in local news stories anticipated the variations that people began telling and were the source of the ballad treatment by those singing Lounge Lizards. "The Plant's Revenge" may not be a full-blown legend yet, but it seems to be on its way.

Incidentally, you need not send me information or clippings about the Arizona glider pilot who crash-landed into a 2,000 pound saguaro on July 16, 1986. I already have plenty of documentation about this accident, including a front-page story from the *Republic*. The pilot survived the crash landing but was killed when the cactus toppled into the cockpit. A passenger survived both accidents.

It's no wonder that we so readily believe urban legends, when the news includes stories as strange as these!

Death and Danger in the Air

Some of the best urban legends began as stories that circulated among members of a particular trade or social group. Actors, for instance, first told the now-classic story of the leading man in a play who was surprised when the prop telephone on stage rang at the wrong time. The actor, nonplussed, picked up the phone, turned to his co-star and said, "It's for you!"

If a story about a particular group of people is especially funny, suspenseful, or profound, insiders are bound to share it with the rest of the world. Here are two horror stories that have slipped out of their usual orbits. Both involve danger and airplanes.

The first was told to me by a friend of mine, who heard it from a friend of his. His friend is a scuba diver and said the story is "popular lore among divers."

It is the day after a forest fire, and a ranger is examining the fire and water damage caused by the blaze when he notices a human body tangled in the branches of a blackened tree. A rescue team retrieves the corpse and shows it to the ranger, who is shocked by what he sees. It is the body of a scuba diver wearing a wet suit, a mask, flippers, and an oxygen tank.

Yes, a scuba diver found dead in a tree. Incredible.

The puzzled ranger finally comes up with an explanation. To put out the fire, firefighting planes scooped water from a nearby lake and then dumped it on the blaze. The diver, the ranger figured, accidentally became part of the plane's cargo.

But the details of the story give it away. Could a firefighting plane swoop close enough to the water to scoop up a diver swimming beneath the surface? Does such a plane discharge water through an opening large enough for a man to pass through? And would any pilot both pick up and drop a diver without being aware of it?

My initial suspicion of the story was confirmed by a letter I received recently from England. The writer had heard that the scuba-diver accident had happened in Australia, where water was scooped from the sea to extinguish a raging bushfire. He said that although the accident was reported by the British press, it was later debunked by *Diver* magazine.

Among scuba divers, the story probably reflects the anxiety that naturally results from swimming in dark, silent waters, unaware of the world above. But in telling the story to outsiders, scuba divers share a wacky and suspenseful urban legend and convey an idea of the possible (or impossible) dangers.

The second airplane story was sent to me by a pilot for United Airlines, who was told that it happened on a plane owned by another airline.

This plane is a DC-9, a two-pilot aircraft. Midway through the flight, the copilot leaves the cockpit to use the lavatory. A long time passes, and the captain grows concerned. He calls the flight attendants on the intercom and asks them to check on the copilot.

But both attendants are at the rear of the cabin, and a beverage cart is blocking the aisle, making it impossible for them to go to the forward lavatory.

Since it is the middle of the flight, the captain decides to check on the copilot himself. He activates the automatic pilot, steps out of the cockpit, and closes the door behind him.

Just then the copilot emerges from the lavatory. Both of them realize with dismay that neither has the key to the cockpit door. The two pilots have to smash the door with a fire ax in front of the horrified passengers.

The United pilot first heard the story in 1978 and thought it was an unlikely scenario. No pilot would leave the cockpit unattended, he said, and flight attendants can always get to the front of the cabin, even if it means climbing over a seat.

I have heard similar lockout stories from other pilots, all of whom tell their tale as happening to "another airline." In some versions, the captain leaves the cockpit to greet the passengers or to get sugar for his coffee. In others, turbulence causes the door to shut on its own.

I have also heard the story from air travelers, who tell it with a different emphasis. They lead in with the supposed ineptitude of a particular airline, tell the locked-out-pilot story, and conclude, "I'll never fly with them again!"

Another typical way that such legends are circulated is via newspaper columnists, who sometimes repeat entertaining stories they have heard without establishing their truth. Readers of the *Seattle Times* on December 30, 1987, for example, found "The Locked-out Pilot" story in Rick Anderson's triweekly column under the headline "Next Time You Fly, Make Sure the Pilot Has an Ax."

Anderson's version concerned a Boeing commercial jet operated by a Far East carrier. (Notice how subtle criticism of foreigners creeps into this one.) Anderson credited the story to "a Boeing representative, based on a first-hand account from one of Boeing's Far East agents." That, my friends, is a FOAF* if I ever met one.

And it's a familiar variation of the legend as well: two pilots stroll down the aisle to greet passengers, the cockpit door gets stuck, and "they used an ax on the door."

I wonder if it ever occurred to the Boeing rep either to

---

*Friend of a friend.

double-check the story or—as a matter of general interest—to have someone at the assembly plant experiment
in order to see just how long it takes to use a fire ax to
break down a well-designed security door on a jumbo jet.

And what is an airplane-company rep doing telling
such stories to a journalist anyway? The whole thing
smells of urban legend to yours truly.

"Halloween Sadists"

Just as surely as we can expect American children to trick-or-treat every Halloween, so we can expect well-meaning adults to raise the specter of what I and other folklorists call "Halloween sadists"—stories about people who prey upon costumed kids by giving them tainted treats.

School and police authorities issue their annual warnings against tampered foods; and hospitals, hoping to placate anxious parents, will X-ray their children's bags of sugar-coated Halloween loot.

What they look for each Halloween is danger—razor blades, needles, poisons, or drugs inserted into or concealed in apples and candy.

What they find, if history continues to run true to course, is nothing. While caution about the hazards of our Halloween customs is wise, statistics suggest that the kind of nasty-neighbor story that incites such fear at Halloween time is just another urban legend.

The existence of large-scale threats to children from Halloween sadists is taken for granted by most parents. But this belief, and the fear that results, is based largely on hearsay and exaggerated reporting, not on documented attacks on children.

As Joel Best, a sociologist at California State University, Fresno, has written in 1985 in *Psychology Today* magazine: "Everyone knows that Halloween sadists have been responsible for countless deaths and serious injuries. Fortunately, everyone is wrong."

In order to assess the threat of Halloween sadists, Best and his colleague Gerald T. Horiuchi reviewed all the Halloween-related stories reported by four newspapers—the *New York Times,* the *Los Angeles Times,* the *Chi-cago Tribune,* and the *Sacramento Bee*—between 1958 and 1984. They reported their findings in the sociology journal *Social Problems* in June 1985.

Best and Horiuchi found only 76 reported incidents in the twenty-seven-year period. Many of the incidents turned out to be unverifiable or to be hoaxes perpetrated by children in the spirit of Halloween misbehavior. And no report described an incident in which death or serious injury was caused by adulterated goodies.

There is a prototype for later Halloween sadist stories. A rumor that spread in the 1940s described a prankster who heated pennies on a skillet, then offered them to unwitting trick-or-treaters.

But Best and Horiuchi's survey suggests that a fear of more lethal Halloween sadists developed in the early 1970s. Of the 76 news reports, 31 were published between 1969 and 1971, with a second peak of 12 reports coming in 1982.

The pair contend that the first peak might be attributed to "heightened social strains of that period." The 1982 cases, however, were directly related to reports of the seven deaths caused by cyanide-laced Extra-Strength Tylenol sold in the Chicago area, and of several similar incidents that followed.

That year, the Food and Drug Administration studied 270 potential candy-adulteration cases and found that only 5 percent indicated any actual tampering. An FDA official described the fear of Halloween sadists as a case of "psychosomatic mass hysteria."

Even though crime reports and reliable news stories do not support the fear of Halloween sadists, oral tradition keeps the concern alive.

These rumors and stories combine two familiar themes of urban legends: dangers to children and the contamination of foods. And just as urban legends like

"The Microwaved Baby" or "The Batter-fried Rat" seem almost plausible, the Halloween-sadist rumors appear to make sense when compared to crimes described daily in the news.

Unlike most urban legends, there is no well-defined "text" of these rumors. They may take the form of warnings to parents to check their children's treats before allowing the children to eat them. Or it may be one child's warning to another: "You shouldn't go to that house because of what happened to a kid there once."

The razor blade and the apple, however, appear regularly in accounts of the legend. The apple may recur because of its Biblical status as a forbidden fruit or, more likely, because apples are in season at the time of Halloween. The razor blade may recur because its size would make it easy to conceal within a snack or because its blade—sharper than a needle or pin—makes it especially menacing.

The media play a large part in keeping the idea of a wave of annual treat tampering alive. A typical article in a parents' magazine in 1974 called Halloween the "Holiday for sadists." *Newsweek,* in a 1975 article, went so far as to claim that "several children have died and hundreds have narrowly escaped injury from razor blades, sewing needles and shards of glass purposefully put into their goodies by adults."

Another influence on the rumor is "slasher" films, such as *Halloween* (1979) and *Halloween II* (1981), in which random attacks by maniacs are directed against helpless young people. One such film, *Halloween III: Season of the Witch* (1983), depicts a maniac's plot to murder millions of children. These films are usually shown on or near Halloween, often at midnight, making the fear of Halloween sadists all too fresh in viewers' minds when they set out trick-or-treating.

Mostly, however, the Halloween-sadist rumors seem

to combine the fears that we naturally associate with the holiday: a fear of strangers, a fear of the night, and fear for our children's welfare that is wholly justified, considering the myriad types of mischief that are given license on Halloween.

There is one case in which a child was killed by a contaminated Halloween treat. On Halloween, in 1974, eight-year-old Timothy O'Bryan of Houston, Texas, died from cyanide poisoning after eating a package of Pixie Stix candy that had been adulterated with the poison. But the person convicted for the murder was not a random sadist, but the boy's father, Ronald Clark O'Bryan, who inserted the tainted candy into Timmy's bag after he had returned from trick-or-treating.

Sylvia Grider, a folklorist at Texas A&M University, studied this case and concluded that Mr. O'Bryan was "the only person ever convicted of acting out an urban legend and carrying it to the ultimate conclusion—murder."

It is usually a version of the "Candyman murder" incident, as the press dubbed the O'Bryan case, that people retell when they pass on a Halloween-sadist story.

Of course, the evidence against the threat of Halloween sadists does not mean that parents should not warn children about the hazards of taking candy from strangers or eating it without inspection. After all, urban legends often give good advice in a fictional framework. But the Halloween-sadist rumor shows that just as we've got to be careful about what we eat, so, too, must we be careful about what we believe.

"Blue Star Acid"

LSD may be more a part of the 1960s than the 1980s, having largely died out as a drug of choice. However, a long-discredited rumor about the drug reappeared in a big way during late 1986. I got dozens of reports—from four states in one week alone in early 1987—about a kind of LSD called "Blue Star acid." The story just wasn't true, but the flashbacks continued.

Here are the contents of a flier that one reader sent me: "A WARNING TO ALL PARENTS. According to police, a form of tattoo—BLUE STAR—is readily available to young children. It is a small sheet of white paper containing blue stars the size of a pencil eraser. Each STAR is impregnated with LSD and can be removed from the paper to be placed in the mouth. Absorption can occur through the skin by simply handling the paper tattoo!"

The spurious information, and even the capitalized words, vary only slightly among many photocopies of this warning circulated around the country. Sometimes a specific source, such as the San Diego police or a Kansas "drug squad," is mentioned. Most warnings also include references to small colored paper "tabs" in circulation, likewise impregnated with acid and bearing the likeness of Mickey Mouse, Superman, or other cartoon characters.

It is tricky to disprove the "Blue Star acid" rumors definitively, since some forms of what narcotics agents call "blotter acid" or "paper acid"—paper impregnated with LSD did, in fact, circulate during the 1960s and 1970s. Some were imprinted with cartoon characters, and police sometimes refer to them as "Snoopies." Occasionally, even today, blotter acid shows up in drug-enforcement efforts.

But seldom, if ever, was blotter acid distributed to children, and never was an actual paper tattoo or transfer used to transport LSD.

A 1980 New Jersey State Police Narcotic Bureau bulletin did warn, "Children may be susceptible to this type of cartoon stamp *believing it a tattoo transfer*" (my emphasis). But there is no evidence that any actual cartoon "tattoos" containing LSD have circulated among children.

In the November 24, 1986, issue of *Newsweek,* reporters investigated rumors in New York, New Jersey, Texas, Georgia, Kansas, and Nebraska before concluding only that some "microdots" of LSD resembling the Blue Stars "may have existed" about fifteen years earlier.

Here are the four reports that I received in 1987, all in a single week:

One of the fliers warning of the current "threat" circulated in the schools of Great Neck, New York, during early February 1987. The Nassau County Department of Drug and Alcohol Addiction checked into it and issued a statement saying that there was "no validity to this letter at this time."

On February 9, the *Columbia* (South Carolina) *Record* published a carefully researched article on virtually the same scare letter, which was making the rounds in schools and day-care centers. Law-enforcement authorities pronounced the flier to be bogus. A local agent of the federal Drug Enforcement Administration said, "We haven't heard of LSD being circulated this way in years."

On February 11, the *Tacoma* (Washington) *News Tribune,* impelled by "hundreds of frightened parents" who had called the Washington State Highway Patrol headquarters, assured readers that Blue Star LSD-impregnated tattoos or decals were not, as rumor claimed, being sold in any area schools. The newspaper quoted a police spokesman: "We could not substantiate one case anywhere in the country."

The following week, I heard reports of the flier circulating in a number of cities in Illinois and Indiana. The *Richmond* (Indiana) *Palladium-Item* even quoted from a past study that I had made of a version of the legend, which was common in 1981 to 1982.

Back then, I called it "Mickey Mouse acid" because this character was most often named in the warnings. But even at that time, the term "Blue Star" had begun appearing in many fliers. Lately, the Blue Stars are getting first mention, and the cartoon characters come into subsequent paragraphs. In addition, the warnings are becoming more elaborate.

In August 1986, the *Baltimore Evening Sun* had reported hundreds of warning notices being distributed by teachers, pediatricians, and even in a Baltimore police-precinct bulletin. One version of the story described a brain-damaged child dying in a Baltimore hospital after handling the Blue Stars.

In an attempt to trace the rumor, the *Sun* followed up references on the fliers to San Diego, to an Elks lodge in Idaho, and to several organizations throughout Maryland. The newspaper found not a shred of evidence that Blue Star acid ever existed. Needless to say, the story about the brain-damaged child turned out to be false.

Another major study of the rumor was reported in the *Philadelphia Inquirer* in December 1986. "Blue Star tattoo," the article conceded, "was something everybody has heard about [and] no one has actually seen."

It's possible that some genuine police bulletins were misread by citizens and that the rumors, already in circulation, took off from there. In the Tacoma case, it appears that a police query—apparently itself a response to the rumor—was worded "Have you seen any drug-laced tattoos?" This was then mistakenly repeated as "We have seen many drug-laced tattoos!" That's one way these stories build up steam.

Shortly after I wrote my original column, as above, in late February 1987, virtually the same "Blue Star" warnings dated in early March came to me from Richmond, Virginia; Lancaster, Pennsylvania; and Seattle, Washington. About a year and a half after my original column, the story was still going strong and, in response to a midwestern reader's question, I devoted a second column to the subject, which follows below.

AM I SPREADING BLUE STAR ACID?

A reader who follows "Urban Legends" in the Milwaukee Journal *wrote to me a while back to ask, "Do you think your column may have started a rumor about 'Blue Star Acid'? Or was my experience just one of those things?"*

I wish I felt as confident deciphering the signature on this letter as I feel in answering these questions.

No, I do not think my column spawned a Milwaukee-area rumor about the supposed deadly drug called "Blue Star Acid," since the "Blue Star" story proliferated both before and after I debunked it here a year and one-half ago.

I quoted then from crudely typewritten and photocopied fliers that I had collected in communities from coast to coast.

The fliers, most of them titled "A Warning to Parents," purported to be factual bulletins about a local rash of LSD addiction. They claimed that the drug was given to children on the surface of paper tattoos or transfers imprinted with blue stars and other designs.

The warnings urged parents to watch for "Blue Star Acid" in the hands of their kids, claiming that addiction and even death could result from children licking, or even just touching, the stars as they removed them from the paper. (LSD, incidentally, is not considered to be an addictive drug.)

Wherever the "Blue Star" rumor has begun to circulate, local police have disclaimed any knowledge of the fliers' source, and denied that LSD in this form was a problem in their community. And there are no records of any child licking a tab of "Blue Star," thinking it was a lick-and-stick tattoo.

Why was I suspected of starting the local rumor? Well, my Wisconsin reader had never heard the story until reading about it in my column. Then, some weeks later, the reader said, a woman working in the same factory came up with "something very important" to be inserted into the plant newsletter.

The important thing was a "Blue Star Acid" warning flier, worded just as I had described it.

Could I have unwittingly spawned the story in Wisconsin? It's not likely, considering that I quoted only a small part of an entire flier in the first column. Besides, the "Blue Star" story has done very well on its own, despite my debunking attempt.

Since the column appeared, I have received twenty-seven pieces of mail from several states and Canada documenting further "Blue Star Acid" scares. The letters contained either new versions of the same old flier or copies of local newspaper stories, quoting law-enforcement authorities, that debunk the rumors.

I've been sent fliers issued by day-care centers, schools, lodges, and churches. Many of them are reproduced almost verbatim from earlier warnings, sometimes superimposed on a new group's letterhead.

Most of the texts make heavy use of capital letters, underlining, and exclamation points, and they tend to include vague references like "The Valley Childrens Hospital" or "according to Police Authorities." The fliers often begin, "We have been informed," without stating who has informed whom. Many fliers use the phrase—in reference to drug pushers—that they hope to "cultivate new customers."

Channels of distribution include school and company newsletters, office bulletin boards, and even computer networks. Titles on typical fliers are "Blue Star Alert!" "Fatal Tattoo," and "Attention Parents!"

One flier sent to me from the Midwest begins, "The following notice is appearing in many offices and publications." What an understatement!

Unfortunately, several newspapers have printed such fliers without comment, assuming they were an official warning of some kind. These papers include the August 26, 1987, issue of the Griffin (Georgia) Daily News, the November 19, 1987, issue of the Governors Island Gazette, and the June 1988 issue of Oregon Education.

Newspapers that assigned reporters to investigate "Blue Star Acid" rumors all over the country, however, found no verification, and headlined their stories accordingly: "No Cause for Alarm" (Washington Post, June 2, 1988); "Only a Folk Tale" (Dubuque Telegraph-Herald, October 6, 1987); "Tattoo Tripped Up" (Chicago Sun-Times, May 20, 1987).

But folklorists, journalists, and police authorities all saying there is no epidemic of "Blue Star Acid" among children, does not convince everyone. In the same period I have received three letters from people asserting that the story must be true because blotter acid actually exists.

Two of these letters came from prisoners, who may

have a prejudiced view of police information; the third
letter merely claimed without evidence that "drug-laced
tattoos ARE NOT an urban legend."

OK, prove it, then. Blotter acid (which I KNOW
exists!) is not a "tattoo"; and tattoos or transfers are
what these fliers claim is running rampant in dozens of
communities. The designs on blotter acid cannot be
peeled off; merely handling these sheets is highly
unlikely to pose serious health hazards. There would be
very little profit potential in giving free LSD to
youngsters.

It's one thing to oppose (as I assure you, I do) sales of
illicit drugs and the personal and social problems such
drugs cause. But it's quite another matter to base your
opposition on scare tactics and fantasy, which is what
these ubiquitous "Blue Star Acid" fliers represent.

The most authoritative proof of the folkloric nature of
the "Blue Star Acid" fliers that I have found came not
from a folklorist, but from a drug expert. Recently I
spoke to William Hopkins, director of the Bureau of Research for the State of New York Division of Substance
Abuse Services, who described a statewide survey that
his unit conducted in February and March 1988 in which
the unit looked for problems with the stuff. A question-
naire was sent to 405 New York law-enforcement agencies after thousands of anonymous letters were circulated throughout the state suggesting that "Blue Star
Acid" was "an impending disaster." The survey asked
the agencies to report their cases involving LSD—particularly acid in the "Blue Star" form—during the period
1985 through 1987.

"And I'll bet you found very little "Blue Star Acid," I
said.

"Next to nothing—almost nothing at all!" Mr. Hopkins replied.

What "next to nothing" translates into in terms of statistics—for example, in 1987—was that out of the 405 law-enforcement agencies surveyed, 342 (84.4 percent) had no cases involving LSD of any type, and only 3 departments (1.0 percent) had more than twenty LSD cases. In the very few instances where LSD cases were reported, less than half involved a blue star or cartoon imprinted on absorbent paper. The figures for 1985 and 1986 were comparable.

The cautiously worded conclusion that Hopkins's office drew from the results of the survey was that these results "tend to support our initial impression that the anonymous letters warning about Blue Star LSD was a hoax and should be treated as such." In the cover letter transmitting the survey results, the advice furnished to the state's drug agencies was to "discourage the reprinting and circulation" of the fliers because "the rumored spread of LSD is generally unfounded."

A particular concern of drug-abuse officers, Hopkins told me, is that fliers of this kind could actually create a problem where none exists. Drug users may learn about "Blue Star Acid" from the fliers themselves and then begin to ask for it from their suppliers. Where there's demand, a supply can be created. Ironically, then, the "Blue Star Acid" fliers have the potential of bringing about the very situation that they purport to be fighting. So come on, folks. Please, stop duplicating and distributing these spurious notices.*

Although law-enforcement officials, journalists, and

---

*By the way, William Hopkins also has access to the finest collection of authentic blotter-acid artwork that I know of. He sent me a full-color reproduction of samples from his division's stash of captured sheets; there's just one Mickey Mouse and no blue stars among the many psychedelic and symbolic images.

folklorists continue to debunk the Blue Star acid rumor, as this book goes to press the fliers continue to proliferate and the rumor still spreads. In autumn 1988, I received copies of the by-now-familiar drug alert from readers in Massachusetts, Connecticut, Vermont, Wisconsin, Indiana, Delaware, Ohio, and Kentucky. In the New York–New Jersey area, the fliers became so widespread that the *New York Times* ran a story on December 9, 1988, debunking the rumor. (See also my letter responding to their story, published on December 24.)

In November and December, I received a flurry of calls from Alaska about the story, the first one coming from a woman in Fairbanks who was disturbed by a "Safety and Health Alert" notice that her first-grader brought home from school. Some Alaskan authorities assumed that Blue Star acid was a genuine problem in the lower Forty-eight, but merely a rumor (so far) in Alaska. Not so.

At around the same time, an employee of the U. S. Agency for International Development in Lima, Peru, saw virtually the same notice, written in Spanish, posted in the U.S. embassy and USAID offices. The Lima newspaper *La República* later picked up the warning and published an article cautioning parents against "estrella azul"—Blue Star acid.

Neither woman gave any credence to these apparently official warnings, though. Both had read about the Blue Star acid rumor in my 1984 book *The Choking Doberman,* and they knew that it was untrue.

Early in the new year, I received a call from David Mannweiler, columnist for the *Indianapolis News:* Blue Star acid rumors were still rife in that city, with fliers coming home from school with the kiddies. As Mannweiler quoted Captain Michael Sherman, head of the Indianapolis Police Department narcotics division, in his column on January 10: "We have not had that first seizure of this kind of transfer patches for LSD. I haven't received any concrete evidence that this has happened. We haven't found any of those transfers."

Where have I heard that kind of explanation before?

Are We Paranoid?

"Why do we tell such gruesome stories?" I am often asked. "Are Americans incurably morbid, or are we tortured by groundless fears?"

You don't have to be an urban folklorist to realize that there is, of course, no single answer to such a question. But we folklorists work from the premise that people's reasons for telling horror stories are often revealed by the details of the stories and by the contexts in which the stories are told. People who tell scary stories are not necessarily paranoid.

Some horror stories actually sound more like jokes, and people accept them for their entertainment value without objecting to unsavory details. Few listeners object to the implied suffering in legends about microwaved pets or exploding toilets, because these stories are often thought of as "just jokes."

Other stories are told deliberately to make a point. Legends about hidden assailants or poisoned Halloween candy are often cautionary tales and make the hearers feel uneasy, even if they know that the story is just an oral tradition.

Further examples of the latter type are two stories about accidental deaths that I have heard lately. Each describes death caused by a hazard unique to modern life.

The first one, which I call "The Fatal Tee," was told to my source by an acquaintance who lives in the East in an apartment overlooking a country club. The acquaintance had heard it from a classmate who claims to have read it in a newspaper. While the story's ostensible subject is golf, it deals in a general way with the danger of pesticides polluting the environment.

In the classmate's version of the story, an army officer took a four-day leave, planning to spend all the time playing golf at the very club that adjoined the acquaintance's apartment.

From the first day, the officer got into the habit of putting the tee into his mouth after he teed off, and leaving it there as he played the course. After two days of play, he began to feel sick; and on the fourth day, he dropped dead. The course had been sprayed so heavily with pesticides that sucking on the tee had caused the officer to ingest a fatal dose of poison.

My source says that after hearing the story, his acquaintance's classmate decided not to play at the club any longer, despite the convenience of living next door.

This story's conclusion is much like that in the legend I call "The Snake at the Discount Store," in which the teller vows never to shop in a certain store because of an unverified story that describes a poisonous snake sewn into the lining of an imported coat or blanket.

An interesting sidelight on "The Fatal Tee" story is that it apparently is based on an actual case that likely did receive press coverage. An article on pesticide dangers at golf courses in the November 1987 issue of *Audubon* magazine describes a golfer's death traced to exposure to a compound called Daconil (which eradicates brown spots on the turf) while playing at the same course. There is no mention in the article of sucking on a tee, and the man died two weeks after checking into a hospital. This incident occurred in 1982.

As it passed into the oral tradition, "The Fatal Tee" story became more specific in some details while slighting other facts that contribute less to the teller's reason for telling it.

The second story, "The Second Death," was told to me by a student of mine, who had heard it from a fellow student who was enrolled in a "Death and Dying" class at the University of Utah, where I teach.

The class toured a mortuary, and an employee there told a story that "one of our drivers heard had happened to a friend of his in the same kind of job."

The mortuary employee was sent out in a hearse to pick up the body of an elderly woman who had died in the night. While the employee was returning to the mortuary, he heard a gurgling noise in the back of the hearse.

At first, he thought it was merely the sound of an air bubble escaping from the corpse, which had been jostled about when the hearse drove over potholes in the road. But when the noise continued, the employee stopped the vehicle and went around to the back to check. He unzipped the body bag and found that the "corpse" was actually still alive. The bumpy ride had aroused the woman from a coma.

The employee immediately called a nearby hospital, relayed his location, and was instructed to drive toward the hospital. An ambulance would meet him en route, and the woman would be transferred to it for emergency treatment.

But in his excitement, the employee drove too fast, and the hearse collided with a vehicle in the other lane— the oncoming ambulance. In a twist worthy of O. Henry, the woman in the back of the hearse was killed.

A dead elderly woman . . . a revived corpse . . . a coincidental collision . . . a thirdhand anonymous source! These are definitely the stuff of urban legends. By itself, any of these details might be credible—but together, they give the story away as apocryphal. When told by a mortuary employee, the message seems to be: "Look what a weird business I'm in!"

Like "The Fatal Tee," the second-death story is based on irony. In both stories, procedures that are intended to be helpful—like pest control—become fatal instead. In both stories, deaths result from plausible causes—poisoning and an auto accident—but death comes about in implausible ways. And while one story is very nearly amusing and the other is indisputably morbid, they both warn us of the hazards of even the most helpful actions.

Who says urban legends are just jokes?

And here's a further example of a comical horror story that I call "Dental Death" as sent to me by a reader, followed by one more on the same theme as I heard it shortly afterwards:

Dear Professor:

I heard this one just this morning: A dentist was horrified to discover that one of his patients had died while he was working on his teeth. Fearing the consequences, he hoisted the man onto his shoulder and carried him down a flight of stairs to a restroom on the floor below. He left the corpse on a toilet and returned to his office.

Imagine his surprise when, about a half hour later, the door opened and in walked the "dead" man. It seems that in carrying the man down the stairs over his shoulder, the dentist inadvertently had given him CPR and brought him back to life.

M.M.
Newport Beach, California

Dear M.M.:

When I told that to my dentist, he said that it's a standard dental-school joke that if a patient dies in the chair you could dispose of him in this way. He hadn't heard about the CPR surprise, but he liked it.

A friend then told me a story he had heard regarding a dentist who lost two patients when he tried to put both under gas at the same time and work on them alternately. When he turned to tend to the first patient, who was reacting badly to anesthesia, he neglected the second one, and both died.

It looks like the trauma of dentistry touches both driller and drillee, so that horror legends circulate on both sides.

"The Last Kiss"

I know they have urban legends in Oz, but what about in New Zealand?

I suppose I had better explain.

"Oz" is the nickname that New Zealanders like to use for Australia. Many Aussies—or is it "Ozzies"—have sent me urban legends, but I've come across only a few from New Zealand. So, when I visited there in early 1988, I wondered if I would find legends similar to the American and Australian ones circulating in the land of Kiwis.

I found plenty of legends, some new and some recycled. These are scattered through this book according to their general topics. But first, some background.

It happened that my earlier book *The Choking Doberman* had arrived in New Zealand in a paperback edition at just about the time I did. Upon looking at the title legend, which I had traced to ancient European legends and documented as existing all over the United States, an executive of my New Zealand publisher told me that he had heard the same story in his health club in Auckland.

He proceeded to recount "The Choking Doberman," in which a burglar is discovered after a huge dog, having bitten off the intruder's fingers, goes into convulsions. A veterinarian extracts the fingers from the dog's throat, and the police find the intruder hiding in the house. The New Zealander's version supposedly happened in Wellington to a friend of the brother of the man in the gym.

That was just the first of many legends I heard there. Evidently word-of-mouth stories about bizarre incidents are as popular all over Down Under as they are throughout Up Over (or whatever our half of the planet should be called).

One New Zealander told me about three middle-aged ladies from his country who, while on holiday in the States, had suffered a most embarrassing experience in an elevator in Los Angeles (or was it Las Vegas?—he wasn't sure). While they were on a lift, a tall black man leading a big dog on a leash stepped on and said, "Sit."

The three women sat down and waited fearfully to have their money stolen or worse.

"Don't tell me," I interrupted. "The man was Reggie Jackson, but he was speaking to his dog, right?"

"Who's Reggie Jackson?" my informant said. "It was Lionel Richie, the pop singer. He *was* speaking to his dog, though. I heard it from this bloke who knows the bloke whose mother was one of the ladies."

I made a note that "The Elevator Incident," a common legend in the United States and England, is also known in New Zealand.

Then there was the Kiwi who told me about a bridegroom who abruptly called off his wedding at the end of the ceremony, telling all those assembled that the bride had slept with the best man the night before. The incident occurred in Hamilton, he said, or maybe Christchurch.

I hated to tell him that I have collected versions of the legend I call "The Bothered Bride" from all over the United States. In most American versions, however, the groom had slept with the maid of honor.

Every legend I heard had some tiny wee New Zealand twist to it. (New Zealanders, especially those on the South Island, say "tiny wee" a lot. It seems to be the settlers' Scottish background showing through.)

Now and then I also heard legends that sounded rare or local, such as the horror story of the man caught in "the Petone shingle crusher."

Petone is a city near Wellington, and "shingle" is gravel used for road surfacing. The crusher is a huge piece of machinery that makes little rocks out of big ones.

One day, I was told, a man became trapped in the Petone shingle crusher, and there was no way to dismantle it to free him. Whether they started the machine again or left it idling, the man would die.

So they called his wife to come over and kiss him goodby, gave him a heavy dose of painkillers, and sorrowfully restarted the machine.

Excuse me for feeling gleeful about hearing such a horrible story—but I had filed another version of "The Last Kiss" told to me back home in Salt Lake City a year or so ago, wondering if its very unlikely plot would turn out to be traditional. I traveled a long way to find an answer. When I got home, I united the two versions in the "Horrors, miscellaneous" folder.

The only difference between the accounts was that in the American one the man was trapped in a piece of steel-rolling equipment. Of course, neither the Kiwi nor American informants for these two stories knew anyone personally who witnessed the accident.

Hearing these legends, I felt right at home in New Zealand, even if they do drive on the left, place the hot water taps on the right, arrange numbers counterclockwise on the telephone dial, mount their light switches upside down, put salt in the shaker with one hole, and add spaghetti to their list of pizza toppings.

All those things are true and not urban legends, I assure you.

"The Message under the Stamp"

"I don't know whether wartime propaganda meets your criteria for legends or not," writes Lewis S. English of Wilmington, Delaware, sending me a story of wartime atrocity that he heard back in the 1940s.

Of course, it does. As it happens, that old archetype "the war story" has produced its share of urban legends, including the one Mr. English sent me—"The Message Under the Stamp."

During World War II, English served with the Merchant Marine on an oil tanker stationed in the Pacific. In 1943, his mother recounted in a letter a story that was going around about another sailor stationed in the Pacific.

The sailor was a regular, punctual letter writer, and his mother eagerly awaited his news from the Far East. But after a time, his letters suddenly stopped coming.

The mother was distraught. And she was well-nigh inconsolable after Navy authorities contacted her and reported that her son had been taken prisoner by the enemy.

The mother eventually received a letter from her son. He was confined to a Japanese prison camp, he said, but he was safe and was being treated well.

When the mother steamed the stamp off the envelope, though, she found a hidden message from him: "They've cut off my hands!"

"Right away I was suspicious of the story," English says. If the man's hands had been cut off, how was he able to write the letter, especially the secret message? And what prompted the woman to steam off the stamp?

Sure enough, while on leave a year later, he overheard

two men in a tavern talk about the war. One was telling the other about a man who had received such a letter from his son, a prisoner of war in Germany.

This time, the Gestapo was said to have cut off the prisoner's hands after trying unsuccessfully to extract top-secret information from him.

The story meets all the criteria for an urban legend. It's an unusually tidy tale, it was passed on orally, variations were heard in different times and places. And its verity depends on several questionable details.

I've heard versions of the story that try to explain what led the mother to remove the stamp. In these versions, the son suggests in his letter that she should steam off the stamp for "little Alf" or "little Johnny" to add to his collection. But there is no little Alf or Johnny in the family. Nor are there any stamp collectors. The mother finally realizes that this is a clue and steams the stamp off the envelope, finding the message.

Given its wartime setting, it's not surprising that one variation pushes the origin of the story back from the Second World War to the First.

In his autobiography *Exit Laughing,* published in 1941, journalist and humorist Irwin S. Cobb described a "sad little tale which sprang up 24 years ago and now is enjoying a popular revival. It's the heart-moving one about the German housewife who writes a letter to her kinfolks in America that everything is just dandy in the Vaterland but suggests that the stamp be soaked off the envelope for a souvenir, and when the stamp is soaked off there underneath are the words, 'We are starving.' I don't know how we'd get along without that standby every time war breaks out in Europe," Cobb added. He clearly disbelieved the heart-moving tale.

It's interesting that between the wars, the story seems to turn inside out. When told during World War I, the story condemned the conditions endured by civilians.

But during World War II, it accused the enemy of mistreating their prisoners.

In debunking "The Message under the Stamp," I worked out all the fallacies in the story except one, which several readers of my column were quick to grasp. The major flaw in the story is that during World War II all soldiers and prisoners of war were granted free mailing privileges. Stamps were not required for these postings—so there were none to be steamed off letters "for little Johnny's collection," revealing mysterious messages.

The only mystery remaining is: Why did so many people believe the story?

Probably because the legend is so intriguing that we fail to question it closely.

"The Fatal Boot"

Dear Professor—
Might I suggest that you consider a companion
column, "Rural Legends," to be published alternately?
                                        Carl Frith
                                        Sylmar, California

Dear Carl—
That's a great idea. Several readers have sent me old
stories that I would love to tell, but that scarcely fit my
idea of urban lore.
The premise of this column is that the ancient art of
oral storytelling continues in the present, with updated
subject matter. So while I cannot simply alternate
archaic and contemporary legends, I will devote an
occasional column to a timeworn traditional legend that
continues to circulate in new variations.
I begin with the story of "The Fatal Boot," an
American frontier legend which three readers have sent
me recently.
J.E. of Raleigh, North Carolina, heard this version of
the story out West:
"There is a rancher or cowboy who stomps the head
of a rattlesnake after stunning it with a rope or quirt.
The man sickens and dies within days.
"The man's son or nephew inherits the boots, and he
too soon sickens and dies. Then yet another male
relative begins to wear the boots, then dies. And so it
goes until someone takes a good look at the heels on
the boots and discovers the rattlesnake's fangs broken
off and still seeping venom!"
T.R. of San Antonio, Texas, says that he heard "The

*Fatal Boot" from his stepgrandfather, who was born in
Kentucky. This version concerns hunting boots rather
than cowboy boots. Three brothers are killed by the
snake's venom beginning with the oldest and
proceeding to the youngest, just as adventures occur to
three siblings in sequence in European fairy tales.*

*Speaking of the number of the deaths, T.R.
remarked, "That has to be a record for one snake."*

*K.H. of Pasadena, California, received the story in a
letter from a friend in New Mexico. A cowboy is killed
by the rattler biting through the boot, and returns from
a day of herding, dead in the saddle. It is assumed that
he died of a heart attack.*

*In this variation, the cowboy's older son dies next.
But the boots are too large for the younger son, so he
survives. Eventually the old boots are examined closely,
and the lethal rattlesnake fang is discovered.*

*The variations in these three "Fatal Boot" stories, as
well as the neat pattern of three generations or three
brothers dying, mark this amazing yarn as folklore.*

*To check whether rattlesnake venom actually remains
potent for years, I consulted Laurence M. Klauber's
definitive two-volume work* Rattlesnakes: Their Habits,
Life Histories, and Influence on Mankind *(2nd edn.,
University of California Press, 1972), which tells all
there is to know about rattlesnakes.*

*Debunking "The Fatal Boot," Klauber examines both
the structure of rattlesnake fangs and data from some
actual experiments made with skin scratches from dried
fangs. He contends that the legend wildly exaggerates
the slim possibility of being poisoned from a broken
fang of a rattler. The flaw in the story, he writes, is "the
belief that the point of a fang could contain enough
dried venom to do serious damage."*

*Klauber collected dozens of versions of "The Fatal
Boot" legend from several Western states. But the*

earliest American example he found surfaced in the East, appearing in St. Jean de Crèvecoeur's book Letters from an American Farmer *published in 1782. There are also foreign antecedents for the story.*

An updated American tall-tale version, collected in Texas, brings "The Fatal Boot" into the realm of modern folklore. A cowboy drives his pickup truck over a rattler, and one of the snake's fangs becomes embedded in one of the tires. The driver takes the truck to a garage, where two mechanics die after being scratched by the lethal fang.

Folklore slithers on!

"The Graveyard Wager"

Here's another old horror legend remembered by a reader. This one was sent to me by Vonnie Shepherd of Bloomington, Indiana, who writes, "I grew up hearing this story in a small town in central Kentucky:

"Several girls were sleeping over at one girl's home while the parents were away. After the lights were out, they started talking about the recent burial of an old man in the nearby cemetery. A rumor was going around that the man had been buried alive and had been heard trying to claw his way out.

"One girl laughed at the idea, so they dared her to go out and visit the grave. As proof that she had gone, she was to drive a stake into the earth above the grave.

"They sent their friend off on her errand and shut off the lights again, expecting her to return right away.

"But an hour passed, and then another, without any sign of the girl. The others lay awake, gradually growing terrified. Morning came, and she still hadn't returned.

"Later that day, the girl's parents arrived home, and parents and friends went together to the cemetery.

"They found the girl lying on the grave—dead. When she squatted down to push the wooden stake into the ground, she drove it through the hem of her skirt. When she tried to stand up and couldn't, she thought the dead man had grabbed hold of her—and she died instantly of fright."

This is a nicely modernized version of a narrative that is so old and widespread that we folklorists even have a number for it.

In *The Types of the Folktale,* a standard index of folk-narrative plots, the story is listed as "Type 1676B, Clothing Caught in Graveyard." Usually, though, we folklorists just call it "The Graveyard Wager."

Variations on the basic theme have been recorded since the Middle Ages in Europe and have migrated to much of the world. It's one of those stories that no one really believes—would anyone actually die "of fright"? But the story keeps going around, nevertheless.

In some versions, a soldier bets that he has the courage to remain overnight in a cemetery, but he dies from fright after plunging his sword through his long cloak. In others, a drunken man drives his dagger through the hem of his overcoat. Sometimes the person visiting the grave is told to drive a nail into a wooden cross, and the nail goes through part of his garment.

In a few versions the graveyard visitor suffers just a good scare and a cold night in the cemetery, rather than death.

Vonnie Shepherd's version updates the story so it depicts girls at a sleepover party. It is convincing: a rumor about a man buried alive is the kind of thing teen-agers will talk about once the lights are out.

The references to a person buried alive and a stake plunged into a grave, though, make it sound as if these girls have been reading too much Edgar Allen Poe or watching vampire films.

A more elaborate update of "The Graveyard Wager" story was sent to me recently by G. L. Maclean, a professor at the University of Natal, Republic of South Africa. He says he first heard it twenty or thirty years ago, when university students there were still required to wear academic gowns at their evening meals.

"One evening at dinner," Professor Maclean wrote, "three medical students at the University of Cape Town were talking about a body they had seen lying on the mortuary slab at the hospital adjacent to the medical school.

"They dared each other to take a knife, sneak into the mortuary in the dark, and plunge the knife into the corpse. One student accepted the dare, and the others waited outside while he went in.

"A few minutes after he entered the mortuary, they heard a scream, and fled in terror.

"The next morning their colleague was found lying dead on the floor, the knife firmly plunged into the corpse, and also through the long sleeve of his black academic gown. The fright of thinking he was being pulled back by the corpse caused him to die of a heart attack."

Professor Maclean suggests that by substituting a white lab coat for the academic gown, the story might fit medical students anywhere in the world.

Although I have never encountered such a form of "The Graveyard Wager," I won't be surprised if I do. This traditional story has successfully made the leap into urban legendhood.

And, as several readers pointed out to me, "The Graveyard Wager" was also the inspiration for an episode of the popular television series "Twilight Zone." I am endebted to Michael A. Garoutte of Belmont, California, for sending me photocopies of pages 219–220 of *The Twilight Zone Companion* (New York: Bantam, 1982), which indicate that the episode was originally broadcast on October 27, 1961, and included Lee Marvin in the role of the man found dead beside the grave with his knife stuck through his coat and into the earth above a grave.

"The Snake in the Strawberry Patch"

In my continuing crusade to promote truth and de-bunk error—at least insofar as error is masked as urban legend—I considered the story told in the following letter from Mrs. B.G. of Raleigh, North Carolina.

Dear Professor:

I am sending you a tale I heard at the beauty shop. This supposedly happened to a friend of a friend, etc., but nobody could tell who the people involved were. It sounds totally fantastic. Please research this for me, as I have a bet on that this didn't happen.

A woman fed her small baby some milk and then took the child with her to a nearby field to pick strawberries. The child was asleep, so she pulled the car very close to the area in which she was picking. It was a fairly cool day, and she left the windows open, both for ventilation and in order to hear.

A snake crawled into the car and down the child's throat after the milk and strangled the child. Snakes are known to do this, so the story goes. What do you think?

Dear Reader:

I think you win your bet; this account has several hallmarks of an old rural snake legend gone suburban, if not literally urban. Besides, I heard the story a couple of other times this past summer [1987] from your region, as well as picking up echoes of it elsewhere.

There is a connection here to an old legend called the "bosom serpent." In this legend, a snake enters the body, usually in the form of unhatched eggs, and injures the person. Typically, the smell of milk is said to be

*used to lure the hatched snake out of the body. In the
updated version you heard, the lure of milk is what
attracts the snake into the baby's mouth to begin with.*

*A few of the old "bosom serpent" stories found in
Europe describe a field worker falling asleep during a
lunch break. A snake creeps into the person's open
mouth, taking up residence in the stomach until lured
forth.*

*As for recent parallels to Mrs. B.G.'s story, in June,
1987, William A. Dennis, Managing Editor of the
Henderson, North Carolina,* Daily Dispatch *reported
the same strawberry-patch legend to me. He wrote: "A
friend of mind who operates a pick-your-own
strawberry farm was quite disturbed because someone
had started a rumor about an incident at her farm."*

*It turned out to be the snake and baby story—said to
have happened just thirty miles or so up Interstate 85
from the Raleigh-Durham area, in the town of
Henderson. The only variations were that the child was
said to be left in an infant seat, instead of a car, at the
end of the strawberry row, and that the snake had either
entered its mouth or strangled it from the outside.*

*Dennis found no evidence that such a thing had
happened and advised his friend "that she shouldn't
worry about it." He wrote to me expressing strong
disbelief in the incident, though he hadn't gone so far as
to bet on it.*

*About a month later I got a call from a journalist a
little further up the pike (still Interstate 85, actually) in
Richmond, Virginia. She was taken aback when I
finished her strawberry-patch story for her after hearing
her tell just a few opening details. I told her to call Bill
Dennis down in Henderson to learn more about the
snake story, and to say hello for me.*

*Whether she called Henderson or not, this
reporter—Eileen Barrett of the* Richmond News

Leader—*did contact a snake expert at the University of Richmond who told her, "Snakes don't drink milk. They're carnivorous. Snakes wouldn't even be attracted to milk, so that tale is crazy and totally beyond the known biology of snakes."*

Meanwhile in mid-July I got an interesting letter from E.S. of Torrance, California. She remembered a frightening story from her high school days in the early 1970s about a young couple leaving their sleeping baby in its crib. A large snake they kept for a pet crept into the nursery and devoured the baby. A really large snake, I suppose.

But, E.S. added, just a couple of weeks ago she heard virtually the same snake/baby story told by a checker in a supermarket, except that in this instance the couple arrived back home just in time to rescue the baby.

The latest non-news of this event—as I am sure it is—appeared in a United Press International story, datelined Moscow, that ran in my local newspaper on August 20, 1987. Paraphrasing from the Communist Party newspaper Pravda, *UPI described an eleven-year-old girl "known only by her first name, Matanet," who fell asleep in a tomato patch where she was working one hot day and suffered a two-foot-long snake creeping down her throat and choking her.*

Doctors, the story concluded, in the Soviet Caucasian republic of Azerbaijan, where the event allegedly occurred, were able to remove the snake. I'll bet I know how they did it.

Speaking of bets, I'd also be willing to put money on my belief that this is nothing more than a Russian village version of the old "bosom serpent" legend that somehow came to a Moscow reporter's ear and thence crept into print during a slow news week in the summer of '87.

"The Mutilated Bride"—a Tourist Horror Story

Although the Japanese are enthusiastic tourists today, their xenophobic past is still reflected by an urban legend they tell.

I got this one from Professor Robert Bethke of the University of Delaware, who came across it in a folklore term paper written by Sachiko Shudo, a Japanese-born student there. Shudo recounts the legend as she heard it from a cousin:

"A Japanese newlywed couple went to Europe for their honeymoon. In Paris, the wife spent hours shopping for clothes. At one trendy boutique, she wanted to try on several dresses. So the husband waited outside the dressing room.

"A long while passed and the wife didn't come out. So the husband began to wonder what was keeping her. He inquired of one of the shopgirls; she checked, then told him, to his surprise, that the dressing room was empty.

"His initial reaction was that his wife was playing a practical joke on him. So he went back to their hotel. But she was not there. Still thinking it a joke, he sat down to wait for her.

"As the hours passed, he became more and more anxious. And when she had not returned by the following morning, he was distraught. He called the police, the boutique, and all the Paris hospitals. There was no trace of her anywhere.

"The police did what they could, but after three weeks, there wasn't a single clue. Exhausted and in despair, the husband returned to Japan.

"Five years passed. And then the husband, finally having gotten over the loss of his wife, received a phone call from a friend who had just returned from a trip to the Philippines. The friend told him that he had seen the wife in Manila—as the featured attraction of a freak show.

"When the husband asked how his beautiful bride could possibly be exhibited this way, the friend explained, with great sadness, that her arms and legs had been mutilated."

How was the wife removed from the dressing room?

In one variation, Shudo says, the wife is kidnaped through a trap door in the dressing-room floor. In another, the setting is a restaurant in New York City, and the bride is abducted in a restroom.

Why does this story appeal to the Japanese? Shudo points out that the country has only one race of people, who for centuries were intentionally isolated from the rest of the world. While the isolationism has passed, distrust of foreigners may linger.

Shudo mentions a Japanese children's song called "The Red Shoes," which was popular in the years before World War II. One line goes, "A girl wearing red shoes was taken away by an *ijinsan* [foreigner]."

Also, Shudo says, Japanese parents customarily discipline their children by telling them that they will be sold to a circus if they don't behave. Circuses in Japan are run by foreigners, Shudo says, and most of them do have freak shows.

I would add to these speculations that the mention of the Philippines as the place where the mutilated bride is found may reveal the tellers' antagonism toward Filipinos (Japanese forces occupied the Philippines during the war). Or it may reveal their guilty feelings.

Tourist horror tales like this one are told elsewhere, of course. The one I've heard most often describes a woman traveler, usually from Scandinavia or the United States, who disappears from her tour group while traveling in Turkey. Several days later her clothes turn up at a bazaar in Istanbul. What has happened to the woman is never discovered.

Another one describes a couple backpacking in the Far East. One morning, according to the story, they are found dead in their sleeping bags; their heads have been cut off and switched with each other.

And we worry about lost luggage!

2

Automobile Legends

"The Smashed VW Bug"

A Columbus, Ohio, dentist writes to me that he heard of an accident on the Autobahn (the German freeway system) when he was stationed at a military dental clinic in Germany in 1976. The horrible details that came to him via oral tradition were never confirmed by any press reports he saw.

"Whadaya think?" wrote the dentist, a specialist in prosthodontics. (There may be something about urban legends that makes even highly trained professionals adopt a folksy tone.) Here's his story:

Late one night, two tractor trailers collided head on at a very high speed. Nobody witnessed the collision. The force of the impact welded or fused the two cabs together, killing the drivers. After the bodies were pried out, the wrecks were towed away in one piece to a wrecking yard.

A couple of weeks later, the cabs were pulled apart to salvage the scrap metal. Between them, they found a very thin Volkswagen Bug, flattened by the force of the collision, as well as the unrecognizable remains of what was assumed to be the driver of the car.

This certainly sounds like an urban legend, because I have three other versions of it, with significant variations. One sent to me from Arizona says that the accident occurred on the Interstate between Phoenix and Los Angeles. A terrible smell at the wrecking yard some weeks after the accident led salvagers to separate the fused cabs, using four huge tow trucks. Between the cabs, they found a VW Bug with four corpses crushed inside.

Another smashed-Bug story from San Francisco says that the two trucks were in the mountains, one going up and the other down. The accident occurred when the downward-moving vehicle began to pass a car.

These trucks, after the collision, were left by the side of the road, still fused together, until local residents complained of a smell. After bulldozers separate the cabs, a VW Bug with—count them if you can—*five* corpses was found flattened between them.

This is probably as great as the tragedy can become, since I doubt that more than five people can be squeezed into a Beetle that is actually driven on a highway, even in a legend. Funny that nobody hearing the stories ever seems to question the idea that four or five motorists are missing and not searched for sooner along their route of travel.

Incidentally, I've heard another, slightly different story about a horrible VW accident. An Iowa resident told me that on a narrow, foggy road, a trucker driving a giant eighteen-wheeler stopped for coffee and walked around his rig to check the tires. To his shock, he discovered a VW Bug stuck to his right front fender; the occupants inside the Bug were dead. Apparently, he hadn't even noticed the accident while driving. This one, it seems to me, is related to another story (discussed in the following section) about a small child that a drunken motorist finds embedded in the grill of his car.

I have sent accounts of these smashed-bug stories to

several government and private traffic safety and accident offices. While safety officials say they have heard similar stories, they have been unable to confirm that any of them actually occurred. The accidents in which smaller cars were crushed by collisions with trucks, say officials, never involve the wreckage of the vehicles being left for days or weeks before being checked for human remains.

Gruesome automobile accidents surely do happen, and the larger vehicles nearly always suffer less damage than smaller ones. Yet—up to now—I have found no verifiable accounts of crushed VW Bugs like the ones in these stories. The smashed-Bug legends seem to be exaggerated tales about the general dangers of driving— especially in compact cars. They put particular emphasis on the car model whose nicknames derive from the creatures that commonly are crushed on car windshields and radiators—"bugs" and "beetles."

"The Body on the Car"

The question is: Was Ann Landers taken in by a horrifying urban legend? Many of her readers—at least, those who are also *my* readers—seem to think she was, and they wrote to ask my opinion.

People from coast to coast, plus a few from abroad, sent me Ann's column dated September 24, 1986. In it, a reader relates a tragic story of drunken driving.

It seems that a woman's husband came home from work at 2:00 A.M., cockeyed drunk. He managed to get up for work in time, though, and began pulling his car out of the garage, into the driveway. His wife realized that he had forgotten to take his lunch and began running out to give it to him. She got "as far as the porch and fainted." The husband got out of the car to see what was the matter. There, embedded in the grill of his car, was the lifeless body of an eight-year-old girl.

The letter was signed "Still Horrified in Portland."

Ann Landers replied, "What a grisly story! Bone-chilling, to say the least. I hope it makes an impact on drivers who chance 'a few' and don't think it will make any difference."

I also hope it has an impact, but not because I think it's true. Until someone can offer conclusive proof that this cautionary tale really happened, I'll have to say that that's just what it is: a mini–morality play that got started up and gained currency because it demonstrates our rising concern with the dangers of drunken driving.

There are a number of questionable elements here. For one thing, there are no corroborating details of time or place. The letter writer simply begins, "I would like to tell you about another woman who had a nervous breakdown because of the same problem"—i.e., her husband's drunken driving, discussed in a previous Ann Landers column.

I called Mothers against Drunk Driving (MADD) in Houston, Texas, which keeps track of alcohol-related accidents. They told me that they assumed the story to be true—but even they could provide no further details.

Yet, in April 1987—seven months after the Ann Landers's column—I received a letter from a Covina, California, reader who had heard a variation of "The Body on the Car" told at a Students against Drunk Driving (SADD) presentation. In this version, the wife goes out for the morning newspaper and discovers the "embedded" body, while her husband, still passed out from the night before, is lying on the living-room couch. Either other versions of the story had been circulating, or the one in the Ann Landers column was acquiring variations from repetitions.

Another letter sent in the spring of '87 reported "The Body on the Car" told in Carbondale, Illinois. One slight variation here: she was a seven-year-old girl.

The notion implied in all versions that a young child was out on the streets at 2:00 A.M. seems farfetched. We're asked to believe that the girl became integrated with the car's grillwork (like the VW Bug in the preceding legend) instead of being hurled through the air, which is what normally happens in a head-on collision with a pedestrian. We're also supposed to accept the idea that the driver was so drunk, he didn't notice that he'd just hit a young child—nor did anyone else on the road— as he drove around town with her riding on his car like a hood ornament. Yet, this semiconscious man was still alert enough to park his car in the garage without incident.

The fainting woman is another familiar touch of urban-legend fantasy, as is the unlikely detail that the driver was up bright and early for work the day after his adventurous night.

One reader sending me the clip added the footnote, "Please, Ann, tell us it's just a story." Several others sent me copies of their own letters to Ann Landers, tipping her off that it smelled like a legend to them. But as far as I know, there has been no disclaimer for this one in any subsequent Ann Landers column.

I suppose I cannot blame Ann; she really wasn't the first to spread the story. A reader wrote to me some weeks before the Ann Landers column (letter dated August 27, 1986) that she had heard it told in Santa Monica, California. At this time, it was attributed to the traditional "friend of a friend" and had the variation of the man himself making the discovery. He goes to a party, where he gets drunk. His host and hostess try to make him stay over, but he insists on driving home. In the morning, he returns to his car and sees "draped across the hood . . . a dead body."

The day after most of the above discussion appeared in my column (in late March 1987), Professor Malcolm K. Shuman of the Museum of Geoscience at Lousiana State University in Baton Rouge wrote. He remembers reading a story very similar to the legend while browsing through the comic-book collection of a younger cousin some thirty years ago ("ca. 1953, give or take a couple of years").

As Professor Shuman recalls the horror-comic episode, a man driving on a highway (fast, but not under the influence) is well aware that he has struck a pedestrian but decides to ignore the accident and drive on. But in the next town, an angry crowd stops him when they see the dead pedestrian caught between bumper and grill. So the hit-and-run element of the story seems to have existed much earlier than the 1980s, although the ultimate source of all details in "The Body on the Car" is still obscure.

Considering all these references to "The Body on the Car"—yes, folks, I do believe that Ann Landers fell for a legend, although her motives were only the best. After all, the reason so many grisly urban legends like this one continue to circulate is that they teach us worthwhile lessons in highly dramatic ways. The warning contained in "The Body on the Car" story should certainly be heeded, but that does not mean that the incident is true.

Moral(s): Don't drink and drive. But don't believe all the scare stories you hear, either.

"Fear of Frying"

One reason people give for not buckling their automobile seat belts is fear of the belt itself.

What keeps them from buckling up, they explain, is the dread of being trapped by the belt in a burning or submerged car. They say they have heard of many such accidents in which needless deaths occurred because victims could not unbuckle their seat belts and escape the danger.

This fear, authorities on the subject tell me, is largely unwarranted. But it lives on, perpetuated by what I call the "Doomed by Their Seat Belt" or "Fear of Frying" stories, which circulate in the manner of urban legends.

In a study conducted at the University of North Carolina in 1981, for example, a typical excuse given for not wearing seat belts was this one: "I've seen too many people burn up because they couldn't get out."

But Dr. B. J. Campbell, director of the University's Highway Safety Research Center, notes that this claim has little, if any, basis in fact.

"This myth of being trapped in a burning car remains, yet no scientific study has ever shown this to be true, Campbell says. "In fact, a person wearing a seat belt and involved in a fiery crash is more likely to be conscious and able to escape than someone not wearing a seat belt."

When my home state of Utah passed a law in 1986 requiring motorists to wear seat belts, similar fears were expressed. Opponents of the law offered unsubstantial references to "people I know who would have died in a burning wreck if they had been wearing seat belts."

When the Wisconsin state senate approved a manda-

tory seat-belt bill in 1987, the *Milwauke Journal* referred
to one such story as folklore in reporting citizens' reac-
tions to the proposed law.

"I don't want to be confined in anything like that," the
Journal quoted one woman as saying. It then reported
that she justified her fear by "telling an urban legend she
heard years ago of five bridesmaids killed when they
couldn't get out of a burning automobile."

Having heard vague references to similar shocking
deaths, I wrote to several automobile-safety agencies,
asking if there is any truth to the "Doomed by Their Seat
Belts" story.

All of the agencies emphatically denied that the stories
were true.

B. Grace Hazzard, an aptly named information-man-
agement specialist for the National Highway Traffic
Safety Administration, replied, "There are some very
few instances in which people who were wearing safety
belts suffered injury or death in unusual kinds of accidents, but there is overwhelming evidence on the other
side of the numbers of people whose lives have been
saved because they were buckled up." According to this
agency, less than one-half of 1 percent of all injury-pro-
ducing collisions involve fire or submersion.

The National Transportation Safety Board, another
government agency that promotes seat-belt use, sent me
a detailed study published in 1986 entitled "The Performance of Lap Belts in 26 Frontal Crashes." I warn you
that if you look up this technical tome in the documents
section of a major library, the illustrations of wrecks and
the descriptions of injuries are awful.

The study shows that while the consequences of auto
accidents are truly frightening, the fear of burning or
drowning as a result of wearing a safety belt should be
among the least of our worries. There is little chance that
a seat-belt wearer can be trapped by the belt. And in all

the most likely forms of car accidents, seat belts are life-savers.

Robert B. Overend, editor of *Traffic Safety* magazine published by the National Safety Council, echoed the comments of the other authorities. But he also called my attention to a device called "The Life Hammer," introduced recently by a West German manufacturer.

The Life Hammer, a combination hammer and cutting tool, is designed to cut through a jammed safety belt and smash a car window in order to help passengers escape. The market for the device is obviously people who fear being trapped in a car wreck by a seat belt.

This may be the first time a new product has been designed in direct response to an urban legend.

There is some good news about the "Doomed by Their Seat Belts" legend: it appears that fewer and fewer people are believing it. A Gallup poll survey, released in October 1987, showed that seat-belt use in the United States has quadrupled during the last five years. In 1987, 65 percent of those polled said they wore seat belts, versus just 17 percent in 1982.

Perhaps the fear of frying is finally subsiding.

"The Lost Wreck"

A good story can remain for decades, even centuries, in the collective memory, changing as it passes from generation to generation to suit different times and places.

Sometimes you can dig beneath a legend's modern veneer to discover its ancient ancestor.

Take the legend called "The Lost Wreck," which I know best from a version that circulates in Canada. It's a legend in which an old story is buried—literally—within a new one.

A clipping of the story that appeared in the *Edmonton Journal* on December 15, 1985, was sent to me by Professor John Johansen of the Department of English at Camrose (Alberta) Lutheran College. The story, dateline Jasper (Alberta), is headlined: "Miette Skeleton Mystery As Real As Mountain Mist."

Sounds like old news already? You ain't heard nuthin' yet.

According to the news article, a resident of Jasper, "who preferred to remain nameless," tells that "a friend of a friend heard about a gruesome discovery made by a work crew widening the road to Miette Hot Springs over the summer."

While on a lunch break, the story goes, members of a work crew were idly shoving boulders over the edge of the steep road when they suddenly heard the sound of a rock hitting metal.

It turned out that buried among the jagged rocks of the roadside was a wrecked old car with 1950s Canadian license plates. Inside, still looking straight ahead, were the skeletons of four unfortunate passengers.

Local police—named as Chief Dumpleton and Staff

Sergeant Rumple—were quoted in the 1985 news story denying that any such discovery had been made. But I didn't need Dumpleton and Rumple to tell me that this was a very old legend, since I'd heard that clang of rock upon metal somewhere before. "The Fatal Wreck" seems to be a modern version of a Norwegian story from the nineteenth century.

There's a good translation of the story in Reidar Th. Christiansen's book *Folktales of Norway* (Chicago: University of Chicago Press, 1964), where it is entitled "The Church Found in the Woods."

The time of the original story is the Middle Ages, during the period when the bubonic plague ("Black Death") was ravaging Europe. And the setting, Christiansen writes, "is always a remote valley which the Black Death had struck with overwhelming force."

The buried object in the older story isn't a car, of course. It's a church.

Here's how the Norwegian legend begins:

"Once there was a hunter who was out shooting grouse. It must have been a long time ago, for he was using a bow and arrow. He caught sight of a bird sitting in a tree and shot at it, but a strange clang was heard as though the arrow had struck a metal object. The hunter went over to see what it was, and underneath some huge trees stood an ancient church."

The hunter has discovered the site of a village apparently completely wiped out by the plague. The metal his arrow had struck was the old churchbell.

How did this story of long ago and far away move to Canada?

I suspect that it was retold by Norwegian immigrants in Alberta, then updated to describe a forgotten auto accident in the mountains.

It just goes to show: You can't keep a good story down!

"The Arrest"

Dear Professor:

This was told to me by a guy from Torrington, Connecticut.

A man was driving home late one evening going south on I–91. He had taken several drinks earlier, and this was so obvious that he was soon pulled over.

As the state cop approached the car, an accident occurred in a northbound lane, so the cop told him to get out of the car and wait. The cop crossed the median to see if he could be of any help.

The drunk waited a while, and then decided the hell with it. He hopped in the car and took off home. There he told his wife to tell the police, if they should call, that he had been home all night, as sober as a judge.

The next morning the doorbell rang, and when he answered it, two state cops were standing there, including the one who had stopped him. Naturally, he claimed he had been home all night. "Just ask my wife," he said.

His wife backed up the story, but the cops asked if they could look in the garage. The man, not sure what was going on, said "Sure." And when they opened the garage, there was the police cruiser, its lights still flashing.

> *John Ruckes*
> *Branford, Conn.*

Gullible Reader:

A new urban legend often seems to become popular simultaneously in different locations. Your story, which I call "The Arrest," demonstrates how this happened in the space of a few months recently.

Even without the proof furnished by two earlier versions of this tale that I heard—supposedly it happened in other locales—I would have suspected this one to be a legend. It has just the right mix of believability, irony, and humor to suggest that it's a "true" story that's too good to be true (which is not a bad definition of "urban legend").

Ruckes's letter is dated July 14, 1986, but I have a cousin of "The Arrest" on file from the Washington Post *column "Bob Levey's Washington" of April 7, 1986. Levey heard that the motorist had been pulled over by the police in Fairfax County, Virginia. It was said that the cruiser found in the man's garage still had the motor running.*

The police spokesman Levey consulted, however, denied any knowledge of the event, except in the form of a story he had heard going around some eighteen months before. As another police authority sagely commented, "Certain stories develop, and they seem to get a life of their own."

I've practically based my whole career on that principle.

A version of the same legend was sent to me in mid-May 1986 by Suzanne Timbers of Henley-on-Thames, England. It's full of wonderfully specific details.

The driver's car is a Ford Escort, and the incident was alleged to have happened "down the Bath Road in Reading." When the first driver gets home, in the English variation, he has a couple more drinks so he can honestly claim he drank after driving. The police arrive the same day to discover their own cruiser—also a Ford Escort—in the garage.

In September 1986 I received two further versions of "The Arrest" from Gainesville, Florida, and Ottawa

(Ontario), Canada. Both writers recalled having seen the story in a local newspaper, and both letters expressed some skepticism about the truth of the tale. "Something tells me you may have heard the story before," wrote the Canadian; and "You gotta admit it sounds unlikely," commented the Floridian. Right you are, both of you!

"The Unstealable Car"

I thought this story, which I had heard from just one person, sounded too good to be true, so I asked readers if they had heard it. It reminded me of the legends about people who have neighbors involved with organized crime, who are able to retrieve some valuable stolen property for them just by making a phone call.

A student in Oregon had sent my original version of "The Unstealable Car." He had heard it told about someone's lovingly restored Corvette.

A man has this classic sports car that he labored for years to restore to mint condition. He keeps it parked in his garage with the wheels on cardboard sheets, taking it out only on special occasions and in perfect weather.

Fearful of thieves, he devises a foolproof way to secure his treasure. He has thick steel staples sunk into the concrete of the garage floor, and he attaches the car using heavy chains passed through the staples and around the car's frame and secured with several locks.

The car is thus parked and locked, facing into the garage, and covered with a tarp.

The next time he removes the tarp preparing to drive his sports car, he finds the vehicle still solidly chained down and locked—but now facing outward. Under a wiper blade is this note: "If we want this car, we'll take it."

The lesson: No matter how we contrive to foil thieves, the true professionals among them can easily outwit us. And even thieves take pride in their work and have a sense of humor about it.

The first part of the story, I suppose, is believable enough. But the second part depends on two suspicious twists. Would thieves go to the trouble of bypassing such safeguards just to shift the car's position? And would they risk capture by leaving such a note?

Following my query in the column, several people in the Midwest sent me versions of "The Unstealable Car." Each was a little different from the others, and although all of the respondents had been told that the story was true, the sources were merely friends of friends. None of them sent me reliable evidence of the story's authenticity—a copy of the note, say, or a news clipping describing the event.

V.R. of Hobart, Indiana, wrote that she distrusted the story, when she heard it from an English professor at Purdue University a year ago. The teacher claimed to know someone who knew the person to whom it happened.

In this version, a visitor from the South leaves his fancy sports car overnight on a dead-end street in the Gary-Hammond, Indiana, area, because the person he is visiting has no garage. He parks the car at the end of the street, closely surrounded by other cars. In the morning, he finds his car turned around, with the note on the windshield.

But R.W., in the same region of Indiana, recounted a version of the story told by an insurance agent who declined to insure R.W.'s new Corvette because he lacked a garage for it. This time the sports car was said to have been parked tightly between two other vehicles, plus chained down solidly to heavy staples in the concrete paving. All to no avail, of course, since all three cars are rearranged overnight with the locks reclosed, and the usual note is attached.

A third reader in the same region located the incident precisely in lot No. 40 of the Inland Steel Company at the East Chicago Works. He said that the event supposedly took place "back in the 1970's."

Each day this Corvette owner parked his car in the last row of the lot, chained it to a guard rail, and set a burglar alarm. Coming out of work one day, he found the car still in place, but with the chains and locks lying on the front seat along with a note, "If we want it, we'll take it."

Since these versions come from the northern Indiana-Illinois area, they may stem from an actual incident in the region. But none has come to my attention in the course of my research.

M.R., reading my column in the *Milwaukee Journal,* knew a variant attributed to the region. A friend in Chicago had heard it from someone who supposedly lives in the neighborhood where it happened.

In this version, yet another Corvette is parked each day in the street, locked and safeguarded by seven different alarm systems. But despite these precautions, one morning the car is found parked across the street, facing the other way, and decorated with a note that I don't need to quote.

I received only one response that placed the incident elsewhere (though still in the Midwest) and also introduced a significant variation. J.C. of Warrenville, Illinois, remembers hearing the story in 1976 in Milwaukee.

A graduating high-school student got a new Corvette as a present from his parents and, fearing thieves but lacking a garage, parked the car each night wedged tightly between two large trees in his yard. He supposedly had to jockey the car back and forth twenty-two times to fit it in.

Then he chained and locked the car to the trees using the largest size available of key-operated Masterlocks (a Milwaukee company).

But one day he came out to his car to find it facing the wrong way and with a note under the wiper blade: "When we want it, we'll come and get it."

A story similar to all of these appears to have originated in the East, casting doubt on the possibility of an actual Midwestern event underlying the story.

S.K. of California recalled a story she heard in New York City some fifteen years ago about a woman who had elaborately burglar-proofed her midtown Manhattan apartment. One day she returned home to find all her furniture rearranged. Nothing was missing, but she found a note that read, "If we want to get you, we will."

In this version the threat is a personal one. The discovery of the moved furniture conjures up the fear anyone might feel when spotting clues that an unknown person has entered his or her property.

"The Two Hitchhikers"

Here is another car story with a twist that I queried my readers on. I had found it just once—in a feature article by Erik Lacitis of the *Seattle Daily Times,* published on February 10, 1983. Lacitis wrote that he got it from a reader of that newspaper who had sent it in response to a request in the newspaper for further urban legends.

Although it's a wonderfully ironic story, to qualify for true legendary status, this tale would need wider distribution and evidence that it had appeared with variations. Otherwise, it could be an original story or an unmodified report of an actual event.

So I asked whether my readers had already heard the same or a similar story about two hitchhikers. I got into the urban-legend business some years ago when I studied a story about a hitchhiker, so this one intrigued me.

In the Seattle version, a traveling salesman is driving alone on a long haul between Seattle and Spokane and decides to pick up a hitchhiker to keep him company. But the rider immediately makes him uneasy. The man is middle-aged, scruffy, poorly dressed, and keeps turning around in the front seat as if looking for something to steal.

The driver decides to stop for a second hitchhiker, this time for security. He picks one who is young, clean-cut, well dressed, and who looks thoroughly respectable. This young man gets into the back seat.

Appearances are deceptive, however. As soon as the car with the three occupants is underway again, the young man in back pulls out a gun, points it at the driver, and orders him to stop. As the car slows to a halt, he gestures with the gun for the two to get out.

The moment the gun is moved off its target, however, the older hitchhiker in the front seat takes advantage of the situation, jumps at the would-be mugger, and, with a quick, powerful blow, knocks him cold. Then, to the driver's astonishment, he extracts the young man's wallet and offers to split evenly with the driver the two twenty dollar bills he finds there

"He's new in the business," the hitchhiker says. "He'll have to learn that a gun ain't a pointer. I've been in the business twenty years, and I don't make dumb mistakes anymore."

The driver is aghast. He numbly refuses the money, and he looks frightened enough so that his rescuer finally understands his thoughts.

"Oh, I ain't working today," the man says. "I'm just going to Spokane on a visit."

Unfortunately, no readers responded to my query about "The Two Hitchhikers," but several months later I got an unexpected letter from Claytor W. Allred of Tooele, Utah, who related two stories he remembered hearing about fifty years ago.

His first story, to my surprise, was the hoped-for variation of "The Two Hitchhikers." As Allred tells it: "Back when there were no such things as interstate highways, and traffic was very sparse in the wide-open spaces of the West, a prominent Salt Lake City doctor was returning from a convention in California. Driving across the lonely stretches of Nevada, he came upon a hitchhiker and stopped to offer him a ride in the back seat.

"Shortly, he began to think he had made a mistake. The man was dirty, smelly, and evil looking—a bum. The doctor began to worry as he occasionally took a look at the bum in the back seat. 'What would I do if he held me up?' the doctor wondered. 'I'd better be prepared, just in case.'

"A few miles along the desolate road, the doctor encountered another hitchhiker, this time what appeared to be a nice, clean-cut, college student. Because this seemed to be an answer to his worries, the doctor picked him up and had him get into the front seat by him.

"Not long after, without warning, the clean-cut young man pulled a gun and stuck it into the doctor's ribs. 'Pull over and get out,' he ordered, 'I want your money and your car, and I don't want any foolishness.'

"The doctor pulled off to the side of the road as ordered and was in the process of getting out when the bum in the back seat 'cold cocked' the young holdup man. He opened the doors on the right, dragged the unconscious young fellow out of the car, and picked up his gun, wallet, and watch. As he took the money from the wallet, he said, 'Here, Doc, half of this is yours. Let's get out of here.' "

Allred remembers only that it was his older sister, who died in 1968, who told him the story one Thanksgiving when he was home from college. The sister worked as a nurse, and the impression she gave was that the incident was supposed to have happened to one of the doctors in her clinic.

"This story may not fit into today's pattern," Allred wrote, "but it was quite interesting to me when I first heard it." Judging from the recent Seattle version still being told, "The Two Hitchhikers" still has an appeal among tellers of urban legends.

Mr. Allred's version also taught me an idiom I had not known before: "cold cocked," which evidently means "got the drop on him and knocked him for a loop," or something like that.

Thanks, pal!

"The Stolen Speed Trap" and Other Car Crimes

Cars plus crime form a typical combination in urban legends. Here are three recent car/crime stories. Each comes from a different country and involves some kind of faulty assumption.

The first, which I call "The Stolen Speed Trap," is of British origin. While driving home on the highway one afternoon, a woman sees what looks like a microwave oven left on the roadside. Assuming that someone has abandoned it, she stops and picks it up. Maybe her husband, an electrician, will be able to restore it to working order.

She hurries home with her prize, but she exceeds the speed limit and is stopped by the police. While writing the ticket, the officers notice the microwavelike unit in the back of her car. It is a radar speed-checking device. In spite of the woman's protestations, they arrest her for stealing government property.

In a variation, the woman mistakenly picks up the first unit of a two-part speed trap. Though she drives very carefully, the paired radar units are disrupted because one part is moving in her car. The units miscalculate her speed and electronically alert the police to stop her. While the woman is trying to talk her way out of a speeding ticket, the police spot the stolen speed trap in her car and book her for theft as well.

The second story, called "Stripping the Car," has been described as the classic New York City driving legend. It commonly spreads in large cities, where cars that are abandoned by the side of the road become prey of semiprofessional "strippers," who move from car to car, stripping them of tires, accessories, and other parts of value. Oddly, the people who recount this story to me usually say something like, "I don't know about your part of the country, but in ours . . ." as if car-stripping thieves are unique to their city or region.

In New York, I am told, the story goes like this:

In the middle of traffic on the Long Island Expressway (or the Bronx River Parkway), a man's car breaks down. He steers it onto the shoulder, gets out, and opens the hood. As he bends over the engine searching for the trouble, another car pulls up. The driver of the car gets out, offers to help—then walks to the back of the car and expertly jimmies open the trunk. He shouts around to the driver, "Okay, Buddy. What's under the hood is yours, but I get what's in the trunk."

In a variation of this legend, the stranded motorist is jacking up the rear end of his car to change a tire when he becomes aware that someone is jacking up the front. He walks around the car to investigate, and the stripper says to him, "You take the back wheels, Mac, and I'll take the front ones."

In a variation, the car stripper says, "Take it easy! There's enough here for the both of us!"

The third story, "Stopping the Detroit Car," takes place in Canada. An officer of the Royal Canadian Mounted Police's highway patrol is cruising for speeders on the TransCanada Highway in Saskatchewan, where the road is straight as an arrow for many miles. He spots a large luxury auto with U.S. license plates and signals for the driver to pull over.

The car, perhaps a long white Cadillac or Lincoln Continental, is usually said to have Michigan plates. Its occupants supposedly have driven north from Detroit, though in some versions their place of origin is some other notoriously crime-ridden city—generally Chicago, Miami, or New York.

Both cars stop, and the Mountie walks up to the huge

vehicle to speak with the driver. He merely intends to issue a warning about some minor infraction—a loose license plate, for instance, or a burned-out headlight.

But all four of the car's doors fly open, and four very large men in dark suits and pointy-toed, expensive shoes slowly emerge. The driver and his three passengers turn to face their car, lean over it, move their legs into the spread-eagle position, and place their hands on top.

The Mountie is astonished, since he is not used to the current arrest routine of high-crime U.S. cities. And the four men from Detroit are astonished, too: they are accustomed to being stopped and given a thorough going-over, not just a warning for a minor violation.

Aside from the obvious pattern of theme and variations in all three stories, it is the stereotyped characters in them that most clearly suggest that they are urban legends. "Woman drivers," victimized New Yorkers, naïve country police—these are common clichés that urban legends so often arise around.

What remains puzzling, though, is the way that all three of these stories arrive at a dramatic moment, and then abruptly leave us hanging. What happens to the wrongly charged woman? The car stripper and the owner of the car? The mysterious travelers from Detroit? We'll never know, since these are folklore, not fact. It seems that the endings to these car-crime stories have headed for the open road and stolen away in the night.

"The Celebrity's Car Breakdown"

How many times have you hoped to have a chance meeting like this one?

While traveling on a highway, a driver spots a person whose car is pulled over by the side of the road and stops to help. The stranded motorist turns out to be a celebrity. Grateful for the help, the celebrity later buys the Good Samaritan a new car as a thank-you gift.

In the most common version of this legend, the driver stops to help a woman stranded on the shoulder of a Los Angeles freeway. The woman turns out to be Mrs. Nat King Cole, who later sends the driver a new car—a Cadillac, a Lincoln, or even a Rolls-Royce.

Another celebrity whose car is always breaking down, in legends at least, is Perry Como. One report of Como's car troubles comes from Toronto, where a stranger allegedly changed a flat tire for the crooner and received a set of car keys in the mail a few days later. And I've collected accounts of other Como breakdowns on highways all over the United States.

In one, it's Como's wife who winds up stranded on a highway in Georgia while on her way to join her husband at an engagement in Florida. She sends the helpful driver a color TV or tickets to an upcoming concert.

A reader in Ann Arbor, Michigan, heard, while living in Minneapolis in the 1960s, that someone driving there late at night stopped to help a stranded motorist and later received a TV set from a grateful Louis Armstrong.

And a reader in Des Moines, Iowa, heard one about a truck driver in Nebraska who helped two women change a flat tire on a brand-new Cadillac. The driver politely refused any payment, even after one of the women identified herself as Mrs. Leon Spinks. She later sent him two tickets for her husband's upcoming fight in New Orleans.

All these variations ought to convince you that "The Celebrity's Car Breakdown" is an urban legend. Even if it resembles real life—Elvis Presley, for instance, was known to give new Cadillacs to strangers—such an incident hardly could have happened to all these celebrities, in all these places.

This legend may also borrow from the popular "Elevator Incident" story in which a sports or entertainment star—usually black—pays for someone's meal or hotel room in apology for giving her a fright when he enters an elevator with his dog.

The most detailed account of a roadside brush with fame comes from T.S. of Fairbanks, Alaska, who heard this story a decade ago in Butte, Montana. This time it's the celebrity who renders the aid:

"Sometime in early 1978 I was hitchhiking near Butte when I received a ride from a man in a large black American car," T.S. remembers. "The conversation got around to [motorcycle daredevil] Evel Knievel, a Butte boy.

"The man claimed that one day he had had a flat tire on a back road near Butte. Lacking a spare, he had been at a loss as to what to do next—until Knievel miraculously appeared on his motorcycle and offered to help.

"Around Butte, this guy told me, Evel was a sort of Robin Hood figure. He was a real hell-raiser, but also a protector of those in a jam.

"Evel told the driver to wait for him, saying he would be back soon. Sure enough, some time later he returned with a shiny wheel and tire to match those on the car. Tossing them onto the ground, Evel wished the driver good luck and roared off down the road."

This one nicely updates the Old West tradition of the mysterious stranger who comes out of nowhere to the rescue, then rides off into the sunset. But how did Knievel find matching parts?

"He had cruised around until he found the car he needed, then swiped the tire and wheel," T.S. explains. "Since the car he took them from was in town, the inconvenience would be minimal."

Still, the Evel Knievel story has a few holes in it. Why would the driver of a big car not carry a spare tire? How could Evel manage to jack up a car in town undetected and steal the spare? And if Evel made a habit of helping people in this way, wouldn't he have alienated the folks around Butte from whom he stole car parts to the same degree that he impressed other folks whom he rescued?

But urban legend plots need not be airtight and logical, merely plausible and entertaining.

" 'R' Is for Race"

I was reminded of an old story about car troubles after writing a column about "Push-starting the Car," an even older legend, which is about starting a stalled car with automatic transmission.

In that story, a driver (usually said to be a woman) offers to push-start a stalled automobile with the front end of her own car. "Get it up to thirty-five mph or she won't start," the driver of the stalled car tells her. So she backs off in her car and comes at the other car from half a block away at 35 miles per hour.

After reading my account of that one, J.W. of Kenney, Illinois, sent me this story about a similar automotive misunderstanding. He heard it from a friend in New Hampshire, and I remember hearing it in high school in Michigan many years ago.

"He knew someone who had just received a brand-new Camaro as a birthday present from his wealthy parents," J.W. begins. "One day the kid was racing with a Ford Mustang, and when the Mustang pulled ahead, the Camaro driver shifted his automatic transmission into 'R' for 'Race.'

"Needless to say, disastrous results ensued."

I'll bet they ensued!

"R" on the array of choices for automatic shifting stands for "reverse gear."

You should also notice that this version—in common with one variation of "The Unstealable Car" discussed previously—begins with a young man being given a fancy new car. Maybe there's a secondary warning here against excessive parental generosity.

Are there similar stories about "D" for "Drag," perhaps, or "L" for "Leap"?

"The Dishonest Note"

A number of urban legends urge people to take some action. Legends inspire people to oppose a proposed ban on religious broadcasting, to apply for a veterans insurance dividend, and to save pop tops from aluminum cans for a supposed redemption offer. People hear the stories, then do what they suggest, not realizing that the stories' claims are completely spurious.

A more subtle pattern of suggestion is found in the urban legend that I call "The Dishonest Note." The story describes a course of action that is both illegal and unethical but apparently has been taken by at least four people.

Here's what happens. A man accidentally drives into a parked vehicle, causing a big dent in the rear fender. Though several bystanders have witnessed the accident, the owner of the damaged car is not around. The guilty driver writes a note, slips it under the wiper blade, and drives off. Presumably, the note is an apology and supplies the guilty driver's name, address, and insurance company. But when the owner of the damaged car returns, he finds this note: "The people watching me think I am leaving my name and address. But I'm not."

The earliest example I have of the Dishonest Note appeared in the *San Francisco Examiner* in the summer of 1963, in a column written by Herb Caen. Then in the fall, Caen reported a variation he had read in the *London Daily Mirror*. In the variation, British car terminology was used—"wing" for "fender," "windscreen" for "windshield," etc.—and the note was a bit longer. Caen commented: "Here we have incontrovertible evidence of a new legend that seems destined to go 'round the world and pass into the folklore of our time."

I agree, because I have heard versions of the story from at least a dozen people, most of whom clearly regarded the story as fictional. Some said that they had heard it God-knows-where—perhaps on the radio (Paul Harvey was mentioned). Some thought they remembered reading it in *Reader's Digest*. One person identified the story as occurring in a scene of the TV detective series "The Outsider," which aired in 1968 and 1969. His letter furnished so many specific details from the actual episode that I felt he was a true television buff and couch potato and knew whereof he spoke, though I could not track down the episode.

So it seemed that the print and broadcast media had interacted with oral tradition to spread the story of the dishonest note. There's nothing unusual about that.

But I was surprised to also hear recently from four people who described real-life events resembling the legend, occurring in different parts of the country over more than a decade. All of them purported to be first-hand or secondhand accounts.

One man, writing from southern California said that his father's car had been hit and damaged by another driver's vehicle at a Little League baseball game in 1968. Fans in the stands witnessed the accident. The note under the wiper blade said, simply, "Sorry."

An attorney in Alaska wrote that in the early 1970s he had represented a young man in a hit-and-run case. The man had left a note reading, "Sorry, you lose! Ha, ha!" on a car that he had accidentally damaged. But a witness, for some reason suspicious of the young man, had jotted down his license number, and the hit-and-run driver was apprehended.

Another Alaskan offered a variant, dating from the late 1970s. A policeman whom he knew had witnessed a fender-bender on the highway. The policeman was too far away to read the license number, but when he arrived at the scene of the accident and read the dishonest note, he radioed to an officer parked on the highway ahead, describing the getaway car and telling him to pull the offender over.

The fourth respondent claimed that the incident happened to his cousin at a ski area in New England. The cousin found his car damaged in the parking lot, and the usual dishonest note was attached.

The behavior described in "The Dishonest Note" is such a nasty thing to do that one hopes the story is just a legend. But the expense and embarrassment caused by auto accidents are perhaps great enough to compel some people to leave such a note.

So far, nobody has shown me the actual note or even a photocopy of it. But—come to think of it—what would that prove?

What seems most likely is that "The Dishonest Note" first spread as a plausible legend, aided by the print and broadcast media. Later, people who had heard the legend acted in the same way when they found themselves in a similar situation.

"The Ice-Cream Car"

A reader in Milwaukee sent me a weird story about a car. She believed the story to be true and commented that, in this instance, truth proved to be stranger than fiction. I wonder.

Midway through a scorching Texas summer, a local auto dealer sold a woman a new car. Within a week the woman returned to the dealership with a very odd complaint. The car, she explained, sometimes refused to start. Not just now and then, though. In fact, the car gave her problems only when she drove to the ice-cream parlor to buy a carton of vanilla ice cream.

If she bought chocolate ice cream, or strawberry, or pistachio—any flavor but vanilla—the car started right up without any trouble. But consistently, whenever she bought vanilla ice cream, the engine turned over but refused to start when she came out of the store.

At first the dealer thought the woman was putting him on. But she insisted that she was serious, and eventually the dealer was curious enough to send a mechanic to check her story.

The mechanic drove to the store and bought strawberry ice cream, and the car started fine. But when he bought vanilla, he had to have the car towed to the shop.

He concluded that the problem was a very special mechanical one. What was making the car stall, he figured, was this: Most flavors of ice cream were sold prepacked and took just a few minutes to purchase. But vanilla ice cream was hand-packed for each customer. While the woman waited for her order to be made up, the hot Texas sun created a vapor lock in her car's engine, which caused it not to start.

My suspicions were aroused by the number of times the story made me suspend my disbelief. Did the woman take her car out of the garage only to buy ice cream? Did she never leave the car in the sun at any other time? Would anyone make enough separate trips to the ice cream parlor in one week to discover the nature of the problem?

Besides, wouldn't any Texas-based car dealer worth the plaques on his showroom wall adjust a new car to prevent vapor lock? After all, I can't remember any of the characters in "Dallas" experiencing any problems with stalled cars.

My incredulity, it turns out, was warranted. In my files, under the heading "Miscellaneous Car Legends," I uncovered one other version of "The Ice-Cream Car."

The June 1978 issue of *Traffic Safety* magazine printed the story, citing as its source the car magazine *Automotive Engineering*. In this version, also set in Texas, pistachio ice cream causes the car to stall, since pistachio is the only flavor the shop sells in hand-packed form.

It is possible that the incident did happen, but it seems unlikely. If nothing else, the appearance of two versions of the story with minor variations indicates that it is an automobile legend in the making.

Postscript: My column prompted a note from Betsy Henley, who does not give her exact address, but writes:

"I have heard the 'Ice Cream Car' story, but don't remember it being associated with Texas or a new car. The flavor of the ice cream was pistachio. I can't remember where I heard it. We live in Indiana now, but it might have been Tennessee, California, or Georgia."

"The Bargain Sports Car"

A friend of mine who lives in the San Francisco Bay Area recently bought her dream car—a mint condition year-old Chrysler LeBaron convertible with very low mileage. The reason why the car is in perfect shape, she told me, is that it had belonged to a Chrysler executive who used it only to drive homecoming queens around football stadiums and in parades.

You'd think I would know better, but I believed her story at first. I fell for that homecoming queen, forgetting all the urban legends I had collected about car bargains.

There's the legend I call "The Death Car," which describes a nearly new car that the owner sells cheaply because a deathly smell permeates the upholstery. And there's the one I call "The $75 Porsche," about a sports car sold for a song because the owner ran off with his secretary and foolishly trusted his wife to sell the car and send him the money.

Only after I had repeated my friend's story a few times as an example of the ultimate car-dealer's sales pitch did she admit that, yes, she had made up the part about the homecoming queens.

A bargain sports car and a made-up story also came together in a letter I received recently from Susan P. McKiernan of Medina, Ohio.

"In 1961, my brother told me about a new Corvette which was being sold for $500 because the owner was killed in it and the mother just wanted to get rid of it," McKiernan writes. "I told my brother that this made no sense." She was quicker than I in recognizing a legend. She reasoned that the mother would *give* the car away,

not sell it so cheaply, or she would charge whatever figure was still owed the bank. Her sales offer would only
have called extra attention to the death, further distress-
ing the mother. And besides, the first person to hear of
this deal would have snapped it up anyway.

"My brother, of course, called me an idiot," McKiernan continues. "But in 1963 I heard the same story
again. And my sister and I, thinking that we were the first
to discover this phenomenon of traveling stories, made
one up which came back to us in only two days.

"But my sister and I want you to know that we are
retired from the business of inventing legends," she concludes. "And I'm sorry to say that I can't even remember
now what story we created."

I'm not surprised that you gave up the legend-invent-
ing business. While there are a few instances of deliberately contrived urban legends passing into oral tradition,
I've found that it's much easier to collect and repeat
urban legends than to make up new ones.

Incidentally, you scored perfectly in debunking the
version of "The Bargain Sports Car" told by your
brother. As all the flaws in its plot suggested to you, the
story is apocryphal.

Yet, nearly thirty years later, the legend is still going
strong. And the car involved is still nearly always a vintage Corvette.

In the most common version, an elderly woman whose
son is missing in action in Vietnam wants to sell the old
car he left behind. She asks just $500 for what turns out
to be a 1967 Corvette that is stored on blocks of wood in
her garage with all motor fluids drained. In other words,
a real cream puff.

Sometimes the mother has called a car dealer to find
out how much she should charge for a 1967 Chevy. Not
realizing that she means a classic Corvette, the dealer
suggests that she ask a few hundred dollars at most.

Since it's a legend based on wishful thinking, you seldom hear about anyone actually buying the car. The legend usually ends with the woman explaining the reasons
for the unbelievably low price: after all, it's a small car,
and besides, it's ten years old—so it can't be worth much.

In the most poignant version I've heard so far, a man
spots a newspaper ad offering a 1965 Chevy for $200,
and he decides to take a look at it as a possible second car
for his family. Just as he arrives at the address listed, he
sees a beautiful vintage Corvette driving away. He asks
the elderly lady who answers to his knock on the door if
by any chance that was the car she had advertised.

"Oh, yes, that was it," she says. "I sold it to the first
person who answered my ad."

None of the versions in my files report how the would-
be buyer reacted.

You might guess that he has had nightmares ever since
about missing the buy of a lifetime. I don't believe he
does. There are too many holes in this legend for it to be
anything but a fantasy. But we can dream, can't we?

"The Wife Left Behind"

Here is a real-life news story about a travel mishap that sounds as if it were straight out of urban legend. Perhaps real legends spring from such incidents.

Just before Christmas 1986, Pat and Kenneth Zimmer of Eugene, Oregon, and their five children were driving home on Interstate Route 5 after spending the holiday in California. Mr. Zimmer was at the wheel of their van, while his wife slept in back. At Red Bluff, California, he stopped for a hamburger. Unknown to him, his wife got out a few minutes later to go to the restroom. He got back in and drove away, leaving her with the sight of the disappearing van and just 23 cents in her purse. When the family arrived home, one of the kids asked where Mom was. With the help of California state police, Mrs. Zimmer got on a bus and arrived home the next day.

In reporting the story, the *Eugene Register-Guard* published a front-page photograph of the reunited Zimmers and their van.

I guess history repeats itself, because there is a popular apocryphal story about a very similar incident. In this story, which was circulating long before this real-life incident, a man is riding nude or half-dressed in a trailer while his wife drives the car towing it. When she stops, the man steps out momentarily—a fact that the wife is unaware of. She drives off, and he is stranded by the roadside. The police or a truck driver assist him in getting home.

The only difference between these stories is that in the real story, names, dates, and places are given. The apocryphal, story is—well—apocryphal.

"The Pig on the Road"

Maybe Eugene, Oregon (see the preceding section), is a center of automobile mishaps and legends. At any rate, here is a wonderful automobile story that I got in 1984 from Eugene via fellow folklorist Sharon Sherman of the University of Oregon. She clipped it from Don Bishoff's column in the *Register-Guard,* where it was attributed to an acquaintance of the writer.

I put the story into my book *The Mexican Pet* in 1986 and into a newspaper column in July 1987, wondering whether readers would verify that it was told in other places. And, sure enough, they did.

As Bishoff told the story: A guy is driving down the street and passes a car that has just come around the corner from the opposite direction. The woman driver in the other car shouts "Pig!" at the guy. He promptly retorts, "You're not so great-looking yourself!" Then he turns the corner and runs over a pig in the street.

Incidentally, few newspapers carrying my column about this story could resist a punning headline reference to "road hogs."

Eventually, "The Pig on the Road" was confirmed as a wandering legend, thanks to a reader in California, the Associated Press, and radio commentator Paul Harvey.

B. T. Miller of San Luis Obispo sent me a clipping of an Associated Press news item, datelined Waurika, Oklahoma, that retells a version recounted by Harvey in January 1988.

As Paul Harvey told it, Oklahoma State Highway patrolman Bill Runyan was driving his patrol car in the country near Waurika, when he spotted a farmer jumping up and down by the roadside shouting, "Pig! pig!"

According to Harvey, Runyan leaned out the patrol car window and shouted back, "Redneck! Redneck!" Then, just beyond the next hill, he ran smack into a huge hog that had strayed into the middle of the road.

But, according to the AP, Runyan denied that the anecdote was true. The story, he said, came from his cousin—a newspaper editor—with whom he often trades "war stories" that they jokingly pass off as actual experiences.

My guess is that the Oregon version is older than Harvey's, which picks up the slang usage of "pig" as an insulting term for policeman. This guess, in turn, was supported by the two latest letters I've received about "The Pig on the Road." One contained just the bare memory of a similar item being in the *Reader's Digest* twenty years or so ago; this time, supposedly, the incident was set in England.

The second letter, from O. V. Barlow of Nashua, New Hampshire, provided the following summary of a version told by an Englishman of his acquaintance:

"A lorry driver is negotiating a twisting rough road with numerous blind curves and switchbacks. Rounding a particularly sharp turn, he is suddenly confronted by a woman in an open car who waves her fist and shouts out, 'Bloody pig!'

"Leaning from the window, the driver shouts out, 'Bloody cow!' as she departs in a cloud of dust.

"Then he swerves his attention back to the road just in time to collide with a quite genuinely bloody pig, the victim of a previous mishap."

The oddest thing about Mr. Barlow's letter is that he mentions remembering the first version of "The Pig on the Road" that he heard in 1979 or early 1980. He was—of all things—working for the *Eugene* (Oregon) *Register-Guard* at the time. This is where I came in!

Now, who's going to be first with the *Reader's Digest* clipping?

3

Animal Legends

"The Pet Nabber"

I always say, "Never trust a dead-cat story." That principle applies to suffering-pet stories in general and to small-pet nabbings in particular.

Tales abound about small pets getting grabbed and devoured by carnivorous creatures. A few of them are undoubtedly true, and they contribute a kernel of believability to the genre. For instance, the resurgence of the now-protected alligator population in Florida is said to have led to the demise of a number of small domestic animals. That seems plausible.

But so many other variations of these stories appear so often and in so many alleged settings, that even if they are true, the stories that are told must be many times removed from their original sources.

Betsy James, an illustrator in Albuquerque, New Mexico, sent me a story in this genre that she heard from a friend in Santa Fe. It supposedly happened to a friend of a friend of *her* friend. In Ms. James's own words: "A well-to-do New York designer, unmarried, has a cat that is everything to him. The cat is getting old and stiff and asthmatic, and the designer decides that it would be better for kitty if he moved out west to a high, dry climate, where the cat could spend its declining years in comfort.

"After much research, he buys a quarter-of-a-million-dollar custom adobe in the sagebrush hills east of Santa Fe, loads up the cat to travel, and arrives in town.

"The first afternoon in his new home, he puts the cat gently out on the back patio to wander around in the sagebrush and inspect its new quarters. A few minutes later, he looks out the sliding doors just in time to see an enormous owl come sailing in. The owl picks up the cat in its claws and goes soaring off into the sunset."

Before I could decide whether that story was true or not, folklorist Bill Scott of Australia supplied me with another variation, clipped from the *Brisbane Courier Mail*. As the paper reported it, a woman was walking her dog, a Chihuahua, on the beach in the costal town of Kalbarri, when a pelican landed and gobbled up the poor creature right on the spot.

Here in my home town of Salt Lake City, where two peregrine falcons nesting on a downtown hotel have attracted much attention, I've been trying to start a similar story about a visitor touring the Mormon Temple Square who has a pet parakeet riding around on his shoulder. Suddenly there's a swoop of wings, and . . . no more birdy. Another small pet is carried off.

It could have happened, since the peregrines subsist on pigeons and other captured birds. But, so far, no pet parakeets are missing, and my contrived legend has not caught on.

There is yet another traditional nabbed-pet story, however, in which a dog is taken by its owner to Florida's Marineland amusement park. The pampered pup, wearing a jeweled collar, is being held up on the railing by its owner to watch the show. Then, when the animal keepers toss some meat into the shark tank, the doggy leaps in after it. Guess who's coming to dinner at the sharks' house?

While many people treasure small, defenseless animals as pets, others regard them as ugly, obnoxious, and useless. It's possible that the toy-poodle–haters are the ones who tell these stories with the greatest glee. Maybe it's their revenge for being yapped at daily by their neighbors' pampered Fifi.

And speaking of Fifi-type dogs, please see the following legend.

"Fifi Spills the Paint"

Dear Professor:

I recently heard about a friend of a friend—what you call a FOAF—who is an interior decorator with a thriving business on Chicago's wealthy North Shore. He had just finished painting an elegant home in Wilmette, and was going around with a can of touch-up paint, making sure everything was perfect.

He finished the last brush stroke, stepped back to admire his work, and kicked the paint can over onto the priceless Oriental rug. What to do?

At that moment the client's yappy, snappy, obnoxious toy poodle, Fifi, trotted into the room. Thinking quickly, the decorator scooped her up and dropped her into the puddle of paint, at the same time exclaiming loudly, "Fifi! Bad Dog! What have you done?"

Sounds like a legend to me.

> Susan Levin Kraykowski
> Crystal Lake, Illinois

Dear Susan:

That story is certainly suspicious, and I suspect it is a legend. It has the typical friend-of-a-friend source and depicts an innocent pet suffering for a human's mistake, another common legend ingredient. There's an unlikely twist in the plot in the decorator immediately converting his own error into someone else's problem.

I received Susan Kraykowski's letter in September 1986 and wrote the above as part of a column that ran the week of June 1, 1987. One month later I received the information used in the following epilogue.

The durability of folk stories and storytelling has been brought home to me in much of my mail from readers of this column. Here's one excellent example.

Clint Lovell of San Diego responded to my account of the story of how "Fifi Spilled the Paint." He wrote:

"Regarding your spilled paint/dog story, I can tell you that for damn sure this is a legend.

"In 1929, at the age of 18 years, I joined the 186th Inf. National Guard Band in Portland, Oregon. We had a Sousaphone player, name of Bert Junken.

"You question my memory on this? I later became Company Clerk and could type the monthly attendance reports and payrolls from memory."

I believe you, Clint!

"Bert was a painter by trade. He told some of us the same story. Except, it happened in Portland Heights, on a wooden railing, on a stairway.

"It does go to show you, however, that these small house mutts might sometime serve some useful purpose."

Lovell's letter reflects several fundamental truths about the folk-narrative tradition. It demonstrates the superior memory, sharp wit, and vigorous language that are signs of a talented storyteller. He phrases his letter in the same lively terms that he would use in telling the story orally.

We also learn here about the probable use of the spilled paint/dog story by professional painters, either as just a tale they like to tell or perhaps as an occasional prank resorted to if a paint can is in fact accidentally tipped over.

Most of all, these two versions of "Fifi Spills the Paint" demonstrate the ways that urban legends vary with repeated tellings. It is unlikely that the 1929 Portland story is the direct ancestor of the legend told in Chicago in 1986; probably many other versions have been told over the years as well. But, as happens so often with urban legends, these two texts show how the essential elements of a plot may remain constant, while details are changed to suit each teller's own situation.

"The Crushed Dog"

Shortly after I started writing "Urban Legends," I received a query from a California reader about a story I call "The Crushed Dog." Feeling sure I would see the story again, I filed the letter under "Animals—Miscellaneous."

But it wasn't until fifteen months later that I found two similar stories. I still can't say for sure whether "The Crushed Dog" is a legend, but I'm beginning to believe it is.

The Californian remembered hearing the story told about a friend of a friend ten or fifteen years ago. Its plot is an unusual one for a legend: instead of a single memorable incident, there are two episodes separated by a time gap.

The first episode describes a young man, new in town, who is invited to a party at an expensive home. He falls asleep after drinking heavily and awakens in a dark room. While fumbling for the light switch, he accidentally sticks his fingers into an open ink well and leaves stains and fingerprints all over the room.

Embarrassed by the damage he has done, the young man slips away unnoticed. The next day he decides to return and apologize.

The conclusion of the Californian's story is what sounds like a legend to me: "He was admitted by a servant, who led him to a dim library to await his host or hostess. He entered the library, and sank into the nearest comfortable chair, only to hear and feel a mind-boggling *CRUNCH!* The young man leapt to his feet to discover that he had crushed a delicate Chihuahua to death. He fled again, and never returned."

Sometimes a story like this haunts me for months—even years—before I discover whether it is an urban legend, a true incident, or a literary invention. I usually assume that such a bizarre but believable story just has to be a legend, but I need some evidence—other versions that reveal an oral tradition and plot variations. And although I have lots of suffering-pet legends on file, I lacked another version of this one.

Then, a few weeks ago, I read Tom Robbins's novel *Still Life with Woodpecker* (New York: Bantam, 1980), and there I found my story!

Early in Robbins's book there's a scene in which a nervous suitor calls on his beloved's parents. The young woman's mother has a cherished pet Chihuahua. Here's what happens to the suitor:

"He went into the music room and took a seat on the couch. As he sat, he felt something warm and heard a soft dry snap/crackle/pop, like a singular oversized Rice Krispy being bitten into by a crocodile. He stood up slowly. . . . Beneath him was the beloved Chihuahua. He had sat on it. And broken its neck."

The young man put the dog into the piano, placed the roses he had brought on top, and left quickly.

Robbins must have heard a version of "The Crushed Dog" and adapted it for his novel. And the book, which was a best seller, helped to spread the story to a large audience. But does the story really have an oral tradition?

As I pondered this question, an English acquaintance of mine who now lives in the States called to ask me about a story concerning a Scottish lad.

It seems that the lad was invited somewhere and accidentally sat on the host's Pekingese. Embarrassed, he hid the dog's body in a coal scuttle and fled.

I asked my acquaintance to repeat the story so I could take notes, she said, "Wait, there's more." She wasn't absolutely sure about the details, but she remembered something about his coming back to apologize and accidentally upsetting an open inkwell.

Now I know I'm onto something!

"Shooting the Bull"

Animals come out unhappily in many urban legends. We hear about dead cats, microwaved poodles, deep-fried rats, and the like in some ghastly stories. But the humans who encounter animals in modern legends don't have such happy endings either. There are, for starters, tourists in the Orient served their own pet—roasted; divers working in reservoirs scared witless by giant catfish; and people bitten by poisonous snakes sewn into imported garments.

Here is a typical modern legend that tells about both the hunters and the hunted. It was sent in by a reader in Durham, North Carolina, who began: "I heard this story when I was punching cowboys in Colorado. (I was a bouncer in a tough bar.) A man from Denver went hunting on the western slope, and he asked a rancher if he could hunt on his property.

" 'Fine,' said the rancher, 'but be careful. My prize bull is up in the pasture, and if you kill him it will cost you $2,300.'

"The hunter returned with the sad news that he had indeed killed the rancher's prize bull. He wrote a check for $2,300. So the rancher got into his tractor to bring the meat down, and when he got to the pasture, he found the bull sedately grazing. Looking around he found a beautiful buck cleanly shot by the hunter who had been too stupid to tell the difference between a deer and a bull.

"The check cleared the bank five days later."

Thanks, sir, for a fine example of an updated traditional Western tale! For decades, stories of stupid hunters mistaking domestic cattle for game have been told out here where I live.

Some are merely jokes, but others are believed as gospel. It seems reasonable to many farmers and ranchers that wealthy sportsmen from the big city would make such an error and be quick to pay the price, though perhaps there's some wishful thinking in that last detail.

To warn greenhorn hunters against shooting their stock, some owners actually paint the word "COW" or "HORSE" in day-glo colors on the sides of the animals.

Most of the dumb-hunter stories in my state of Utah, whether believed or not, are told about a mythical California hunter. When he drives up to a state game-checking station, the checker on duty immediately knows that a terrible mistake has been made, because he sees that the "elk" feet sticking over the side of the pickup truck have horseshoes on them. Legions of local hunters have heard and believed that story, but no one seems to have been an eyewitness. The legend is revived every season but never verified.

A popular variation of "shooting the bull" appeared in Don Boxmeyer's column in the *Pioneer Press and Dispatch* of St. Paul, Minnesota, in October 1985. He heard it from a colleague who swore that it happened to a friend of a friend of his.

Three Minnesota hunters drove into a farmyard, and one went up to ask the farmer's permission to hunt his fields. The farmer approved on the condition that the hunters shoot an old bull that he had been planning to get rid of.

The hunter went back to the car and pulled a little gag on his buddies. He told them that the farmer was a rotten old coot who refused them permission to hunt. Then he had the driver stop when they passed the old bull.

He climbed out, very deliberately took aim and shot the bull, and then said, "That'll take care of the rotten old coot."

Whereupon his two companions each shot a cow, commenting, "That'll *really* take care of that rotten old coot."

Boxmeyer added that later he was told virtually the same story by a friend from South Africa, who assured him that it had really happened in that country.

On April 16, 1987, former (several times) New York Yankees manager Billy Martin, appearing on "Late Night with David Letterman," told virtually the same incident as a true story. Martin claimed it was a prank that Mickey Mantle and Whitey Ford had played on him when the three of them were hunting in Texas. Martin said that Mantle, at the rancher's request, shot an old mule, pretending that this was revenge for not getting permission to hunt on his land. Martin claimed that he himself then shot two of the rancher's cows and had to pay $800 to replace them.

Thanks to Giles Daeger of the Department of English, Marquette University, Milwaukee, I have another version of "Shooting the Bull," this one published in 1945 in Morton Thompson's book *Joe, the Wounded Tennis Player* (New York: Doubleday Doran). According to Thompson, the farmer's words are, "While you're at it, you can do me a favor. When you come to the third pasture you'll see an old white horse in it. Poor old devil's got the bots. He's dropping from old age. Been meaning to knock him on the head. I'll take it as a favor if you'll shoot him for me."

I have also heard an English version of the story in which a horse is the animal shot—an old mare of the farmer's that is sharing a field with a valuable milch cow. In this version, the English farmer, speaking in a thick country dialect, remarks, " 'Er's served me well—can't bear to think of her sent off to the knackers." As a favor to the farmer, the hunter shoots the old mare; his hunting companion, misunderstanding the motive, follows suit and shoots the milch cow.

The Englishman who told me this one commented, "I heard this in the pub four times this past summer," reminding me again of the Colorado bar where my American correspondent got his version. It seems that when hunters gather the world around, such stories are told. The urban outsider becomes an object of ridicule in the local legends.

So, when the conversation in a Western bar or an English pub frequented by hunters turns to the topic of "shooting the bull," don't believe a thing you hear.

"Lawn Order in New Zealand (and Elsewhere)"

During my 1988 visit to New Zealand, I came across an article with the wonderful headline "Lawn Order" in *Listener,* the weekly Kiwi television and radio program guide. The article asked whether "a bottle filled with water and placed on your lawn will deter passing dogs from leaving a calling card."

Sounds ridiculous, right? But this bottle-on-the-lawn tactic is serious stuff Down Under, having spread swiftly from Australia to New Zealand and become an article of faith in both countries. It may not be exactly an urban legend, but it certainly is modern folklore.

Everywhere I went in New Zealand I saw bottles of water scattered about on the neatly tended lawns. And everyone I asked about this told me that he or she had heard from someone that it was a sure-fire way to prevent dogs from doing their business on the lawn.

The bottles were the familiar 1¼ liter plastic soft-drink containers. Only clear bottles seemed to be used, though sometimes the paper labels had been left on them. I was told that residents of some of the ritzy suburbs put out water in glass bottles that originally held expensive wines and liquors.

To me, the water-bottle idea seems almost as silly as the preventive used by some people in the States: if they see a dog coming onto their lawn, they stand near the front window and cross their fingers, then supposedly the dog will refrain from relieving itself.

The crossing of the fingers has an air of what anthropologists used to call "sympathetic magic." Like the effects of the water-filled bottles, so the crossed fingers symbolically lock up the dog's functions, as if the pooch had crossed its own back legs.

The usual reason given for the supposed success of the bottle technique is that a dog will not foul its own drinking water.

But dogs know nothing of water in plastic bottles. So some people who scatter the bottles across their lawns say that it's the glitter of the bottle or the dog's seeing its own reflection in the water that does the trick. Others claim that the bottles themselves repel dogs, and the water is just there to keep the wind from blowing the bottles off the lawn.

In search of the truth, *Listener* sent reporter Denis Welch out to study the matter. Welch chose the town of Napier on Hawke's Bay, North Island, as the site for his research. "The answer to all life's problems can ultimately be found in Napier," he explained. "And it also has the best Italian restaurant in the country."

I, too, visited Napier. I couldn't find the restaurant, but I saw plenty of water bottles on tidy lawns. But then I saw water bottles in virtually every New Zealand town I visited. Lawn order seemed to be a national mania, though perhaps not quite a sign of the "uptight anal-repressive tendencies of small-town New Zealand," as Denis Welch suggested.

A letter to the editor of the *Auckland Herald* suggested that the message of the water bottles was directed not to the dogs, but to dog owners: "I don't want your dog fouling my yard!"

At another point in my visit, the *Wellington Evening Post* ran a more serious piece on the subject. They quoted one veterinarian who called it "one of the most stupid things he has ever heard" and another who said that "he saw one hound present his offering on top of a bottle."

But one Australian vet who was also quoted insisted that the tactic works, if done properly: "The full territory has to be enclosed with bottles, the water must not become stale, and it must be shaken regularly to give off the right vibrations.''

As I read the article, I wondered aloud whether the litter of plastic water bottles scattered so liberally about a lawn wouldn't be just as offensive as an occasional doggy dropping. I commented to my wife on the remarkable naïveté of local people, wondering how anyone could think that bottles of water on the lawn would have any power over the neighbor's doggy.

And my wife said, "But I'm sure I saw water bottles on lawns in our neighborhood back home!"

I don't recall every seeing such a thing, although we used to have a big dog that our neighbors probably would have liked to ward off.

I left it to my readers, asking if any of them had heard of this lawn-order stuff. Does it work? And if so—why?

Postscript: I immediately got four letters from California in response to this column. One reported glass and plastic water bottles used on lawns as a dog deterrent in San Diego in 1983 and 1984; no explanation of how (or even *if*) they worked. The second letter described bottles of water scattered on lawns in Santa Cruz during the late 1970s, the "bottle of choice" being institutional-sized condiment jars placed in the approximate center of yards. Walking to work in San Jose the morning he wrote me, my correspondent spotted a row of water bottles on just one lawn there. Letter number 3 was from Los Gatos (which seems like a town with a funny name to have a *dog* problem); same thing there, though: glass and plastic jugs filled with water are thought to repel canines. The fourth letter, from Wayne Bernhardson of Oakland, reported as follows:

After hearing of your research with water bottles on lawns in New Zealand and elsewhere, I thought I should

inform you of my own brief field experiment on this
topic in West Berkeley, where such bottles were fairly
common, several years ago. While walking my dog, a
90-pound Alaskan malamute, through the
neighborhood, I asked a middle-aged black woman her
rationale for having them, and she replied that they
were indeed intended to keep dogs off her lawn. One
subtlety she brought up, however, was that to do so one
had to place either mothballs or ammonia in the bottles
to discourage the dog, which, of course, has an
extraordinarily acute sense of smell.

This seemed at least plausible, although I was not
completely convinced of the efficacy of such a system.
My skepticism proved justified when, a block later, my
dog backed directly onto one of the plastic bottles and
left one large turd delicately balanced on top of it.

So far, I got just one reply from elsewhere, a note
from Dr. Reinhold Aman of Waukesha, Wisconsin, who
reports water bottles used to repel *rabbits* in his
neighborhood.

I've walked a lot around Salt Lake City since my
return from New Zealand and still have not seen this
particular form of lawn order in operation here. But I
have a feeling that my findings on this matter will not
end with these few facts.

"Not My Dog"

Pets and people frequently clash in urban legends, usually with some resulting embarrassment or danger to one or the other. This is illustrated in several of the pet legends that I have discussed or mentioned already.

Another such dog story that has circulated for years centers on a question of etiquette. Although I have heard it as an anonymous friend-of-a-friend story, this comic gem seems to have literary origins. I call the story "Not My Dog," which gives the plot away, but what the heck.

A woman is invited to call at the home of a woman who is wealthier than she is (or, in variations, older or socially superior). From the moment she is invited, the caller is unsure about how to behave—how to sit, how to take tea, etc. And matters are made worse when the time of the visit arrives. A large, lively, dirty beast of a dog is sitting in the front yard, and when the hostess welcomes the caller into the house, the dog follows her inside. While the caller tries to respect the social amenities, that darn dog does not. It tracks mud about the room, sniffs the cookies, and paws the furniture. The caller makes small talk, but the conversation becomes strained. Still, both parties keep a stiff upper lip, observing proper etiquette.

Finally the visit comes to an end. As the caller rises to leave, the hostess, with one eye on the wreckage, remarks icily, "And don't forget to take your dog!"

"My dog?" the caller says. "I thought it was yours!"

Once, when I retold that story at home, a small child (one of my daughters) cried out: "That same story is in one of my *Emily* books!"

Indeed, it is. Lucy Maud Montgomery, author of *Anne of Green Gables* and other popular children's books, wrote three novels about the life and adventures of a girl named Emily Starr. In the third book, *Emily Climbs,* published in 1924, we find the "Not My Dog" story in Chapter 22.

Young Emily calls on Miss Janet Royal, a "brilliant, successful woman," whose very name projects an aristocratic bearing. When the girl arrives for the visit, a large muddy dog, thought by Emily to be Miss Royal's pet chow Chu-Chin, follows her into the elegant parlor of the house and makes an awful mess.

Only when the embarrassed Emily is ready to depart from the uncomfortable interview does she learn that this is not her hostess's dog, which had been locked up in the bedroom to prevent him from chasing a cat. Miss Royal, of course, had assumed that the dog is Emily's. And Emily simply had no idea what a chow dog looks like.

The story may have been a traditional one on Prince Edward Island, Canada, where Montgomery grew up and set most of her fiction. Or it may have become a folktale only later, as a result of its appearance in *Emily Climbs,* which has been read by countless children over the years. Either way, it's now an urban legend.

Another version of "Not My Dog" surfaced recently in Ed Regis's book *Who Got Einstein's Office? Eccentricity and Genius at the Institute for Advanced Study* (Reading, Mass.: Addison-Wesley, 1987, p. 110). This time the participants are the famous mathematicians John von Neumann and Julian Bigelow.

In 1946, Bigelow, according to his quoted account, came to Princeton to meet von Neuman. Arriving late, Bigelow was followed into von Neumann's elegant house by a frisky Great Dane, presumably his host's pet. The dog roamed the house during the interview, at the conclusion of which von Neumann politely asked Bigelow whether he always brought his dog along. "But of course, it wasn't my dog," Bigelow is quoted, "and it wasn't his either." So now we have a variation on the punchline.

Could it be that these eminent scientists—or perhaps author Ed Regis—were readers of *Emily Climbs?* Or is this particular problem of doggy etiquette so common that independent folk stories have sprung up?

A final mystery: Several readers clipped the *Smithsonian* magazine review (February 1988) of *Who Got Einstein's Office* in which the dog episode was summarized, sending it to me with notes indicating that they had within the past year heard Burt Reynolds tell virtually the same story to Johnny Carson on "The Tonight Show." Reynolds, according to my readers, claimed that he himself was the visitor.

If you're reading this, Burt, would you give me a call and explain yourself?

"The Leashed Dogs"

As a modern folklorist—urban legendist, legend ur-
banologist, or what have you—I gather a great many bits
and pieces of stories that may or may not be urban legends. But I never throw anything away too quickly, since
sometimes the least promising and most obscure frag-
ments suddenly blossom as legends.

What makes these oddments seem to be possible
pieces of modern folklore is some weird or comical plot
twist in a tale that is said to be true. What's often lacking,
however, is enough reports of a story—different versions
from different sources.

Here are a couple of examples of suspicious animal
stories—wild plots that just may be true but have a fictional flavor. Both stories concern a dog on a leash.

The first story, which I call "The Leashed Dog No. 1,"
is one I've heard just a few times so far. As the story goes,
a family is on vacation with the kids and the dog when
they stop for refreshments. One of the kids sets a dish of
water for the dog behind the car or camper trailer, and
ties the pet's leash to the rear bumper. But the child fails
to mention this to Dad, who is driving. When the family
starts out again, the leashed dog is dragged to death behind the camper. The kids become hysterical, but all of
them deny leashing the pet to the camper.

I suppose such an accident could have happened, then
been talked about enough to bring it to my ears as a
doubtful story. In fact, after I mentioned this story in a
column, I heard from two people—one in Maryland, one
in Indiana—who had personally witnessed similar mishaps—one in 1954, the other in 1976. Neither dog died,
I am happy to report.

At the same time, though, "The Leashed Dog No. 1" sounds a great deal like the urban legend I call "The Nude in the RV," in which a husband or wife is left behind after stepping, nearly naked, out of a camper or travel trailer when his or her spouse pulls over to the side of the road.

Also, the dog story (as numerous readers reminded me) was also worked into the slapstick plot of the film *National Lampoon's Vacation* released in 1983. The oral circulation of the story precedes the movie use, but the filming of the incident may well have given a new boost to the legend.

"The Leashed Dog No. 2" is either a variant of the other legend or another strange-but-true occurrence. I was sent the story a couple of years ago by a reader who said the incident occurred in Laguna Beach, California. For all I know, it really did happen. But it seems to be a particularly close relative of the first story.

One member of a family takes the family dog outside of the house for some fresh air and leaves it there, tying its leash to the handle of the garage door. Not long afterward, another member of the family comes driving home. A block or so away, he or she hits the remote control that opens the garage door. As the door opens, it pulls the leashed dog into the air, lynching it.

The key to this story, whether it is truth or legend, is a garage door that opens by remote control. As with legends about microwave ovens, sun-tanning lamps, and cruise control, the problems that might arise from a modern gadget are dramatized in a wild story.

1988—Year of the Rabbit—"The Hare Drier"

As far as urban legends went, 1988 was the Year of the Rabbit—or at least it included the Season of the Rabbit. The hottest story going around that spring and summer was one about a dead rabbit that got blow-dried. I dubbed the legend "The Hare Drier." (Yes, I know there's a difference between hares and rabbits, but the pun was irresistible.)

I included the story, as I first heard it in April, in a column released the week of July 4, 1988, little realizing how popular it was becoming. When I opened my back-logged mail in early June, after returning from New Zealand, other versions of "The Hare Drier" came hopping out like multiplying bunnies in a magician's act.

The usual story goes about like this: One day a woman is horrified to see her dog holding a dead rabbit in its mouth. Her neighbors have always kept a pet rabbit in a cage behind the house, and she recognizes the dead animal as their pet. The woman takes the rabbit from her dog, cleans it up as best she can, blow-dries its fur, and—her neighbors being gone—sneaks into their yard and replaces the restored rabbit in its cage in a lifelike posture. The next day, she sees a police car parked in front of her neighbors' house. Curious, she goes outside and asks what's going on. "A nuisance call," the officer says. "Their pet rabbit died yesterday, and some weirdo dug it up and put it back in its cage."

If you haven't heard this one yet, you must lead a sheltered life.

In the dozens of versions I've collected, details vary—the kind of dog, or the state of relations between the neighbors—but nearly all versions agree that the dead bunny was blow-dried and returned to its hutch.

Often the police are absent from the story, and the two neighbors simply meet across the backyard fence. The rabbit owner either assumes that human intervention has brought the bunny home (a "sicko, weirdo, deviant, or creep . . ."), or else the owner believes that the rabbit had accidentally been buried alive, then clawed its way out of the grave, and crept exhausted back to its hutch, only to die there from the exertion. It's not a pretty story.

My first letter on the story arrived in April, from Michelle Moon of Red Bank, New Jersey. She heard it from a friend who claimed, unconvincingly says Michelle, that it happened to his sister.

But on Father's Day (June 19), the *San Diego Union* awarded first prize in their "Embarrassing Dads" contest to a reader who told the returned rabbit story on her father, claiming it had happened twenty-two years ago. The published story in the paper that day had everything the recent oral story includes except a blow drier—this dead bunny was simply hosed off and rubbed down with a towel.

Philomene d'Ursin of La Jolla, California, clipped the *Union*'s article to send to me because she didn't believe it was true. Her sister, living in Birmingham, England, had told her the rabbit story back in January, insisting that it happened to a co-worker of hers. Commented d'Ursin, "Either fluffing up dead rabbits is an international pastime or we've got an urban legend." In February, d'Ursin had sent the story to *Reader's Digest,* and in June she sent it to me.

Versions of "The Hare Drier" kept coming all summer and into early fall, and I'll bet the *Digest* got its share as well. Many who sent it to me were very specific about where they had heard the story and how it was told. For example, Chris Key of Hurst, Texas, got the story in early June from a writer for a Fort Worth paper. The incident was supposed to have happened on Long Island, New York, to the sister and nephew of an office-mate of her friend's brother. FOAF behind FOAF behind FOAF right there.

The earliest printed version I've come across so far appeared in James Dent's column "The Gazetteer" in the *Charleston* (West Virginia) *Gazette* for May 12, 1988. Dent heard it from a woman whose brother in North Carolina, living with two other young bachelors, had supposedly taken the rabbit corpse from his golden retriever's teeth and submitted it to the required shampoo and blow-drying.

"This story sounds a little like an urban fable," Dent commented, "but the reader who told me the tale assures me that it actually happened."

That's pretty much the line I got from the other people in Illinois, Ohio, California, Florida, Pennsylvania, Washington, D.C., Maryland, Massachusetts, and Utah who sent me their versions. Everyone telling the story swore it was true, but then someone hearing the story disbelieved and wrote to me. "The Hare Drier" file got thicker and thicker, eventually including further published accounts from the *Canton* (Ohio) *Repository,* the *Chicago Tribune,* the *Dallas Times Herald,* and the *St. Louis Post-Dispatch.* As you might expect, Roger Rabbit, star of the big movie hit of summer 1988, kept popping up in these newspaper accounts.

I got two letters from England saying that the story was told there in late May. One version featured a dead cat instead of a rabbit. The neighbors take the mangled creature from their Doberman and race to a vet's office, where the cat is pronounced dead and disposed of. The incident costs the Doberman owners fifty pounds in vet's fees plus a speeding ticket. The cat owners wonder who has robbed their pet's grave. The other English version is the straight hare-drier legend, which my correspondent had heard twice. It's hard to guess, from evidence gathered so far, which way "The Hare Drier" migrated.

An American version of the legend involving a cat rather than a dog as the supposed rabbit killer (some cat!) was sent to me by Liz Parkhurst, vice president of August House publishers, Little Rock, Arkansas. Beyond that single variation in detail, her version was pretty standard, blow drier and all. But the circumstances of repeating this Arkansas text are fascinating. Ms. Parkhurst wrote: "The story is so powerful that the friend who told me this (as a true story) also told me this: Her teenage daughter, she said, who had moved out of the house in a fit of rebellion, broke her silence to call home and share the story."

Like I said, the year of the rabbit.

The variations kept rolling in. One afternoon in late June, I got a telephone call from a man named Bruce in Philadelphia. He apologized for the intrusion, but he was dying to know whether a story he'd heard in a bagel shop one morning was an urban legend. I asked him to start telling it, saying I would interrupt when I recognized the story (a technique that saves me a lot of time, though it makes me unpopular at parties).

"Well, in a suburb here called Chestnut Hill," Bruce began, "there's supposed to be this woman who had a large German shepherd as a pet . . ."

"Stop!" I said. "Her neighbor kept a rabbit in her backyard, right?"

Right it was, because Bruce had, of course, heard "The Hare Drier." He said that he had had his doubts about the story from the start, since, he explained, "someone from Chestnut Hill could easily afford to replace one rabbit, or even twenty, if something like that occurred."

"And would someone in Chestnut Hill keep a rabbit in the backyard?" I asked. No matter, since the person in the bagel shop swore it was true.

A couple of days later, the telephone rang right at dinner time—as usual. A radio-talk-show host in Los Angeles who consults me occasionally about urban legends was calling to ask if I would take a question live on the air about a story that was going around L.A.

I was so relieved to learn that the telephone call was not a telemarketer pushing dance lessons or carpet cleaning that I agreed.

It was worth it, since the radio host's version of the story included the unusual detail of the dead rabbit being found by a babysitter, then washed in Woolite, and hung by its ears in the shower to dry. What a scene!

The next afternoon, with rabbits on my mind, I came into the English Department at the University of Utah, where I teach, just as Laurie Spetsas, our department assistant, was sorting the mail. Handing me my letters, Laurie started to tell me about a hilarious dog-and-rabbit story she heard on a local talk show the night before.

So I played a little game with her. "Here are five unopened letters," I said. "I predict that at least one of them contains the same story."

The first four letters lacked the rabbit tale, and I began to fear that my gambit would fail. Then I opened letter number 5.

Presto! It contained a copy of Ron Blankenbaker's June 17 column in the *Salem* (Oregon) *Statesman-Journal* in which he repeated a story about a man whose hunting dog had dragged home the mangled corpse of the neighbor's cat. The cat got a shampoo and blow-dry before being sneaked back to its usual resting place in the neighbor's yard.

I handed Laurie the clipping, very pleased with myself.

But she protested that this was a cat story, not a rabbit story. So I pointed out the concluding words of Blankenbaker's column: "At about the same time I was being told about the kitty cat and the hunting dog, the same story

was being told to a colleague. Only there was a difference
. . . the victim was a neighbor's pet bunny rabbit."

Some days I maintain my reputation just by opening
my mail.

There are several other urban legends about pets, both
dead and alive, getting mixed up by humans. These
older stories probably had an influence on the surprise
appearance of "The Hare Drier" recently.

For example, there's the story about a dog, sent by air
freight, that rises from the dead. Here's how it goes:

Airline baggage handlers working at Chicago's O'-
Hare (that's a nice touch, no?) International Airport discover a dead poodle in a crate bound for Rome. They are
afraid of being accused of mishandling the animal and
causing its death, so they take up a collection, buy a new
poodle, and ship it to Rome in the same crate.

But when the pet's Italian owner comes to collect the
crate at the Rome airport, she faints in shock as the new
poodle bounds out of the crate to greet her.

Her pet had died in Chicago while accompanying her
on a tour of the States, and she was shipping the body
back to Italy for burial.

I've come across other dead-pets-in-package legends
many times before. Usually the animal is sent in a smaller
container than a shipping crate—a suitcase or shoebox,
for instance—which is stolen by a luckless thief. The
story of the transshipped poodle that rose from the dead
sounds to me like a baggage handlers' adaptation of the
usual tale. But this insider's urban legend reached the
general public and also became popular in 1988, as at-
tested to by several letters and clippings I received from
readers after mentioning the story in a column.

Among others who spread the story was former Marine Lieutenant Colonel Oliver North, star of the 1987
Iran-Contra hearings. North went on the lecture circuit

in 1988, and in his speeches he told jokes. One of his jokes turned out to be this same urban legend.

In Portland, Oregon, the *Willamette Week,* in an article published the week of July 28–August 3, 1988, reported that North began his address by telling a socko story that wowed the audience. The paper said that Ollie "had the crowd in stitches with a story about an airline baggage handler who feared he had killed a woman passenger's pet poodle (Poopsie) and so replaced it with an identical dog from a pet store." The baggage handler, who thought the dog had died of neglect, was afraid of losing his job as a result. So he went to the trouble of finding a dog that looked exactly like the original—almost exactly. North closed the story in the usual way, by describing the woman's surprise when she claimed her dog from the baggage carousel. As she opened the container, she fainted, because, as she explained later, she had been shipping her dead dog home for burial.

"The moral of the joke," for Ollie North, the *Willamette Week* explained, "was that trying harder may not be good enough. Ollie said he can relate to that."

I am definitely not claiming that North picked up his version of the story from my column. The same story has been around for at least a dozen years, and it had a spurt of new popularity in the spring of 1988. People wrote to me then from Maryland, New York, Colorado, and California, saying that they had recently heard this supposedly true story. And the *Week* also mentioned that "most of the crowd in Portland was laughing way before Ollie came anywhere near the punch line," which suggests that some of them must have heard the story not long before.

Jim Tilford, an aviation consultant in Mobile, Alabama, sent me an even older version of the baggage handlers' legend. He related a story he heard in the mid-1950s, when he was working for an airline that sometimes shipped pets to South America.

He heard about "a very valuable special breed cat" that was to be shipped to South America via Havana. The priceless feline had to remain overnight in the Havana freight terminal, and a Cuban employee who felt sorry for the animal let it out of its shipping crate for some exercise.

Cats (even purebred ones) being cats, the critter escaped in a flash of fur. Then, supposedly, the Cuban baggage handlers substituted a Havana alley cat in the shipping crate and sent it onward the next morning.

Tilford says that he and his fellow employees were convinced that the story was true and believed that the company would be facing a negligence suit if the champion cat was not found. But Tilford never learned the outcome of the case and now suspects that it was just another version of the dead-dog legend.

Helping to establish further the air-freighted dog or cat story as legendary is a similar account I received from Geoffrey van Dulken of Emsworth, England. He heard his version in New York in the 1960s.

A cargo of several German shepherds, he wrote, was being shipped overseas by air freight, with the plane scheduled to stop in Alaska to refuel. When the plane landed in Anchorage, a kindhearted baggage handler let the dogs out of their kennels for exercise. But when the plane was ready to depart, the handler had great difficulty rounding up the dogs and getting them back in the kennels. When the plane carrying the dogs reached its destination, one dog appeared to be sick. The shipping crew summoned a veterinarian who told them that it wasn't a German shepherd at all, but an Alaskan wolf.

Do I hear an echo of "The Mexican Pet" here? I'm referring to the legend about tourists on vacation in Mexico who "adopt" a cute little stray dog and smuggle it back to the United States, only to learn from their vet that it's actually a sewer rat.

But closer to "The Hare Drier" in its plot than any of these urban legends is a much older story about a farm boy who, neglecting his chores, repeatedly fails to feed the pigs. When a couple of pigs starve to death, the boy prop them up against the pigsty fence so that they appear to be alive when seen from the house. But one day, not long afterward, the boy falls ill and is confined to bed. His father, taking over the pig-feeding chores, discovers his son's ruse.

If any pig farmers are reading this book, could you tell me if this is still an active legend? (It's usually told as a family anecdote from many years ago, as in the version from Purcellville, Virginia, given in *A Celebration of American Family Folklore,* edited by Steven J. Zeitlin, Amy J. Kotkin, and Holly Cutting Baker [New York: Pantheon, 1982], p. 45, which was collected as part of the Smithsonian Institution's Family Folklore project.)

By late summer, the story had reached Australia in an elaborately reworded form. Columnist Jon Carroll in the *San Francisco Chronicle* for August 25, 1988, quoted a version from an unnamed newspaper in Sydney, commenting that the story "has the feel of one of those urban folktales, but, true or not, it is nevertheless a lovely story." The plot details in the Aussie text are not remarkable, but the wording of the story is. A sample: "Stricken with remorse over the predatory antics of his pooch, our red-faced protagonist carried off the bunny's corpse, washed and blow-dried it, before sneaking it back to its once-happy hutch. When our hapless hotelier later came across his neighbor, he nervously ventured an inquiry about how things were going. . . . His child's rabbit, he said, had died and, not wanting the tot upset, he had secretly buried it. Now, he said, it had returned, still dead, but noticeably more fluffy and spruce, to its former home."

Two lessons here: (1) journalists should *know,* not just guess, when a story is apocryphal; and (2) the straightforward wording of an oral story works better than purple prose for telling an urban legend.

A graduate student at the College of William and Mary in Williamsburg, Virginia, C. Ray Gardner, overheard another Australian version told in a restaurant. The teller repeated the story as it was sent to her in a letter from her brother Down Under: it was the standard blow-dried bunny legend. Gardner, who once had taken an undergraduate folklore course with me at the University of Utah, soon heard further versions told in the Williamsburg area (including one attributed to London) and recognized it as an urban legend. Good for you, Ray, and thanks!

At least two American newspaper columnists were late getting on the bunny bandwagon, publishing their discoveries of "The Hare Drier" in Autumn 1988. I spotted a reprint of Joe Murray's column—originally published in the *Lufkin* (Texas) *Daily News*—in the *San Francisco Chronicle* in mid-September. Murray originally heard what he called "Resurrection Rabbit" as an "Aggie" story and commented that "an Aggie by himself isn't nearly so funny as an Aggie with a dead rabbit." After hearing the first version, Murray spotted the same story told for true in newspapers from Dallas and Houston.

In the November 7, 1988, edition of *The Sioux City* (Iowa) *Journal,* in Cal Olson's column "My Turn," there's yet another Hare Drier version—surely not the last, but at least the latest I've found up to the deadline for this book manuscript. Olson heard it told about a woman from Holstein, Iowa, but attributed to her daughter, who "lives in a city with her family." The incident, supposedly, happened to two friends of the daughter's, Phyllis and Barbara; the rabbit's name was "Friskie." Olson, who is editor of the *Journal,* asked readers for advice to pass on to the dog's owner. How much should she admit to her neighbor? I wonder how many readers advised Olson that he simply should not have believed the rabbit story in the first place.

It just shows the risk editors take when they don't subscribe to my syndicated column.

Oops! Here are three more hare-drier versions that showed up the week I was proofreading the book. In February 1989, the story appeared in the Seattle *Weekly,* the *Akron* (Ohio) *Beacon Journal,* and the magazine *Toronto*. The editors of *Toronto* traced it to a version told by a local "theatre movement coach," who had learned it from an architect, who had heard it from someone in Davenport, Iowa, at a business meeting, who had received the story in the mail from his stepdaughter, an Iowa State University crisis-line volunteer who had been told that the incident had happened originally in a town in rural Iowa.

"The Flying Kitten"

This hilarious story was reported on June 1, 1987, in "Bob Levey's Washington," a column that appears in the *Washington Post*. (The same column a year earlier contained the automobile legend "The Arrest," as I mentioned in Chapter 2.) Two readers who sent clippings of Levey's column to me indicated that they had also heard the story repeated orally. I paraphrase:

A couple found a cute stray kitten and decided to keep it as a pet. One day, though, it climbed to the top branch of a birch tree in their backyard and refused to come down. After lots of fruitless coaxing, the couple looped a rope over the branch, hoping to pull the branch low enough for them to reach the stranded pet. But as they pulled, the rope broke and the kitten was launched into orbit. They were unable to find it.

A week later, while grocery shopping, they met one of their neighbors in the checkout line. The neighbor was carrying a bag of cat food.

"We didn't know you had a cat," one of them commented.

"I didn't until last week," the neighbor replied. "But Joe and I were sitting out on the patio the other day when this kitten dropped out of the sky, just like that. Fell right into Joe's lap."

Even though none of the thousands (?) of readers of my newspaper column about "The Flying Kitten" during the week of February 22, 1988, responded to my request for further versions of the story, I still feel sure that it must be a legend. Why? First, because Bob Levey quoted it from a woman who heard it from her Washington hairdresser. And, second, because stories about cats stuck in trees are usually apocryphal. (See the next legend.)

"The Bungled Rescue of the Cat"

Here's another dead-catter, one of that class of apocryphal stories involving a dead cat. I've heard it several
times from sources in different locations.

The latest person to send me this particular cat story is
The Very Rev. John T. Shone, M.A., Dean of the Scottish
Episcopal Church, Diocese of St. Andrews, Perth, Australia. (I quote directly from the reverend's impressive
letterhead.) He remembers having heard it told in several regions of Britain.

"The background facts are these," Dean Shone writes.
"British fire engines are always painted bright red. But
about ten years ago there was a national strike by the
Fire Brigade Union, and while the strike was on, emergency cover was provided by soldiers, sailors, and air-
men.

"They could not use the regular fire engines and had
to use government reserve engines, which were painted
green. The engines became known as 'Green God-
desses,' named after a popular TV personality.

"The story goes that a little old lady, during the strike,
found her cat had got up a tree and couldn't get down.
She dialed the emergency number, and a jolly squad of
soldiers arrived with a green goddess and rescued the
cat.

"The old lady was so delighted that she invited the
soldiers in for a cup of tea.

"After a while the soldiers merrily waved goodbye, got
in their green goddess, and drove off—killing the cat
which was then sitting underneath the fire engine.

"Although the strike has been over for years, the story
is still told, always as having happened locally," Reverend Shone closes. "I have never heard the story told in

relation to the regular fire brigade."

Well, I have. In fact, I had never heard of a Green Goddess until I read this letter. I've heard lots of versions that attribute the same bungled cat rescue to ordinary fire departments. Usually they're set in one part or another of Great Britain or, less commonly, in the United States.

It may well be that such an accident really did occur. But if so, the many subsequent repetitions of the story have adapted it to different times and places.

Several aspects of "The Bungled Rescue of the Cat" smell strongly of legend. For one, there's the matter of actual behavior versus legendary behavior of felines and humans. Few real-life cats will stay up in a tree for long, and few fire departments will respond to cat-up-a-tree calls until the pet has been given a long, long time to come down on its own. Furthermore, most cats will dart from beneath a parked vehicle as soon as it is started up. It's unusual for a normally alert cat to be killed by a car or truck in this way.

I'm sure I'll hear from cat owners disputing these generalizations. But even if such an incident could happen, I still doubt the truth of the story. The notion of a cat caught helplessly in a tree is most familiar to us as a proverbial plot—we all know the situation, but we've never actually seen such a thing. And the neat irony of the rescuers compounding the very problem they set out to solve sounds extremely predictable to me.

The legend seems to me to recycle the motif from a common legend about a mother who, rushing to take one injured child to an emergency room, backs her car over a second toddler playing behind the car.

It could happen, but did it? Probably not—at least not at all the times and in all the places to which the story has been attributed.

In his letter, Dean Shone remarked, "In my profession

we spend a lot of time listening to people." That's true of folklorists as well as clergymen. I am ready to listen to anyone who sends me further versions of "The Bungled Rescue" story or possible facts behind it.

4

Other Legends of Accidents and Mishaps

"The Heel in the Grate"

Frequently in my columns, I will mention a story that supposedly happened to someone and then guess that it's an urban legend because it seems so weird or funny and, plotwise, so neat. I invite readers to send me variations or verification. Sometimes I get nothing, but usually I receive a few letters reporting on different versions of the story from different locations, and that's about it.

"The Heel in the Grate" is my best success story so far in tracing a legend. When I queried readers about that one, I soon found myself flooded with mail and led straight back to its source.

Here's my original reference to the story from a column published the week of February 2, 1987:

Dear Professor:
My aunt told me this story in the late 1950's.
During a local wedding, one of the bridesmaids got the spike-heel of her shoe caught in a ventilation grate in the aisle. The next usher coming down the aisle tried to pick up the shoe; the entire grate came up, so he just took it with him.
Then the bride came down the aisle and fell in the

*hole. Was my aunt suckered by an urban legend? Have
you ever found the sources of such stories in the
Reader's Digest?*

> *Joyce Kehoe*
> *Seattle*

Dear Joyce:
    *I think it's a legend, but I can't prove it—yet. There
are plenty of apocryphal stories involving series of
accidents, and a handful of others exist about mishaps
at weddings. This one sounds like a legend, but I would
need either testimony from a participant in the incident
or further versions of the story from different times and
locations to be sure. It certainly does sound like one of
those* Reader's Digest *items, doesn't it?*
    How about it, readers?

My column spurred several people in Dayton, Ohio, to
guide me to the story's origin. Such discoveries are rare
in urban-legend studies, and tracing an item published
in one of the hundreds of issues of the *Reader's Digest*
takes more time and patience than I possess.

The answers to both of Joyce Kehoe's questions
turned out to be "Yes," and the telling data came from
Dayton because that's where "The Heel in the Grate"
first got into print.

But to begin with, here's the *Digest* connection: "The
Heel in the Grate" appeared there in January 1958
under the headline "Chain Reaction." It told of a young
woman in an Ontario church getting her "needle heel"
stuck in a hot-air register and was attributed to the *Kitch-
ener-Waterloo* (Ontario) *Record,* which had quoted it, in
turn, from the publication *The Lutheran,* where presumably it originated.

In the *Digest*-transmitted version, a choir was beginning the recessional, singing as they marched. The last

woman in the line was the one who lost her shoe, the first man behind her picked it up along with the heating grate, and the following man fell into the opening.

Now, for the truth. The incident did happen, but not in Canada and not in a Lutheran church. Nor was it at a wedding, as in the Seattle version. The story goes back to a mishap that took place a decade or so earlier at the Hanover Presbyterian Church in Hanover, Indiana, at the end of a regular church service, when the choir was marching down the aisle, singing.

I know this because several readers in Dayton, Ohio, said that they knew of the story from their local paper, the *Dayton Journal-Herald,* which had mentioned specific names. I also got a letter from Woodfin ("Woody") Jones, who was a witness to the incident and had been the source of the first printed version. (All this quickly came to me because the *Dayton Journal-Herald* carried my column at that time.)

According to Woody Jones, he and two Beta Theta Pi fraternity brothers at Hanover College, Jim Stuckey and Ed Steiner, were involved in the event, which took place in spring 1949.

According to Jones, Stuckey was the one who picked up the woman's shoe along with the grate; another student behind him stepped over the hole; and Ed Steiner, a baritone, fell into it.

I also checked with Woody's former college classmates. James A. Stuckey, now of Port Chester, New York, backed his two fraternity brothers with this elegant testimonial, which he sent to me: "I, James Albert Stuckey, was a member of the Hanover College Choir in the spring of 1949 who, during the recessional, spied the shoe caught in the grate of the hot air register in the center of the aisle. Being the kind of courteous, thoughtful freshman so highly prized in those days, I stopped to retrieve the shoe . . . and the grate . . . tucked both under my copy of the hymnal and continued down the aisle."

Lest any suspect that this fraternity man is perpetuating a decades-old joke, consider this: Brother Jim is now Reverend James A. Stuckey, pastor of the Presbyterian Church in Port Chester.

Edwin C. Steiner, Hanover class of 1950, now living in Midland, Michigan, also confirmed the story: "Yes, it certainly was I who fell into that hot air duct," he wrote. "I hit the hole cleanly; I didn't even scrape my toe on the edge. It was like stepping off a gigantic stair step, and I went into the hole all the way up to my thigh."

The story surfaced in print when Marj Heyduck, a late *Dayton Journal-Herald* columnist, heard it from Woodfin Jones and published it in her popular column "Third and Main" on August 15, 1957. Jones was at that time executive secretary of the Greenville, Ohio, Chamber of Commerce.

Five months later, finding her story almost verbatim in the *Digest* and, subsequently, in dozens of church newsletters and other small publications, Heyduck doublechecked with Jones to be sure he was not putting her on. He swore he had told the truth. So in a column published on March 8, 1958, Heyduck explained how the true story had taken on a life of its own in oral tradition and in print. As she summed up the case then, "Woody was in the church. Woody told Marj. And Marj printed the story."

Heyduck's theory about how the story was spread—detailed in her book *The Best of Marj* in 1962—was that it might have been repeated widely both from her writings and from the many times she told it in talks she gave.

We can get an idea of how the story became stylized into a true folk legend in some of the variations. Marj herself first specified in her book version that the soprano, the baritone, and the bass were the choir members involved. But a later published version mentioned the soprano, the alto, and the tenor; while a second source said it was the soprano, the tenor, and the minister. The wedding version, like this third choir version, arranges the details for the best possible climax to the story—having the bride herself fall into the hole.

Another embellishment to the story was giving the minister a funny punchline. In one version, for example, the minister, at a loss for the right words, blurts out by way of a benediction, "And now unto Him who will keep us from falling. . . ." Pandemonium followed in the church!

Marj Heyduck died in 1969 and was the subject of an appreciative column in her paper by writer Mickey Davis. "Marj was famous for her hats," Davis wrote, explaining how she was photographed wearing a different hat for each one of her columns. Davis concluded that "she was a reader's delight, but a photographer's nightmare."

I must add to this that she and Woody Jones, Jim Stuckey, and Ed Steiner, and the others who wrote to me are all folklorist's dreams. They included clippings, photocopies, accurate dates, and full names and addresses for all concerned. Thanks to them, for once I found the origin of an urban legend.

There was one more lucky coincidence in tracing the life story of "The Heel in the Grate." My column unraveling the whole business was released the week of July 20, 1987. And, with the subject on my mind, I mentioned it the following week in my summer American Folklore class at the University of Utah, whereupon a student said, "I saw a scene like that in a movie on the Disney Channel last night."

The film, she said, called *The Glass Bottom Boat,* was a 1966 release that included in the cast Doris Day, Rod Taylor, Dick Martin, and Arthur Godfrey. The plot summary in the television listings didn't sound promising, however, and I wondered if the student was remembering correctly. Nobody else in class had seen the broadcast, so I wondered how I could double-check the scene in the film.

"Well," the student said, "you can just borrow my tape and watch it for yourself if you want to." And why, I inquired, had she made a tape of the film? Because, she explained, she's a big Doris Day fan and never misses a chance to capture DD on her VCR. That's why.

Never mind the convoluted plot of the whole film, which I watched strictly in the line of duty that night. The scene we are interested in here is this one: Doris Day steps into a sort of astronauts' clean room to demonstrate its function for a group of people who are touring the space-flight facility where she works. Doris loses her shoe when her spike heel gets caught in the floor grating; Rod picks up the shoe and the grate, and Dick comes along a bit later and falls in.

Evidently a writer working on that script in the mid-1960s had read about "The Heel in the Grate" in the 1958 *Reader's Digest*—or perhaps in a church magazine or newsletter—and then filed the anecdote away for future reference.

Just think, if a rabid Doris Day fan had not enrolled in my folklore class that summer, and if the old film had not been rerun on TV, I may never have located this final piece to the puzzle of "The Heel in the Grate."

Or *is* it the final piece? I think it would be just great to find some more versions of "The Heel in the Grate."

"The Ice-Cream-Cone Caper"

The Great Ice-Cream-Cone-Caper of 1986 was an embarrassing example of news reporting gone awry when confronted with an emerging urban legend. As Art Nauman, ombudsman of the *Sacramento Bee,* wrote in September, "Just when you think journalism has reached a state of perfection, along comes an episode like this to restore your faith."

For a few months that year, the story was everywhere, including local and national newspapers, the wire services, magazines, network television, and radio talk shows coast to coast. A UPI story, circulated on September 12, rightly characterized it as "in the class with contemporary myths like The Vanishing Hitchhiker."

In case you stayed home that summer with the plug pulled on your TV and all the papers canceled, here's how the cone caper went. Either Paul Newman in Wesport, Connecticut (or Jack Nicholson in Cohasset, Massachusets, or Robert Redford in Santa Fe, New Mexico, or even Tom Brokaw somewhere else), is in a local ice-cream store. A woman comes in and recognizes the star. She is on the verge of swooning with ecstasy, but she is determined to remain calm and not disgrace herself or invade the star's privacy. So she buys a cone and departs without saying anything, but outside the store she realizes that, while she has her change, she's missing her ice-cream cone. She goes back in to claim what is rightly hers, whereupon the celebrity—licking his own cone—comments, "You'll find it in your purse, ma'am—right where you put it."

Some journalists made unsuccessful attempts to check the story out with Paul Newman himself (who, by the

way, does live in Westport). Others approached Robert Redford, who was in fact filming a movie in Santa Fe at the time, or Jack Nicholson, who had recently filmed in Cohasset. These grains of truth made the story seem plausible to some, but I recognized at once that it was too good—and had too many variations—to be true.

Yet also, as Steven Slosberg of the *New London* (Connecticut) *Day* commented, it was a story "too good not to share." Numerous papers ran the story, analyzed it (and retracted it), but obviously at the same time enjoyed it tremendously. Headline writers had fun with the story, dreaming up phrases about putting the episode on ice, scooping the competition, providing more poop on the scoop, following a melting story, keeping one's cool, and so forth.

Even the mentioned celebrities eventually got into the act as transmitters of the ice-cream-cone caper, with

Nicholson slyly saying that perhaps it had, indeed, happened to him sometime that summer, and Newman being quoted in *USA Today* saying that he felt like suing Nicholson and Redford because the tale was *his* false story of the summer.

Most people tell such stories as having happened to a friend of a friend (a FOAF, for short). And most of them do, indeed, believe the tale to be true; after all, someone else told them it happened to a FOAF, and so they pass it on, giving a FOAF as the source, as does the next person, and so on. That elusive "friend of a friend," the ultimate source of the story, always seems to be just a few story-tellers back. But if you try to trace it, the trail usually just keeps going and going . . . until it's gone.

A few facts eventually came out showing how the ice-cream-cone caper got into print, though its origin as an oral tale remained hidden.

Hartford (Connecticut) *Courant* reader representative Henry McNulty found the earliest printed version of the ice-cream-cone story in the *Greenwich* (Connecticut) *News* in a June 5, 1986, column mentioning the star as being Paul Newman. The story was written by columnist Jerry Dumas, who heard it from his wife, who heard it from another woman, to whom it supposedly happened. But when Dumas went to check it out, it turned out that the woman actually had heard it from another woman, who heard it from a minister, who heard it from . . . . Well, Dumas never was able to get back to the original source.

In *USA Today,* a reporter is mentioned who heard it at a party from a businessman, who "heard it from a broker, who heard it from a client, whose secretary was supposedly the lady in question."

The *Boston Business Journal* described another reporter who got it from his wife, who got it from a friend, who got it from a minister. And a journalist from St. Louis told me she knew a source who had heard it told at choir practice and was indignant to learn that the story was probably not true.

In late August, Hollywood columnist Marilyn Beck gave national publicity to the Jack Nicholson version. By October, oral transmission had returned the story to California, except that by then it was said to be either Redford in Beverly Hills or Newman *and* Joanne Woodward (his wife) in a Hollywood ice-cream store.

The *Los Angeles Times,* in an editorial published on September 15 headlined "The Stuff of Legends," invoked yours truly as an urban-legend expert and concluded, "Sounds tailor-made for his collection."

I shall restrain myself from drawing from the ice-cream-cone caper any ponderous lessons about the gullibility or deviousness of the press (or, perhaps, press agents). Nor shall I offer a Freudian interpretation of the story, even though at least one other columnist did so ("The cone and purse take on a little obvious symbolism"). Could be, could be. I won't deny it.

However, our star-oriented culture eats up stories like this precisely because they address something that so many of us think about: "Oh, my god! What would I do if I met Paul Newman?" (or Madonna, or Robert Redford, or whomever). The very foolishness of the people in these stories constitutes their appeal. We're so relieved that we weren't personally involved, we remember the story and repeat it, putting the onus of star-struck idiocy on someone else. It's a neat catharsis for our own petty fears.

This all confirms the conclusion of the aforementioned *Los Angeles Times* editorial, that such stories are "just plausible enough to assume a life of their own, even though they are not true."

Amen!

"The Pregnant Shoplifter"

Another one of those news stories that reads like a legend concerned a woman in Arlington, Virginia, who in February 1985 was nine months pregnant. The Associated Press reported that she went shopping at Irving's sporting-goods store in a shopping center in Falls Church, Virginia. Store personnel took a look at her and decided that she was trying to smuggle a basketball out of the store. They detained her, threatened her with arrest, and searched her.

Even the journalistic reports of the incident introduced some variation into the story. The wire service quoted her as saying, "I had to disrobe in front of six male security guards and police officers in the store." The *Baltimore Sun,* however, quoted the woman as describing the search this way: "They made me take off some of my garments. . . . I had to shake out my maternity top."

At any rate, the woman had a son the very next day and named him Darius. She later filed a $600,000 lawsuit against the store.

I at once suspected this story to be an urban legend because I first saw it in a September 1985 newspaper clipping that gave the gist of the incident with none of the above identifying details. It sounded more like an item from the tabloid press than a reliable news report.

Also, I came across some secondhand accounts of radio and TV reports of the incident. Columnist Herb Caen of the *San Francisco Chronicle* had the same impression of it that I initially did and commented "Too neat. Sounds like a fable." In fact, a few generalized retold versions of the story have occasionally been sent to me

more recently by people who do not remember seeing or hearing any actual news report of the incident, but who have learned of it by word of mouth. So, even if the story was not a legend to begin with, it may eventually achieve legendary status.

A turned-around version of this shoplifting story that definitely is a fable of long-standing concerns a man who attempts to smuggle a frozen chicken out of a supermarket by concealing it in his hat. Numbed by the frozen meat sitting atop his head, he faints in the checkout line and is arrested. In another version, it was an old lady who was spotted when a clerk saw the chicken's blood running down her head. This story has been told around the United States, as well as England and Sweden, since the early 1970s.

Yet another older story along these lines has it that a worker in an aircraft plant was trying to steal fifty feet of air hose by wrapping it around his chest. It's said that he passed out while waiting in line to exit the plant because he had wrapped the hose too tightly around himself.

Doubtless, some urban legends spring from real-life incidents and pass into folklore, thus losing their connection with the people to whom they happened. The pregnant-shoplifter story, though, shows that it can work both ways, with the legend coming first and the similar real-life incident occurring later.

"The Barrel of Bricks"

Dear Professor—
Have you heard a story about a man using a pulley
and a barrel to move a load of bricks? I forget the exact
sequence. It was going around about fifteen years ago,
and I think I read it once in National Lampoon.
                                        Adam Granger
                                        Minneapolis (September 1986)

This is typical of the queries that I receive two or three
times a year about the "Barrel of Bricks" story. People
usually remember the plot of the story rather dimly, but
they always recall that the complicated brick-and-pully
incident was hilarious.

I already had a fat file on the story when I wrote this
column in December 1987, but there were several gaps
remaining in the story's history. Reprinting the column
here, I have inserted in square brackets the added material that I subsequently got from my readers or as a result
of their helpful information. But, as my conclusion
shows, I still remain inconclusive about the ultimate origin of this fascinating bit of traditional humor.

Dear Reader—
Yes, I know this legend, which I call "The Barrel of
Bricks." It appears to be an old slapstick plot that keeps
resurfacing as a legend.
Usually the plot takes the form of a letter from a
foreign or poorly-educated workman explaining why he
needs sick leave. In 1966, for example, I clipped a
version with the dateline "Saigon," circulated to
newspapers as a "Chicago Daily News—Post Dispatch
Special Dispatch." The alleged letter from a Vietnamese

workman had six numbered paragraphs, beginning:

(1)*When I arrived at building T-1640 to fix it, I found that the rains had dislodged a large number of tiles on the roof. So I rigged up a beam with a pulley at the top of the building and hoisted up a couple of barrels of tile.*

(2)*When I fixed the building there was a lot of tile left over. I hoisted the barrel back up again and secured the line at the bottom and then went up and filled the barrel with the extra tile. Then I went down to the bottom and cast off the line.*

(3)*Unfortunately the barrel of tile was heavier than I was, and before I knew what was happening the barrel started down and I started up. I decided to hang on, and half way up met the barrel coming down and received a severe blow on the shoulder.*

The hapless workman, continuing his letter, then describes hitting his head on the beam, jamming his fingers in the pulley, starting to fall, being struck by the barrel on his way down, crashing into the bricks on the ground, and finally letting go of the rope and thus releasing the barrel—which falls on him.

All of this is told in the same manner as above, the numbered points and precise language clashing with the absurd events and the workman's assumed naïveté toward dealing with the managerial class, until the story—unbelievable to begin with—is positively ludicrous.

The letter writer concludes: "I respectfully ask for sick leave."

This story has been reprinted in different forms in a wide variety of sources: Playboy *(June 1972),* Games *(May/June 1982), various joke books, the 1967* Turner's Carolina Almanac *(published in Winston-Salem, North Carolina, and retold in the third person), and elsewhere. In June 1978 the barrel of* bricks story was even included in a safety newsletter circulated on my own university campus in Utah. This time the mishap was said to have occurred to a workman during his first day on a construction job, and the newsletter editor added this comment:

"At a time when the language of bureaucracy seems to sink ever deeper into gobbledygook, it is always refreshing and encouraging to find an example of clear, vivid writing where it might be least expected." But the editor did not say where he found the text.

I laughed so hard sitting there in my office reading this version that a couple of colleagues stopped in to see if I had finally lost my mind completely in the search for urban legends.

I doubt that many people actually tell the complicated story as an oral joke. Judging from my mail, the story usually gets around by way of photocopies posted on office bulletin boards. I have several such copies in my files, typed out, but usually with a handwritten heading like "And I thought I had some bad days!"

The same kind of letter also circulates in England. The British version, which often opens with the greeting "Respected Sir—" is frequently set in the West Indies, where roof tiles or bricks can easily be torn loose by hurricanes and where—according to the letter—the replacement is done by a native workman.

English writer Rodney Dale, the man who coined the term FOAF (friend of a friend) in his 1978 book The Tumour in the Whale," credited the story to "the late Gerard Hoffnung" who, wrote Dale, used the bricklayer story as a comic monologue. Dale heard Hoffnung's stage performance on a 1958 Decca record, which I have been unable to locate.

[Howard M. Block of Newark, Delaware, wrote to say that he found my column about "The Barrel of Bricks" especially "striking." I forgive Mr. Block that pun, for *he sent me a tape recording of the long-sought Hoffnung performance.*

Block wrote that he bought the record in England during a United States Air Force tour of duty there in 1959 because he recognized Hoffnung's rendition as a near-exact copy of a story that Block's Uncle Percy used to tell. The uncle was in the building trade in England, and claimed that the incident had happened to one of his mates on the job. Later, after running across the Hoffnung record, Block realized that Uncle Percy was merely carrying on his well-deserved reputation as a storyteller.

The Hoffnung performance as recorded was presented in the form of the comedian reading a letter that he said had appeared in print. The text is an absolutely straightforward rendering of the typical British form of the story ("Respected Sir—" etc.), except for mentioning that the incident supposedly happened in a place called "Golders Green."]

I do have my own copy of another recording of "The Barrel of Bricks," on Bert and I Stem Inflation, *a 1961 album on which Marshall Dodge and Robert Bryant, two storytellers from Maine, tell it in a droll Down East dialect. They add this concluding moral: " 'Bert,' I said, 'that should be a lesson to both of us. If you try to hold on to something of value these days, through all the ups and downs, you'll end up in the barrel for sure, all smashed up and nothing to show for your efforts but a pile of dust.' "*

[J. D. Robbin of San Jose, California, wrote to say that The Clancy Brothers/Live with Robbie O'Connell, *a 1982 Vanguard album, includes a song called "The Boss," which tells "The Barrel of Bricks" story in the form of a folklike ballad. I suppose there may be more of these kinds of adaptations around that I haven't located yet.]*

Other sources make me wonder how far back the story goes.

Scot Morris, in his wonderfully browseable Book of Strange Facts & Useless Information *(Garden City, NY: Doubleday/Dolphin Books, 1979), reprints the same Saigon version of the story that I quoted from above, and he alludes to another told by radio comedian Fred Allen in 1932. Other people have told that they remember Allen using the story on his radio shows.*

[The state of Delaware is a rich source of data on this story. Herman F. Reinhold, Jr., of Wilmington sent me photocopies of pages out of H. Allen Smith's 1945 book Desert Island Decameron *(New York: Pocket Books, 1949) in which appears a Fred Allen routine in hillbilly dialect incorporating "The Barrel of Bricks." In a parody of trial proceedings called "Mountain Justice," a character named "Jolo Tate" sues his insurance company, claiming that he had suffered five accidents and the company will only pay for one.*

Judge Fred Allen's verdict, based on Tate's account of "The Barrel of Bricks" accident, is this: "When ye say 'em slow, ye got five. But reel 'em off and they group up on ye."]

Folklorist Edward D. Ives of the University of Maine tells me that he saw the story acted out in a "Pete Smith Specialty" film short released sometime in the 1940s, another source I am still seeking.

Folklorist Mac Barrick of Shippensburg State University, Pennsylvania, may have discovered the likely ancestor of all the modern retellings of "The Barrel of Bricks" in an Irish dialect version six decades old. The implications in the language of this version of the workman's ignorance and semi-literacy anticipate the theme of racism and ethnic stereotyping found in most of the later examples of "The Barrel of Bricks."

Barrick sent me the text as he copied it from a

jokebook dated 1918 (Percy F. Smith, Memory's
Milestones *[Pittsburgh: privately printed]). This time an
Irish construction worker who is "lowering heavy tile in
a barrel from the top of a 10-story building" suffers just
two stages of the usual accident. The mishap is
witnessed by other workmen looking out the building's
windows, and Pat replies to their question about
whether he is hurt by saying, "Get away wid ye; I passed
you twice in a minute and not one of yez as much as
spoke to me; yez are not a bit sociable."*

*And, finally, yes Dear Reader (returning to the
original question), "The Barrel of Bricks" did appear in*
National Lampoon, *in a feature called "All New True
Facts, 1986." A reader from Honolulu had submitted
the story in all its complicated glory. The editor's
comment was, "This story happened when they were
working on the Pyramids or something even older."*

*[I'm not back to the Pyramids yet in searching out the
presumed origin of "The Barrel of Bricks," but I have
found another printed version, attributing it this time to
the late eighteenth century! The source is Henry D.
Spalding's anthology* The Best of American Jewish
Humor *(New York: Jonathan David, 1976), pp.
109–110.*

*What we have here is a letter allegedly sent on
September 8, 1776, to "Gen. G. Washington" by "Cpl.
Isaac Franks." (Why is a corporal writing to a general?)
The text begins in the traditional way—"Respected
Sir"—and ends similarly—"I respectfully request sick
leave." It contains most of the usual phrases of other
versions: "I rigged up a beam with a pulley at the top of
the building . . . ," etc. So is this letter the source of
"The Barrel of Bricks? I doubt it. In fact, I even doubt
that the letter is authentic.*

*In the language used in the supposed 1776 letter
from Isaac Franks, for example, only the spelling of the*

word "kegge" gives the style a slight tinge of antiquity, but none of the other spellings nor the phraseology is even remotely like that of the time from which it supposedly originates. For example, the phrase "sick leave" would hardly have been used in the hard-pressed revolutionary army, especially not in the fall of 1776 when Washington's army was recovering from the Battle of Long Island. Nor were written dates expressed at that time in the modern "military" format: "8 September 1776."

Editor Spalding introduced the alleged Franks letter in his book by commenting that Isaac Franks's "most comical misadventure . . . earned him a special niche in the humorous folklore of the people." Spalding also refers to the letter as being "surely . . . the most uproariously funny document in the archives of the United States Government."

A source note says this letter was "adapted from" Joseph Mendes's The Franks of Philadelphia, published in 1871.

Unable to locate the Mendes book via the usual Interlibrary Loan sources and bibliographic data bases, I wrote to Henry D. Spalding, who was retired and seventy-five years old when I reached him in October 1988. Spalding was unable to recall where he had consulted the book, nor could he find his source notes for the Isaac Franks version of "The Barrel of Bricks" in his personal files that had been partly destroyed by fire some years earlier.

The elusive Mendes book—for which I am still searching—may have been a family history published only in a limited edition, or it could have been a manuscript work that Spalding once saw during his many years of compiling examples of Jewish humor from a variety of sources. Isaac Franks of Philadelphia was real enough, but even the Special Collections

*Department of the University of Pennsylvania Library
was unable to come up with any information about the
book concerning his family or about its author. Edwin
Wolf II, co-author of the definitive* History of the Jews
of Philadelphia *(1956), wrote to me (on September 31,
1988) that he believed the Franks letter to be a hoax,
and he doubted the existence of the Mendes work, at
least as a published book.*

*If any hoaxing was going on here, I suspect that the
blame rests on the shoulders of Mendes (whoever he
was) or of somebody else faking a reference under that
name. A hoaxer may have inserted into the Frankses'
family history a slightly reworded version of "The
Barrel of Bricks" as if it were an eighteenth-century
document and then passed this doubtful "information"
on to Spalding. Even though Henry Spalding, in his
own words, wrote his books "for their entertainment
value, with authenticity a poor second," he is also a
trained journalist who worked for many years on the*
Los Angeles Daily News. *Spalding seems an unlikely
writer to invent a source. Besides, he frankly stated in*
The Best of American Jewish Humor *that his version
was "adapted." If only we knew in what ways it was
altered and from what source.*

*Not to leave any stone unturned, I inquired from the
National Archives about the surviving records of Isaac
Franks. A single letter from Franks to the Congress
written in 1783 is on file. As for letters from Isaac
Franks to George Washington, Philander D. Chase of
the University of Virginia, editor of the Revolutionary
War Series of the general's papers, kindly searched his
indexes for a Franks letter. He found only one from
March 1782 in which Franks resigned his commission as
an ensign in the Seventh Massachusetts Regiment.
Chase's opinion of the letter that Spalding published
was that although it lacked any "blatant anachronisms,"*

*it still did not sound right for the time. "For instance,"
he wrote, "a Revolutionary soldier would more likely
say 'hospital' than 'infirmary.' "*

*Isaac Franks lived from 1759 to 1822, joined the rebel
army at the age of seventeen (in 1776, which was the
year of the alleged "kegge of brackets" letter), and,
after retiring from active duty, was made a lieutenant
colonel in the Pennsylvania militia in 1794. I have found
no evidence that he ever served in as lowly a rank as
corporal. Franks's letter applying for a veteran's
pension in 1818 is published in* The Jews of the United
States 1790–1840 *(1963). But there's not a word here,
nor in any other source on Isaac Franks and his military
service, about an incident even slightly resembling
"The Barrel of Bricks."*

So that's the story on the man who didn't *write "The
Barrel of Bricks." I put all this stuff in mainly because I
found it interesting. Besides, others will stumble upon
the letter published in Spalding's book, and they will
write to me identifying the supposed "original" of the
story. And now I've got my reply ready in advance!*

*I got another note recently about "The Barrel of
Bricks" from—would you believe—Wilmington,
Delaware, again. Margaret Seramone sent me a
photocopy of a 1982 column she had saved from the*
Louisville *(Kentucky)* Courier-Journal. *The writer,
Byron Crawford, repeats a story that a friend of his
passed on from a small-town newspaper in Georgia,
"alleged to be a copy of a letter written by a client to his
insurance company." Here we go again! Those bricks
and that workman, it seems, are still going up and
down, up and down, up and down . . .]*

"Trouble with Technology"

In modern folklore our present-day technology may substitute for the supernaturalism in myths from earlier epochs. As a result, we hear urban horror stories concerning microwave ovens, fast foods, and elevators rather than monsters, omens, or evil spells.

A case in point are the recent stories about now-familiar technological advances that have been introduced relatively recently. Already there is an emerging body of folklore about them.

For example, I've heard several times from bank personnel about a frustrated robber who they believe tried to hold up an automatic teller machine somewhere. (It was never the storyteller's own bank.) The man allegedly wrote a note saying "Give me all your money, or I'll shoot" and inserted the slip of paper into the bank's ATM. When three such attempts gained him nothing, the man is said to have become so angry that he shot the machine full of holes, thus attracting the police, who arrested him.

I have also heard rumors—but never found verification—of a computer store that was unable to hook up a printer to one customer's computer, whereupon the man became so irate that he shot and killed the salesman. In a variant of that story, the computer store keeps ordering the wrong cables for connecting the parts of the system, and the angry customer strangles a clerk with one of them. (Actually, I almost did that one time myself.)

A more old-fashioned technological legend concerns the proper way to load a dishwashing machine. Some people claim that you should never put knives and forks point up in the silverware basket because a woman who did it one time tripped and fell on an open dishwasher, impaling herself on the sharp points and dying as a result.

In a similar, and probably apocryphal, story that an electrician told me, three-prong grounded wall outlets are supposed to be very dangerous when installed in the usual way—with the two power openings on top and the single ground connector at the bottom. This electrician had heard several times about a nun being electrocuted when her rosary accidentally fell across the power points of a three-prong plug that was leaning slightly out of its wall mounting. Still, the electrician said, she had never heard of anyone actually mounting wall plugs "upside down" so as to avoid killing careless nuns.

My favorite technological legend of late was sent by a reader from Indiana. She heard about "someone's in-laws somewhere" who started hearing a constant peeping sound coming from their basement. Unfortunately, as is usual in these situations, it was a weekend, and no exterminator would come out to check it until Monday. So the homeowners locked the basement door and taped it all around the edges to keep the mysterious creature inside. When the exterminator arrived, he broke the seal and fearfully shut and locked the door behind him as he descended the stairs in search of the dreaded pest. The exterminator, however, came quickly back upstairs and pounded on the door to get out. He had traced the peeping sound to technology, not varmints. "To solve your problem," he reported, "you will just need to go down there and put new batteries in your smoke alarm."

(After the above story appeared in a column, I heard from a reader in Milwaukee whose parents, living in Kansas, had indeed mistaken the chirping sound of their smoke detector for a cricket hiding in the house. This may indicate the actual origin of the apocryphal story, but it also makes me wonder if there are stories about telephones that "chirp" instead of ringing normally in the way that God, and Alexander Graham Bell, intended phones to do.)

Along the same technological lines are what I call "The Tales of Bungling Brides." Although the stereotype of the inept newlywed woman is passé nowadays, some of the old stories still circulate among people who are presumably hearing them for the first time. One such story is represented in the following letter.

Dear Professor—

Have you heard about the bride who cut the bones out of the drumsticks before she baked the Thanksgiving turkey? Her husband asked her why she was doing so, but she didn't really know. Puzzled, she called her mother, who had taught her to prepare a turkey this way.

Her mother explained, "I always did that because our oven at home is too small to put the turkey in with the bones in the drumsticks poking out."

M.B.
Kansas City, Missouri

Dear Reader:

This is a variation on an old standard bungling bride story. More often I used to hear that she is asked by her husband why she always cuts the end off a roast or a ham before putting it into the oven. As in your story, she merely was imitating her mother's practice, not realizing that Mom had simply done it that way in order to make large cuts of meat fit into her small roasting pan.

Another bungling bride story was heard more frequently in the days before home air conditioning was common.

Houses then always had screen doors, and more than

one new husband was said to have been curious when
he observed his bride fastening little balls of cotton to
the screen doors with hair pins. He asked her why she
did that.

"They keep flies out of the house," she answered. But
how, he wondered, could cotton balls on the screen
have any effect on flies. His wife wasn't really sure, so
she called her mother who had taught her this wifely
skill.

Very simple, Mom explained. She always used to stuff
the cotton from pill bottles and the like into holes in the
screen doors to plug them up after kids or collisions had
damaged the screen. It really worked well to keep flies
out of the house!

"Waiting for the Ice Man"
—Another Domestic Drama

Having gotten, in the previous section, to the subject of old wives' tales about wives, I'll include just one more such story that was sent to me by a reader in response to a different housewife-in-trouble legend. But this one never made it into a published column.

Dear Professor—

Your column describing the housewife being accidentally caught in the nude with a football helmet on her head by a repairman reminded me of a variation that was told in the mid to late 1930s in Cincinnati.

The woman I heard about was just about to take a shower when she remembered that she needed to unlock the back door so the ice man could get to her ice box. (This was before everyone had electric refrigerators.)

But as she opened the door the gas-meter reader appeared, and naturally the woman, in her natural state, was taken by surprise.

She blurted out to the meter man, "Oh, I was just waiting for the ice man."

> *R.N.*
> *Munster, Indiana*

Dear Reader—

Stories about affairs with the ice man have been around for decades. Eugene O'Neill's drama The Iceman Cometh, *written in 1939–40, takes its title partly from that notion and stems from about the same period as when you heard the anecdote.*

The punchline conclusion of your story—similar to the ending of the other nude housewife legend ("I hope your team wins, lady")—indicates that both of these items fall somewhere between being legends and jokes.

But it's funny stuff, or was once thought so, no matter how we label it nowadays.

5

Sex and Scandal Legends

"AIDS Mary"

As the epidemic of AIDS spreads, so does a story about a mysterious woman who is intentionally giving the disease to others. The story has shown up on the grapevine virtually everywhere, with only minor variations in detail. Here's one telling of it:

A recently divorced man went to a singles bar, where he met a beautiful woman. They became friendly and ended up going to his place, where they made love all night. The man woke up the next morning, and she was gone. He went into the bathroom. Then he looked at the mirror. Scrawled there, in bright red lipstick, was the message, "WELCOME TO THE WORLD OF AIDS!"

Supposedly the woman had become embittered after catching the disease from an earlier lover and was determined to pass it on to every man she could seduce. This woman has made her deadly appearance in bedrooms from Chicago to Fresno to Dallas and everywhere in between, as well as in Europe—at least according to legends.

One Florida reader wrote in with a much more detailed version, which he claims happened to a friend of his brother's. This fellow was at a nightclub, where he met a pretty, young woman. She went home with him and spent the night. In the morning, he asked if he could drive her home, but she insisted on being dropped off on a street corner.

However, she made a date to meet him at the nightclub again and, again, went home with him. This went on for about a month. One morning, the man woke up to find her gone. He took a shower, emerged from the bathroom, and saw that she had scrawled the chilling message on the bureau mirror.

According to the Florida account, doctors have told the man that he has contracted the disease. He now spends all his time looking for his killer. But no one seems to know her, and she has not returned to the nightclub.

I received a dramatic example of the rapid spread of modern urban legends after I sent an account of "AIDS Mary" in late November 1986 to Bengt af Klintberg, my Swedish folklorist friend who also follows such matters. He responded: "Early in the morning of December 10th a distant acquaintance called me on the telephone and told me the same story. She had heard it from a friend in Växjö in southern Sweden. Then, when I came into my institute at Stockholm University that day, there was a letter waiting for me, written by a journalist in Malmö telling the same story. Both ended with the message, written with lipstick on the mirror, 'WELCOME TO THE AIDS CLUB.' "

The same "AIDS CLUB" version appeared on January 8, 1987, in Rob Morse's column in the *San Francisco Examiner*. But this time it was said to have happened to a French businessman who spent a weekend with a Jamaican woman.

Chuck Fallis, a spokesman for the Centers for Disease Control in Atlanta, the clearinghouse for information on Acquired Immune Deficiency Syndrome and other epidemics, told me that this story is apocryphal—in fact, he called it "an urban legend" without any prompting from me.

This is not to say that there are no actual cases of AIDS sufferers knowingly spreading the disease. Fallis pointed out that [at the time I spoke to him] there have been at least two cases of male prostitutes, one in Texas and one in Georgia, who may have known that they had the disease but who continued to ply their trade.

On February 21, 1987, the *New York Times* reported that police in Nuremberg, West Germany, had arrested a bisexual former U.S. Army sergeant on the suspicion that he had knowingly spread the disease to his sexual partners. And on March 4, 1987, the paper reported on the upcoming trial of a man who allegedly killed his male sexual partner when the man informed him—after sex— that he had AIDS.

The real cases, so far, have all been men, so it is interesting that the person in the apocryphal story is always a woman. In this country, AIDS has been confined mostly to homosexuals and intravenous drug users. But lately, the medical community and the media have voiced a rising concern that the disease will begin spreading throughout the rest of the population via promiscuous heterosexual contact. The mysterious woman may be the personification of this new concern about the invisible killer; the legend of AIDS Mary represents, paraphrasing a popular advertising slogan, AIDS for the rest of us.

Writer Dan Sheridan of the *Chicago Sun-Times* has dubbed the woman in the stories "AIDS Mary" because she reminded him of the famous real-life character "Typhoid Mary." The historical Typhoid Mary was Mary Mallon, an Irish-American cook who spread the disease to more than fifty persons as she worked in New York City in the early 1900s. She apparently knew she had the disease and managed to elude police for eight years, until she was arrested in 1915.

There may be an even earlier prototype for AIDS Mary. In a story called "Bed No. 29" written in 1884, French writer Guy de Maupassant (1850–1893) depicted a woman who deliberately spread syphilis among enemy forces. It is possible that he based the plot on a legend of his time. "Le Lit 29" takes place during the Franco-Prussian War. Irma, beautiful mistress of a French officer, allows her own infection to go untreated so that she may in turn spread syphilis to as many Prussian officers as possible. On her deathbed, she rebukes her disapproving French lover, saying, "I have killed more than you."

One acquaintance told me that he remembers hearing a "Welcome to the syphilis club" version of the plot many years ago, but I have so far been unable to collect other references to this form of the story.

Back to AIDS Mary. An FBI special agent in San Francisco wrote to me to say that the current story has been spreading like wildfire through the bureau. It is said to have happened to an FBI agent either in California or Florida. Supposedly he reported his experiences to a local police department and was told, "You're the eighth (ninth, tenth, etc.) of her victims so far." The agent who wrote to me says that although nobody has met the victim, everyone who tells it assumes that it really happened.

I'm passing on these versions of the story not for the purpose of transmitting any scare messages about AIDS, although it could happen and the disease certainly is spreading. But is there a disappearing woman crisscrossing the country, leaving a trail of death and a series of lipstick messages behind her? As one columnist who reported the tale said, "This is one of those stories that you pray is apocryphal." I think—at least so far—that his prayers have been answered.

My first column on this legend was released the week of March 16, 1987. The above is slightly revised and expanded.

Letters and clippings about "AIDS Mary" continued to flow in, and in her column for July 30, 1987, Ann Landers printed a letter signed "Sleepless Nights in Canada," which contained yet another version. This time, friends arranged for a boy on his fourteenth birthday to spend a night in a motel with "a sexually active girl" in order to initiate him into the "fraternity of manhood." Landers identified the story as fictitious and printed it with a disclaimer because "it illustrates a crucial point" that teen-agers are as susceptible to AIDS as are adults.

For the week of August 31, 1987, I issued the following column as follow-up on "AIDS Mary." Again, the column is slightly revised for this book.

"AIDS MARY" REVISITED

A shocking headline over the advice column in a recent issue of Weekly World News *caught my attention, though all headlines in this tabloid are shocking. This one screamed, "I gave her love—she gave me AIDS!"*

The sensational story, told in a letter signed "Matter of Life and Death," was a variation of the horrific "AIDS Mary" legend that I wrote about in an earlier column.

The letter described what supposedly happened to the writer, a young man who brought a beautiful girl from a party back to his apartment for the night and made love to her. In the morning she was gone, and a note on his pillow explained that she had been infected with Acquired Immune Deficiency Syndrome—AIDS—by a lover and was now revenging herself on men.

Nothing in the Weekly World News *item tips off*

readers that the story is apocryphal. But, in reality, there is no proof whatever that the tale is true. I had checked months earlier with the Centers for Disease Control, which monitors AIDS cases, and they had heard the story too—but they don't believe it.

The popularity of the legend is fueled by fears about AIDS spreading further, and especially by the possibility of deliberate transmission. On June 19, 1987, the New York Times *reported on thirty legal cases that have been filed all across the country against people—usually gay people, prostitutes, or drug addicts—who have been accused of deliberately trying to transmit the virus. Some of the accusations include sexual acts, but others are based on incidents of biting or spitting—methods not known to spread the disease. None of the incidents resembles the "AIDS Mary" story, and most of them involve a person committing one or two acts, not someone roaming the country seeking out victims. The legend exaggerates the fears, however, for (as the* Times *article mentioned) "the chance that the AIDS virus will spread in a single act of heterosexual intercourse is . . . perhaps 1 in 1,000."*

The facts about AIDS have not kept the story from spreading, though. A Bloomington, Indiana, reader wrote saying that her husband heard the story told at a convention in Los Angeles.

A reader in Redwood City, California, was told the story by her office partner, who learned it from her roommate's brother visiting from Oregon who in turn had read it in a church newsletter. I was also told that Billy Graham had told "AIDS Mary" on a nationally televised broadcast.

A Wisconsin student said that the story was told by his boss as something that had happened to the boss's wife's friend when he moved to southern California.

One reader sent a printout from a computer network

*containing a debate about the possible truth of the
"AIDS Mary" tale. Someone had posted a message to
the net claiming that "unfortunately, it is a true story."
Challenged for proof, the claimant could cite only "my
roommate's sister's cousin" as a source.*

*I got letters reporting "AIDS Mary" as "the hottest
story going" in Toronto, and also as the biggest topic of
conversation in Abilene. A letter from abroad reported
the same story being told at the East Glamorgan
General Hospital, Wales, as something that had
happened to a London lad.*

*A letter from Tulsa said the lipstick message on the
mirror from the AIDS carrier was described by a
hairdresser as something that happened in Hollywood.
A Nashville writer heard it there, as well as in Detroit;
while a Houston student listed Texans, Pennsylvanians,
and New Jerseyites telling the story on campus.*

In March 1987 the Seattle Times *reported calls about
the legend coming in on an AIDS Hotline. Clarence
Page, a* Chicago Tribune *columnist repeated the story
in June as being attached to a U.S. Marine stationed in
San Diego, but it matched versions Page heard in
Chicago.*

In the July issue of Playboy, *the legend was quoted
from a woman in Denver who said it had happened to a
friend of someone she works with.*

*I spoke to sociologist Gary Alan Fine of the University
of Minnesota who has studied the "AIDS Mary" story in
his state. He agreed with me that the legend reflects
people's wariness about impersonal sexual contacts, but
felt that it might also be a story about rape, as well as
about AIDS.*

*For women who tell it, Fine suggested, the story may
represent "a subtle revenge against men." In the story,
the male victim is reduced to a state of helplessness and
potential contamination by AIDS Mary, just as a rape*

*victim is debased by her male attacker. Thus, the man in
the story joins the "family" or "club" of victims when
he contracts AIDS.*

*Fine says that men telling the legend perhaps reveal a
"collective paranoia toward women." The victim learns
from the scarlet message scrawled on his mirror that he
was never in control of the female partner whom he
thought he had seduced.*

*But for both sexes, Fine concluded, "the sour truth is
that we all now reside in 'the world of AIDS.' " So, the
legend of "AIDS Mary," although not about real
people, is metaphorically about all of us.*

Gary Alan Fine published these ideas about "AIDS
Mary" in his article "Welcome to the World of AIDS:
Fantasies of Female Revenge," *Western Folklore,* 46
(1987): 192–197.

I returned to the topic of this legend once again, in the
column released for the week of September 7, 1987, part
of which follows.

"The Handwriting on the Wall (or Mirror)"

Adolescent girls' "slumber parties" or "sleepovers"—
where a houseful of youngsters giggle and gossip until
all hours—are favorite times for telling urban horror legends. A classic tale of this genre even has its setting at a
slumber party.

The legend I call "The Licked Hand" (discussed in *The
Choking Doberman*) is certainly horrifying, but barely plausible. The plot dictates that the girls in the story actually
fall asleep during the all-night party. (As a father of three
daughters, I find that idea fantastic.) In the story, a girl's
hand is licked when she awakens several times at night.
She never turns on the light, just dangles her hand over
the bedside. Presumably her faithful pet dog licks the
hand.

But in the morning, she finds all of her little friends
murdered, and in the bathroom her dog, too, lies dead in
a pool of blood. Written in blood across the bathroom
wall is the message "People can lick, too!"

"The Licked Hand" has circulated in the United States
for at least twenty years. Young women telling it never
need to explain that the killer must have been hiding
under the bed licking the hand himself. The handwrit-
ing-on-the-wall motif at the end makes this gruesome
fact perfectly clear.

The old slumber-party story also shows up as a college
tradition. The scene shifts to a women's dorm on campus
in which one student comes home late and quietly goes
to bed without turning on the light or awakening her
roommate. In the morning, she finds her roommate
murdered and a note either left by the body or written
(sometimes in blood) on the wall: "Aren't you glad you

didn't turn on the light last night?"

Sometimes a dog remains in the story—an odd resident for a college dorm—and its spilled blood becomes the writing medium. Occasionally the bloody message is written on a mirror.

If that last detail seems familiar, it's because in the climax of one of the hottest urban legends going around, a variation of the same motif appeared. A man awakes early one morning to find a frightening message scrawled across his bathroom mirror in vivid red lipstick: "Welcome to the world of AIDS." He learns from his doctor and the police that his female sex partner of the night before, an embittered AIDS victim, had deliberately transmitted the deadly disease to him.

This is the legend of "AIDS Mary," a story that is everywhere, though it's completely unverifiable.

The way that "AIDS Mary" leaves her message behind has puzzled several readers. One man wrote, asking, "Why the lipstick? Why didn't she just use a pad and pencil?"

A prosaic penciled note is not as dramatic as the lipstick graffito, which perhaps suggests the overnight guest's scarlet reputation or the sinful nature of the liaison. But probably the real reason that the message is left in red handwriting upon a mirror is that the motif was borrowed from "The Licked Hand."

Urban legends often lift such motifs from each other and are updated to fit the major concerns of the time. Now it is the AIDS epidemic and not an imagined threat by a demented killer that we fear.

The ominous appearance of a message handwritten upon a wall is the subject of the old proverb about someone being able "to read the writing on the wall." The proverb, of course, alludes to the Biblical passage in Daniel 5:5, where during Belshazzar's feast, fingers of a man's hand write strange words upon the plaster of the king's wall. When the Hebrew prophet Daniel, a captive in Babylon, is summoned to interpret this cryptic writing, part of his translation is "Thou art weighed in the balances, and art found wanting."

This idea seems appropriate for the urban legends reviewed here. If only she had not assumed that it was the dog licking her hand! If only she had turned on the light! If only he had taken precautions against AIDS! If only they had not been promiscuous in the first place!

The legends could still have disastrous endings, but at least if their main characters had been weighed and found sufficient, then the victims in the stories might have had a fighting chance.

"White Slavery in Wellington"

When I visited folklorist Moira Smith recently in Wellington, New Zealand's capital city, she gave me a photocopy of a shocking story that was told in a letter to the editor some fifty years ago.

Smith is studying the capping stunts (graduation pranks) of New Zealand students, which I discuss in Chapter 7. Part of her research includes reading back issues of student newspapers. Discovering an early urban legend on the letters page of *Salient,* the Victoria University newspaper, was a bonus.

The letter, published in *Salient* on June 29, 1938, was headlined "True Story," but it was no such thing.

What the story was, as Smith realized when she first came across it, was a widespread urban legend of the time that had somehow wandered far from its usual American and European orbits of circulation.

The letter writer recounted that the week before, a young couple had gone out to a movie, only to be seated several rows apart from each other because the theater was crowded. What happened next, the writer had heard, was "a matter of importance which I think should be brought to the notice of all students. Presently the girl was worried, as she thought, by an insect, and later began to feel rather queer," the writer explained. "The woman next to her, noticing her restlessness, asked the girl if she were quite well and, on being told that she felt sick, the woman offered to go out with the girl." At this point, the young man stepped between them and told the stranger, as the letter so quaintly phrased it, "to go to——." The young man hailed a taxi and rushed the young woman to a doctor. The doctor found that the young woman had been "heavily drugged by means of a hypodermic syringe," and he finally revived her. The letter writer's conclusion: "Evidently White Slave traffic is acting in Wellington."

The fear of "white slavery"—young women forced into prostitution—was strong in the 1930s, and the legend known as "The Attempted Abduction" was a typical scare story, one that I have discussed in *The Choking Doberman*. Such stories frequently turn on the idea of a girl being drugged in a movie theater via a needle stuck through a crack in the folding seat. Invariably, a stranger then steps forward and offers to assist the victim, actually intending to abduct her. However, the girl's escort always saves her from a life of degradation when he bypasses the stranger and insists upon helping the young woman himself.

In the past ten years or so, "The Attempted Abduction" (discussed in the Preface) has popped up again in localized versions all over the United States. Several details of the story have been altered, but the central theme of a foiled abduction is retained.

The incident is now usually attributed to a shopping center or department store in which a little girl is supposedly sedated and then led out from the public restroom by a strange woman who claims to be helping her daughter who has become ill. The girl is saved in the nick of time by her real mother.

Few of these abduction legends are based on actual cases. Rather, they combine well-traveled motifs with imaginative bits of local color, such as the crowded theater and the young man's command to the would-be abductor in the New Zealand version.

Lest you think I have been too quick to disbelieve the 1938 "true story" from Wellington, Smith found that the letter writer wrote again to *Salient* a few days later to retract her story, saying she had found it to be without foundation.

Heck, I could have told her that. Well, not quite, since I was only five years old in 1938 and had never heard of white slavery.

Mistaken Identities

After Halloween every year, I hear new accounts of an old urban legend that involves mistaken identities at a costume party. The events in the story are plausible, but one never meets the participants. The story is usually told as something that happened to the usual friend of a friend. Sometimes, however, it is circulated as a mere joke, printed on a photocopied sheet with the heading parodying an official memo: "Office of the Divorce Counselor. Subject: A Halloween Party."

As the story goes, a married couple is invited to a Halloween costume party, and the wife rents costumes for both of them. On the night of the party, though, she has a severe headache and feels too ill to attend. She urges the husband to go without her, telling him to have a good time. Disappointed, he puts on his costume and leaves, and she takes a couple of aspirin and goes to bed.

But at about nine in the evening, she wakes up without any sign of her headache and decides to attend the party after all. And since her husband hasn't seen her costume, the wife decides to remain incognito and see how he behaves in her absence.

When she arrives at the party, she spots him in his costume, dancing with several different women and openly flirting with them. So the wife, in costume, begins to flirt with her husband. She dances with him and eventually allows him to lead her off to a vacant bedroom where they make love without removing their masks.

Before the midnight unmasking of the guests, the wife slips away and goes home to await the husband's return. She is sitting up in bed reading when he arrives home. He asks her how she is feeling. She says she feels much better now and asks him what kind of time he had at the party.

"Oh, the same old thing," he replies. "I never have much fun when you're not there."

"Did you dance much?"

"No," he says. "In fact, I didn't dance a single dance. I met a few other men who were also there alone, so we went off to the den and played poker. But the guy who borrowed my costume said he had a heck of a good time!"

In its November 1988 issue, under "Laughter, the Best Medicine," *Reader's Digest* reprinted another version of the mistaken-identity legend found in the *Danbury* (Connecticut) *News-Times.* This time it is "the night of the masked ball" rather than Halloween, and the wife's behavior is not described as fully: she merely "whispered sweet nothings in his ear," then "after a long embrace lured him to the garden." Later, at home, the husband identifies the man who borrowed his costume by name as "Charlie."

If you believe that story, you'll probably believe a similar one in my files about two married couples who go on on a camping trip together. This one seems like one of Chaucer's racier tales or something out of Boccaccio's *Decameron,* but it, too, is usually told as a true story.

Two husbands plot a way to try out each other's wives. They decide that after both couples have gone to their separate tents and the wives are asleep, the husbands will slip out and change places with each other.

But after a long, hard drive to the campground, both men are tired and at night they fall asleep right away.

In the middle of the night, one man awakens and remembers the plan. He slips out of his tent and quietly awakens the other man. They climb into each other's tents and have sex with each other's partners.

The next morning, though, each discovers that he is

actually with his own wife. The two wives had also schemed to test each other's mate and had switched places earlier in the evening.

Both of these schemes would seem highly difficult to carry out without a hitch. What's more, it's virtually impossible to believe that marriage partners would not recognize each other, even in the deep, dark woods. Such unlikely occurrences at the core of these stories give them away as urban legends.

More believable, but still legendary, is another camping story involving sex. I heard this one several times in the summer of 1986.

Mom, Dad, and three kids set out for a camping trip with their new pop-up tent trailer. They arrive at the campground in the afternoon and begin to arrange their site.

After the parents get the tent set up, the double bed inside looks very inviting. But they remember that all five of them will be confined to the single small "bedroom" that night. So they send the kids down to the lake to play, and the two of them get into the tent and make love.

Unfortunately, they have not set the unit up properly. At just the wrong moment, it tips over and collapses, spilling them out on the ground in front of all the other campers at the site. The parents set a new record for rapid repacking of a tent trailer, while the children cry and say, "But *why* do we have to go? We just got here!"

While only the first story relates directly to Halloween, all three legends depict unusual sexual encounters that occur outside the normal round of daily life. There's both an air of wishful thinking and a sense of normal everyday problems (like getting a headache or setting up an unfamiliar tent) in the stories.

Halloween, as Professor Alan Dundes of Berkeley pointed out in his recent collection of office-copier lore, is "a festival at which ritual reversals are permitted, which provides a suitable frame for the reversal that is the basis of the Halloween Party story." And on camping trips, too, people revert in part to a more primitive mode of behavior than usual.

"The Blind Man"

You never know how or when a story that you suspect to be an urban legend might be confirmed as such. And sometimes the proof is almost as weird and unexpected as the legend itself.

For example, I've had the story I call "The Blind Man" on file for a couple of years, assuming that it must be a fictional story with a history of retellings behind it. A recent letter from John Pilge of Soquel, California, settled the matter. His evidence went back thirteen years and comes from Down Under.

In 1973, Pilge recalled, he got a short-wave radio for his birthday and began listening to evening broadcasts from faraway places. One night, he wrote to tell me, he heard a funny story on Radio New Zealand, which he reconstructed for me in his letter.

"From the North Island, we received an amusing story," the broadcaster began. "A woman taking a shower hears her door chime and calls out, 'Who is it?' The reply is 'Blind man!' Thinking of a local charity, she grabs some money, and, without bothering to cover herself, opens the door. The man looks at her, quite astonished, and says, 'G'day ma'm. Now where do you want your blinds?' If you hear of this story after 1973," Pilge added, "I may be partly to blame. I told it to all my friends in high school, and I have heard the same yarn many times since, with different locations given. Always I ask them the source. One person I talked to said he heard it on Paul Harvey."

My own note on file for "The Blind Man" story, however, came not from Harvey's syndicated radio broadcast, but from an equally common disseminator of legends, a recent "Ann Landers" column. In this one, dated August 10, 1986, a reader from Paducah, Kentucky, wrote to share a story that she had heard, admitting that "it may or may not be true."

The story is, of course, another version of "The Blind Man." This time, a woman doing her spring cleaning on a hot day decided to finish the housework in the nude—a motif you may recognize from the legend I call "The Nude Housewife." As she was happily working in this free and easy state, the doorbell rang. When the nude woman peeked out through the curtains and saw a man, she called out to see who it was. The reply came back, "Blind man!" You can guess the rest. The only detail that is different from the New Zealand story is that the woman, on hearing the man's reply, called out again: "Are you sure?"

To which the man replied, "Of course, I'm sure!" The blind man can hardly believe his eyes, but he just gulps and asks, "Okay, lady, where do you want me to hang these blinds?"

The unlikelihood of this series of events, plus the familiar theme of nudity and the Paducah woman's own uncertainty, made me immediately suspect the story to be a fictional one that had been passed around by word of mouth. The New Zealand version supported my judgment, as did letters from two readers of this column.

A woman from the West Coast and a man from the East Coast both wrote to say that they remembered hearing and telling "The Blind Man" in the middle or late 1950s, when the punchline specifically mentioned "Venetian blinds." One correspondent commented, "I thought *everyone* knew this old story."

Well, I didn't, and Ann Landers didn't—until our readers sent them to us. I distrusted the story from the start; as for Ann Landers, she relied on her instincts and professional experience for her reply, which was this:

"It's a funny story, whether it's true or not. If you sat where I'm sitting, you would never question the plausibility of any situation. Nothing is so outrageous or bizarre that somebody, somewhere, won't do it."

While I agree that the story is somewhat plausible, it's all too neat and coincidental to be true. And now I have three responses—one all the way from New Zealand—to verify my guess that the story must be an urban legend.

"The Lover's Telephone Revenge"

Folklore keeps up with the times. There has been a story going around lately about a lover's revenge, in which she uses a telephone rather than something traditional like a voodoo curse.

A man wants to dump his current live-in girlfriend and tells her bluntly one morning that he is going away for two weeks, and he wants her to be gone and to have all of her things cleared out of the apartment when he returns.

When he arrives back home, he half-expects to find the apartment trashed or the girlfriend still there, refusing to leave. Instead, he finds to his satisfaction that the woman and all her possessions are gone, and everything is apparently in order. Then he hears some kind of odd sound coming from the next room and finds the telephone off the hook and a voice spouting some kind of gibberish.

He shrugs and hangs up the receiver, only to learn, when his next phone bill comes, that his former lover had called the time/weather number in Tokyo and left the phone off the hook for a week or so. The bill runs to the thousands of dollars.

Serves the male chauvinist pig right! Somehow I have never heard this particular story told about a man pulling the phone prank on a woman.

But I have encountered plenty of other tellings of the story, including one in the form of a comical poem by Felicity Napier, entitled "Natasha Says," that appeared in the English journal *New Statesman*. This time the couple are vegetarians, and the woman doubles her revenge by scattering health-food seeds throughout the apartment and watering down the whole place. The last stanza:

Then she dialled; listened to the New York Speaking
    Clock
and gently laid the receiver on the duvet;
it would lie, like a slug, awaiting the growth
of the bright sprigged pile of mustard and cress—
so good for you—and slammed the door.

This story kind of grows on you after a while, I think.
At least it has a less violent conclusion than other lover's-
revenge urban legends in which cars are filled with concrete, couples are trapped in campers, or husbands' ap-
pendages are immobilized with superglue.

6

Business, Professional, and Government Legends

"The Mrs. Fields Cookie Recipe"

Companies seldom deny a negative rumor about themselves, since there's a risk that people will learn the rumor from the company's publicity and then just repeat it. But starting the first of the year in 1987, the 450 or so outlets of Mrs. Fields chocolate-chip cookies—the scrumptious ones cooked from scratch and sold warm in shopping malls—were displaying this notice: "Mrs. Fields recipe has NEVER been sold. There is a rumor circulating that the Mrs. Fields Cookie recipe was sold to a woman at a cost of $250. A chocolate-chip cookie recipe was attached to the story. I would like to tell all my customers that the story is **not true**, this is not my recipe and I have never sold the recipe to anyone. Mrs. Fields recipe is a delicious trade secret."

The poster is signed by founder and chief executive officer Debbi Fields herself (who, incidentally, dots her *i*'s with tiny hearts).

Here's the rumor: A woman supposedly calls the Mrs. Fields company headquarters in Park City, Utah, and asks for the recipe. She is told that it will be sent for a charge of "two-fifty," which she tells them to put on her credit card. When the recipe and the bill arrive, the

charge is $250—not $2.50, as she expected. For revenge, the outraged woman duplicates the recipe and sends it out to all her friends and relatives.

That woman, if she exists, must have thousands of acquaintances and a very large family, since photocopied sheets telling some version of this story have shown up everywhere, with the recipe appended. The Mrs. Fields telephone lines were kept busy with queries about it.

Many of the fliers refer to "a woman Grace knows" or "a friend of Jean's mother," or mention other women's names in the chain of transmission. Several also make reference to somebody working for the American Bar Association being the overcharged party, which may suggest that lawyers and staffs have been active in spreading the rumor, presumably thinking it to be factual.

Some newspapers speculated that the story was started by competitors of Mrs. Fields to damage the company. But Sally White, a spokeswoman for the company, told me that she doubts that another company began it. She does admit that it "damaged our integrity. We are disappointed," she said, "that anyone would think that Debbi Fields would sell her recipe."

The Mrs. Fields cookie story is typical urban-legend stuff and, in fact, is probably just a new version of an old story called "Red Velvet Cake." Thirty years ago, the story began circulating that the recipe for a bright red cake supposedly served at New York's Waldorf-Astoria hotel had been sold for an outrageous price—as much as $1,000—with similar results. The chef's secret turned out to be the simple addition of red food coloring. The buyer took the same revenge of sending out the recipe.

I've checked with the Waldorf; they say the story is false. But this hasn't stopped the continued circulation of the legend every now and then, along with a multitude of recipes for the supposed cake.

I think it's possible that the cookie legend took shape

right in Utah, where I live. Baking from scratch is an article of faith here, and recipe exchanges via church groups, neighbors, and newspaper columns are a big pastime.

Imagine that someone had a really good chocolate-chip-cookie recipe, which friends said was "almost as good as Mrs. Fields." The recipe got passed around. After a while, people started to say that it really was Mrs. Fields's recipe. Eventually, someone, half-remembering the older legend, unconsciously combined the two stories. If you stir in a telephone, a credit card, some chocolate chips, and adjust for inflation, you have a perfect yuppie legend.

There's further evidence for this theory. The Mrs. Fields company moved to Utah from Palo Alto, California, in 1982, and the following spring was the first time I heard a prototype of the special chocolate-chip recipe—but not yet connected to Mrs. Fields. At that time, in a generic cookie legend, a Utah housewife was said to have received this special recipe from a restaurant (unnamed), but was required to pay an outlandish bill.

In August 1983, I heard the Utah story being plugged into the Mrs. Fields company directly, although without all the details of the later version. The legend probably received its present form in the next couple of years thanks to oral tradition and people's imagination. Besides just word of mouth, people have mailed photocopies to friends or carried them along on visits. Others have posted the story onto computer bulletin boards, where extended discussions of the quality of the recipe have occurred.

By the way, the recipe does make a fairly decent cookie, although some of the ingredients are a bit odd. For example, it usually calls for five cups of oatmeal to be "powderized" in a blender, and for a Hershey bar to be grated in with the chocolate chips. The Mrs. Fields people say this is completely phony advice, and independent tasters agree that the bogus cookies are too dry to be mistaken for Mrs. Fields's originals. (The latter statement is based on a blind taste test conducted by a student who used members of one of my folklore classes as subjects.)

Obviously, the recipe hasn't put Mrs. Fields out of business. Nor has the "Red Velvet Cake" hurt the Waldorf-Astoria. Lately, the hotel has even turned the tables on the legend and started giving out free copies of that infamous "Red Velvet Cake" recipe-that-never-was-for-sale.

Where do such urban legends come from?

Usually, I have found, they evolve from older legends as people tell them again and again.

Okay, you say, but where did these older legends come from?

These generally stem from even earlier stories. Beyond that? Often no one knows. I've pinpointed the origins of several urban legends, but I wind up tracking most of them back merely to older stories—and that's the end of it. Legends beget legends, but where it all starts remains a mystery.

So you can guess how happy I am when I find new sources for legends like the Mrs. Fields recipe rumor. This was one story I thought I had traced as far back as possible, to the "Red Velvet Cake" story of the 1950s. Then I received in the mail an even earlier expensive-recipe story, which had probably evolved into "Red Velvet Cake."

A Cambridge, Massachusetts, a reader photocopied the recipe from a cookbook called *Massachusetts Cooking Rules, Old and New,* published in Boston in 1948 by the Women's Republican Club of Massachusetts.

The recipe in the book for "$25 Fudge Cake" is credited to Mrs. Randall B. Hatch of Whitman, a town south-east of Boston. The ingredients and mixing instructions for the fudge aren't very striking, but the explanation for the name is.

Mrs. Hatch got the recipe from a friend, who got it from a friend. . . . "This friend had to pay $25 upon the receipt of the recipe from the chef of one of the rail-roads," the cookbook explains. "She had asked for the recipe while eating on a train. The chef gladly sent it to her, together with a bill for $25, which her attorney said she had to pay. She then gave the recipe to all her friends, hoping they would get some pleasure from it."

This reference, in turn, when I used it in a column, triggered the memory of a woman in Taylor, Wisconsin, who wrote me to say that she remembered a story going the rounds in Milwaukee in 1949: "Some poor woman had to pay $100 instead of [what she thought was to be] $1.00 for Mrs. Stevens Fudge Recipe."

Another woman wrote from Bloomington, Indiana, to say that many years ago, "probably in the 1940s," she got hold of a chocolate-cake recipe that allegedly some-one "in a restaurant down south somewhere" had been required to pay $25 to acquire. That woman was giving copies to all her friends in revenge for the high cost.

Believe me, I wouldn't be surprised to find out eventually that the story of the expensive dessert recipe goes all the way back to the Pilgrims. I can hear it now: They got a great recipe for pumpkin pie from the Indians but had to pay dearly for it.

In the meantime, the Mrs. Fields story still pops up from time to time, both in anonymous fliers and in publi-cations. The latest example of the latter I have seen was sent to me by Lydia Paley Hume of the American Em-bassy in Vienna. There it was—in the embassy newsletter *Tales of Vienna* dated February 26, 1988—complete with details about the $250 misunderstanding, the blenderized oatmeal, and the Hershey bar. And the editor's source? It was listed as "a true story from the CLO's [Community Liaison Office's] line in Budapest." I hope this story is not a communist plot.

And meanwhile, in the United States, variants of the recipe story continue to spin off. In December 1987, two residents of St. Louis, Missouri, sent me copies of the "$350 Union Station Chocolate Chip Cookie Recipe." (Interestingly, one of them was found posted on the bulletin board of a law firm there.) The station was recently renovated as a luxury hotel and shopping complex, and I strongly suspect that Mrs. Fields has an outlet there.

Another variation from the Midwest sprang up in Chicago, where a recipe alleged to be the very same mint fudge sold by Marshall Fields department store is circulating. Notice the name—Fields. Hmmmm. There's something familiar going on here, too.

But the hottest variation on the recipe story—as of spring 1988—attributes the story and the recipe to a restaurant in a Nieman-Marcus store. This one has come to my attention in a Utah church-group newsletter, in news stories out of Wisconsin and Georgia, and in letters and fliers from several other states. Let's take a look at how columnist Martha Hertz of the *Athens* (Georgia) *Banner-Herald* got taken by this "gotcha story," as she called it.

Hertz wrote in her column on January 25, 1988, about "a friend of mine in Texas [who] periodically escapes reality by browsing through the stores in North Dallas." The "famous chocolate chip cookies" at Nieman-Marcus were her special indulgence, so finally she asked for the recipe.

Hertz then gave readers the usual story associated with Mrs. Fields cookies and essentially the same typical recipe, concluding with another friend's comment on the cookies, "You know, I'm not sure that $250 is all that much for a recipe like this."

Time passes. The mailman brings Martha Hertz a sheaf of photocopies about "Red Velvet Cake" out of *The Vanishing Hitchhiker* from a folklorist at the University of Georgia. In her column for February 29, 1988, she revealed "some rather amazing facts" about the Nieman-Marcus cookie story.

First, her source: "The cookie story was told to me by a close friend I have known for years. She, however, had heard the story from a close friend of hers who knew the lady involved [and] was given the recipe by her friend in a Christmas card."

(I'm hearing "FOAF" there. Aren't you?)

Next, the facts Hertz found: a phone call to Nieman-Marcus brought her the news that the story is untrue and that the store does not even serve or sell cookies.

"Regardless of the facts," Hertz concluded, "it is still one of the best chocolate chip cookie recipes I've ever found."

I think I'll just bake up a batch of the not-really-Mrs.-Fields cookies, then dunk one in cold milk, and think about facts versus folklore a little more.

"Postcards for Little Buddy"

An international urban legend, with roots more than a century old, recently resurfaced in the United States. It has three surefire elements of drama and pathos: a dying child's last wish, an appeal for help, and a simple way for people to contribute.

"Little Buddy," as the story goes, is a poor Scottish lad dying of leukemia (or cancer) in a hospital near Glasgow. His last wish in life is to see his name added to the *Guinness Book of World Records* as the collector of more postcards than anyone else in history. And never mind that the *Guinness Book of World Records* has no such entry, because true believers in such legends never seem to check.

The spurious appeal for cards seems to have begun by word of mouth. From there, it went into CB broadcasts and spread into print. Soon people were sending postcards addressed simply to "Little Buddy, Glasgow" (or sometimes "Little Willy," in Paisley or Aberdeen).

Thousands of cards (some claim "millions") have arrived in the past few years, especially in the town of Paisley, about seven miles from Glasgow, where the sick child is most often supposed to be wasting away. But there *is* no such child, and there never was an official appeal for postcards.

Sometimes, tellers of the story "verify" it by saying that "Buddy" is a common nickname for people from Paisley, or that the boy's real name is "Paul" and his CB handle is "Buddy." (CBers and ham-radio operators do, in fact, often use nicknames, and they send postcards to verify conversations.) Some people maintain that the postcards arrived too late, and poor Little Buddy died without ever realizing how many wonderful, caring people there were in the world.

Most people hearing the story for the first time simply go ahead and send a postcard or several, and often try to persuade members of their churches, clubs, and work groups to join them in the effort.

The "Little Buddy" story began in 1982, when a truck driver in Scotland claimed that he heard of the card appeal on his citizens-band radio, although this alleged broadcast has never been verified.

European newspapers, businesses, and church groups organized campaigns to send postcards to the dying boy. A year later, when the story reached the United States, the inpouring of cards threatened to swamp some Scottish post offices. At times, the rumor has died down, but it continues to bounce back without warning.

Mark Schumacher, a stamp collector in Greensboro, North Carolina, learned how widespread and popular these postcard campaigns were when he submitted the winning bid on an auction lot described in a catalogue as a "mass of modern picture post cards" by a London auction house. He received some thirty pounds of cards—about 2,900 of them—mostly dated April or May 1983 and all addressed to "Little Buddy." In an article in the *American Philatelist* for November 1988, Schumacher listed the sources of the cards: thirty-three different countries, including "nearly all of Western Europe, Malta, Zimbabwe, Japan, Malawi, Malaysia, Dubai, and the Netherlands Antilles, plus several Commonwealth countries." Senders mentioned that they had heard of Little Buddy's appeal for cards from newspapers, club newsletters, and radio broadcasts. Schumacher's article contains reproductions of six sample cards that illustrate matters of philatelic interest, so it appears that the postcard collection is worth something to someone after all, even if it won't merit mention in the *Guinness Book of World Records.*

Scottish postal officials have issued statements denying the story and have placed advertisements in CB magazines urging people to stop sending cards. The hobbyist magazine *Postcard Collector* published similar notices in October 1985 and again in August 1986. The *Paisley Daily Express,* which headlined a story "Breakers Boost Sick Boy's Dream" on September 28, 1982 ["Breakers" being CB radio enthusiasts], by February 1983 was reporting a "Nightmare in the Post" as the "Little Buddy" story caused the card avalanche to begin. In April 1983, the *Express* reported that "Those Cards Are Still Coming in by the Hundreds!" and, in July 1985, "Little Buddy Strikes Again."

Throughout 1986 and into the next year, the Midwest and the Lehigh Valley of Pennsylvania became the hot spots of the Little Buddy postcard appeals.

The *Kansas City Star* investigated the story that was leading dozens of Missourians to send hundreds of cards to poor Little Buddy. When the Scottish post office returned a box of postcards to a woman who donated them, she wrote to ask why. Officials sent her a replay of the disclaimers.

In March 1987, an Associated Press story reported the efforts of people around Bethlehem, Pennsylvania, to grant the little lad's dying wish. One postcard collector in Bethlehem was planning to send her entire personal hoard of more than 800 cards to the boy when she learned that the story was untrue.

There is an American antecedent to the Little Buddy story. This rumor claims that an indigent child, suffering from kidney disease, needs time on a dialysis machine. Supposedly, there is an enormous effort underway to collect enough aluminum soda- and beer-can pull tabs to pay for the life-saving measure.

Another ancestor of the Little Buddy story was located by the English folklorists Peter and Iona Opie. In their book *The Lore and Language of Schoolchildren,* they quote a passage discovered in the *Illustrated London News* for May 18, 1850, that begins, "Some time since, there appeared in the public journals a statement to the effect that a certain young lady, under age, was to be placed in a convent, by her father, if she did not procure, before the 30th of April last, one million of used postage stamps." The article goes on to say that this appeal generated huge quantities of stamps which arrived in "boxes, bales, and packages" to various English post offices.

The Opies were unable to determine whether the nineteenth-century news story had any truth behind it. They suggest that it is "either the tallest story which has appeared in the pages of that respected journal, or one of its most remarkable."

What is more remarkable, perhaps, is that a similar story—with a British reference in it—still circulates internationally in an updated version.

My column, essentially as given above, appeared the week of May 4, 1987; but in the months to follow, Little Buddy appeals continued to circulate while further debunkings showed up in the press. In fact, on a single day one week later (May 13), *The Province* of Vancouver, British Columbia, published a supposed verification of the legend, while United Press International was distributing a denial. The Canadian news item traced the story moving through Air Canada's computer system, then quoted an airline spokesperson saying, "We checked it out with British Airways, and it's true." But the UPI story that day called it a "scam of unknown origin" and claimed that even President Reagan had sent a card to the sick child in 1983.

Shortly afterward in 1987, I heard from a man in Honolulu who had found the Little Buddy appeal posted on a library bulletin board and had entered it on the national educational computer system before he became aware that he was circulating a legend. Two groups pro-viding humanitarian aid to sick children, "Mail for Tots" and "Make a Wish Foundation," were also sending out Little Buddy notices through the spring and summer.

During autumn 1987, debunkings continued to appear in every sort of medium from tabloids to respected big-city dailies. "Please don't send a card to Buddy," pleaded one headline, and "Little Buddy hoax swamps mails," said another. The *New York Post,* on June 26, 1987, quoted an exasperated postal official in Paisley, who said, "I hope they're going to introduce a record for the per-son who handles the largest volume of useless mail." At that time, Little Buddy postcards were still flowing in, not only from the United States, but from Canada, Ger-many, Greece, Turkey, China, Japan, and Australia.

In September 1987, an Associated Press story debunk-ing the Little Buddy legend in detail was widely pub-lished, and papers gave it headlines such as "Hoax about Buddy Finally Laid to Rest." I certainly hope they're right, but I'm not closing my files on the story yet. I've seen too many such legends pop up again months or even years after they seem to have disappeared.

Here's my favorite parody response to a Little Buddy–type appeal. It appeared at the end of a lengthy exchange of opinions during March 1988 on a national computer bulletin board. Participants debated, via their computer screens and modems, about whether an appeal for post-cards for "David a 7 year old boy who is dying from Cancer in England" was legend or fact. Legend won, of course, since many of those on the net had encountered "Little Buddy" debunkings. Then, in a last dig at the true believers, one person added this notice: "I am dying of normal natural causes, and I would like to get into the Guinness Book of World Records for being the youngest person to personally own a Cray. If each of you would send all the money you can to this net address, I'll be able to afford the down payment. . . . Yeah, I know it's crass & tasteless, but at least you know it's a hoax, right? :-) :-)"

Footnote for nonhackers: A "Cray" is the supercomputer of choice at present and extremely expensive. As for the last two little symbols, if you turn this page clockwise, they look like smile faces—the popular computer-net shorthand symbol used for marking jokes and hoaxes.

(Thanks to Jim Davis of the Operations Staff, Center for Scientific Computing, University of Utah, for providing this last example.)

Talk-Show Tales—"Dave's Behind"

People wonder if the mass media will replace oral tradition, making folk stories as obsolete as pet rocks. This may seem plausible, but, in fact, the modern mass media enhance rather than inhibit the spread of urban legends.

Radio and television talk shows—like electronic grapevines—are actually conduits of urban folklore. Radio shows allow many people to call and exchange tales with a vast audience, while the national TV talk shows give us celebrities and hosts who swap gossip and yarns. Among all the chatter, a good deal of folklore is generated.

It's not surprising, then, that there is a whole body of folklore surrounding broadcast talk shows themselves. Most folklore focuses on "The Tonight Show," starring Johnny Carson. Johnny, though not the most daring host in action now, has inherited Groucho Marx's reputation for racy wit, used to the disadvantage of the show's guests.

Unfortunately, I cannot quote many specifics of such stories here without risking the results that are alleged in the same folklore—lawsuits for character defamation—as well as gasps from those who do not appreciate sexually explicit remarks in print. In general, however, I *can* say that in folklore, Johnny is credited—unfairly—with insulting the likes of Ann-Margaret, Zsa Zsa Gabor, and Raquel Welch with double-entendre responses to their accidentally suggestive questions.

Often, Carson's alleged remarks involve a female guest appearing on the show with a cat on her lap. That seems improbable enough to anyone who has tried to make a pussycat sit still on command, not to mention the unlikelihood of the female cat-cuddler asking Johnny just the right loaded question to set up the joke.

It didn't happen, I assure you. Nor did Carson's alleged punning reply to Mrs. Arnold Palmer's claimed remark about how she assures her husband's good luck in tournaments. Funny story, but I can't repeat it here.

On the other side of the coin, certain actresses are attributed in folklore with having shocked Johnny by announcing on his show radical changes in their lives and sexual orientations. (For instance, one sexy star supposedly confessed that she is a lesbian.) But where are the follow-up news stories, I ask you?

Did anything at all like this ever happen on "The Tonight Show"? Not likely, since one only encounters people who know the anecdotes from friends of friends, never firsthand. Besides, all these shows are broadcast on a tape delay, and any such incidents would be edited out. The standard Carson Productions response to questions about such stories is "We cannot verify any of them."

The most persistent "Tonight Show" tradition is that either Carson himself or a famous guest once gave out his personal telephone-credit-card number for viewers to use for unlimited free calls. The number sometimes is circulated in underground newspapers and on college campuses.

That one is apocryphal, too, whether you heard it about Steve McQueen, Paul Newman, Sammy Davis, Jr., Robert Redford, or (the all-time leading favorite), Burt Reynolds. In every version, the claim is made that the star won a gigantic settlement against AT&T—to be paid off in free calls—and invited his fans to help use up the winnings.

This story has been around for nearly twenty years— about as long as telephone credit cards themselves. Each time it appears anew, many people fall for it and begin reaching out to touch someone, charging the calls to good old Burt, or whoever is mentioned in the story. Unfortunately, some of the fourteen-digit credit card numbers are real, as the tiny Wabash Telephone Cooperative of Louisville, Illinois, found out in 1981, when it received more than $100,000 in billings supposedly being charged to Burt Reynolds's number. The telephone company, of course, bills the calls back to the caller whenever possible.

A version of this story appeared in 1986 in Dorothy Herrmann's biography of humorist S. J. Perelman. The book said that Perlman had seen a movie star on TV announcing the free phone calls some time around 1970. Perelman "jumped at the opportunity," reported Herrmann. I suspect that the irrepressible Perelman told this story to his biographer as a gag.

One TV talk-show story that I checked out in person concerns Carson's fellow NBC host David Letterman. The story was that Letterman has a clause in his "Late Night" contract that forbids the showing of his behind on television. That's why, after the opening monologue he always invites the audience to say hello to bandleader Paul Schaefer. The cameras swing to Paul, so that Dave can make his way discreetly to his desk.

I asked Letterman about this when I was a guest on "Late Night" on April 29, 1987. He not only denied the story definitively, but also obligingly raised his coattails and turned a full circle before the live audience and cameras.

"This is the lowest stoop I have ever stooped," Letterman commented.

And this is about as far as I am able to go in giving details about television talk-show folklore.

"The Welfare Letter"
and Other Language Blunders

People who process welfare applications sometimes come across comical mistakes in English usage made by the applicants as they struggle with the paperwork. The funny language slips may be recounted, and the applications passed around. Such blunders may even be gathered onto a list that is posted in the office.

More often, though, the supposed list of grammatical "mistakes" found on the office bulletin board has been compiled not from actual applications to that office, but merely from another list, which in turn was taken from another list . . . and so on. Where these lists began, nobody really knows, and they constitute a popular genre of modern *written* folklore.

Advice columnist Abigail Van Buren headed her column on July 27, 1987, with one such list, a collection of eleven examples of "how some people murder the English language." Sent by an eighty-year-old woman in Far Rockaway, New York, the examples were said to be quoted verbatim from the local welfare office.

Several of the blunders contained double-entendres. "I am very annoyed to find that you brand my son illiterate," read one example from Abby's column, and continued, "this is a dirty lie, as I was married a week before he was born."

Another read, "My husband got his project cut off two weeks ago, and I haven't had any relief since."

A third read, "I have no children as yet as my husband is a truck driver and works day and night."

Dear Abby called the errors "a delightful day-brightener." I call them an urban legend. Virtually the same list—sometimes with seventeen or eighteen items—has been around for at least fifty years. No one has ever proved that any of the silly statements really appeared in welfare applications nor other governmental correspondence files to which they are attributed. Chances are slim that almost exactly the same errors were repeated in welfare applications from separate locations over many years' time.

For example, the last item in the New York list is "I want my money quick as I can get it. I have been in bed with the doctor for two weeks, and he doesn't do me any good." A similar collection published in 1977 in the *National Retired Teacher's Association Journal* and credited to "a small New England village's social welfare office" includes the same sentence. So do lists I have collected from Montgomery County in Alabama and Salt Lake County in Utah.

Welfare workers most likely circulate the lists out of boredom, perhaps hoping that the lists will help them find whatever humor they can in their real clients' written expression. In any case, the lists derive their effect from their implications about clients' low levels of intelligence and education.

Sometimes the lists are entitled "Examples of Unclear Writing," and one sentence even found its way into a manual of prose style written by a titled Englishman. Sir Ernest Gowers's 1955 book *The Complete Plain Words,* after quoting a real example of bureacratic jargon, cites a supposed response from a citizen: "In accordance with your instructions, I have given birth to twins in the enclosed envelope." Abby's list lacked this one, but it is usually present on others.

How far back does "The Welfare Letter" go? Curtis D. MacDougall in his book *Hoaxes* (New York: Dover, 1958; reprint of a 1940 book) prints six familiar "howlers" from a list of fifteen that he says were of World War I origin and attributed then to the War Risk Insurance Bureau. MacDougall traces reprints and variations of the list in publications of 1934 and 1935, some attributing the items to the "Veterans Bureau."

Dale E. Winn of Salt Lake City provided me with a local example from the 1930s. In 1955, for a talk he gave at a high-school class reunion, he drew on a published source then twenty years old—the *Tooele* (Utah) *Transcript-Bulletin* for February 1, 1935. Right there on page 1 the paper reported on "Curious Letters to New Deal Agencies," quoting eighteen of the same examples I have given above, along with this, "You have changed my little boy to a girl. Will it make any difference?"

Besides "The Welfare Letter," other examples of unclear English that people collect supposedly are quoted from parents' letters to teachers, such as this one: "Dear school, Pleas exkuse John for being absent on January 28, 29, 30, 31, 32 and 33." And another, "I had to keep Billie home because she ad to go Christmas shopping because I didn't know what size she ware." And just one more, "Ralph was absent yesterday because of a sore trout." (I've had that problem myself!)

Another variation on this theme claims to be culled from auto-accident reports. These errors usually are attributed to the files of specific insurance companies, but they can never be tracked to a source other than claim processors passing them around the office.

It is likely that the lists of errors reflect the kinds of mistakes that people really make on insurance-company forms. But it's unlikely that even the most beleaguered applicant would write anything as silly as this: "As I reached an intersection, a hedge sprang up obscuring my vision." Or this: "The pedestrian had no idea which direction to go, so I ran over him." Or this: "An invisible car came out of nowhere, struck my car and vanished."

These and similar goofs even show up in newspaper

stories now and then. In 1979, United Press International sent to newspapers a collection of such statements, supposedly supplied by the Metropolitan Life Insurance Company. Three years later, the same news agency circulated virtually the same list, this time crediting it to the York, Nebraska, Police Department.

One of my city's local papers (not the one that carries my column) published both these lists, and I took pleasure in pointing out in a letter to the editor that both the paper and UPI had fallen for an urban legend.

One more variation on this modern folk tradition is a list of funny mistakes headed "That's What You Dictated, Doctor!" These lulus are said to be quoted from doctors' dictated instructions to nurses: "The pelvic examination will be done later on the floor," says one. "Chief complaint: Chronic right ear," says another.

"The Welfare Letter" and its kin in this murdering-the-language tradition reflect our impatience with lengthy and bureacratic jargon, and our insecurity about our own use of English. In a way, all the lists are variations on the remark that English teachers encounter all too often: "Since you teach English, I guess I'd better watch my language."

"Going by the Old-fashioned Rules"

Rule #9: "Any employee who smokes Spanish cigars, uses liquor in any form, gets shaved at a barber shop, or frequents pool halls or public dance halls will give his employer every reason to suspect his integrity, worthy intentions and his all around honesty."

That's just one of the demanding conditions of employment specified on a widely circulated list of rules that people use in order to show what life was *really* like in "The Good Old Days." These lists are usually claimed to date between around 1860 to 1870. I've seen modern copies—never nineteenth-century ones—posted in businesses and published in articles to illustrate how tough things were for the working person way back then.

Here's another item from a typical version of the rules list:

Rule #6: "Men employees will be given an evening off each week for courting purposes, or two evenings a week if they go regularly to church."

The eight to ten other items specify workdays of up to thirteen hours (except the sabbath, when employees are expected to be in church), and they assign office-cleaning chores—everything from a weekly window washing to whittling ones own pen nibs.

After working a long, hard day, it was suggested that employees should spend their evenings "reading the Bible and other good books."

What a life! It makes you glad you didn't have to work for a living in our great-grandparents' time under those slave-driving bosses.

But these lists cannot be proven to be a century old. They exist only in typewritten, photocopied, or professionally printed versions. Could there have been so many nearly identical sets of rules in different parts of the United States? Where, then, are the original copies of the rules?

I also wonder why Spanish cigars were considered worse than those from other places, or what was immoral about a barber-shop shave. And, if bosses gave only their *male* employees a night or two off for courting, how did female workers cope?

Very likely, these lists are modern inventions simply projected back in time by means of archaic-sounding language and vague references to sweatshop conditions. A genuine set of such rules from the past may exist somewhere, but I've not seen one.

A couple of years ago, the *Deseret News* in Salt Lake City published an article about school discipline of the past. The same rule list was included, said to date from 1872. The list contained the usual rules about shaves in barber shops, whittling pen nibs, church attendance, and saving for retirement. There was even a rule promising dismissal of "women teachers who marry," which seemed a very odd attitude for a Mormon pioneer society in which marriage was strongly encouraged and polygamy was still common.

(I did not realize that schoolteachers' marriages were once frowned upon by local authorities until I heard from Mrs. Elizabeth H. Minson of Salt Lake City. She wrote to me, describing her experience while teaching in a small town in Idaho in April 1935, when she decided to get married. She commented, "I did *not* go on bended knee to the school board or the principal. I really didn't even think of it."

But here's what the principal said to her when she came back to teach two days after the wedding: "I came to tell you that the school board called a meeting Monday night to decide if they would allow you to continue

teaching. Since there are only two months left in the
school year, they decided to let you finish out the year."
Thus, Mrs. Minson learned that "my contract was not
worth the paper it was written on!")

Rule #7 in the Utah list was this: "The teacher who
performs his labor faithfully and without fault for five
years will be given an increase of 25 ½ [cents] per week
in his pay, providing the board of education approves."
This item was identical to one in sets of rules I've collected that supposedly applied to office workers, except
that these usually conclude, "providing profits from the
business permit it." Again—as with other details of the
rules list—the merit raises of American businesses a century ago seem to have been remarkably consistent.

The writer of the newspaper feature told me that her
source for the published list was the principal of an ele-
mentary school whom she had interviewed a few years
earlier, when the school was being closed. The principal
had shown her a school scrapbook in which the rules
were pasted. The list had been submitted for the scrapbook by a former teacher.

The principal pointed out that nobody had claimed
that these were rules for this particular school, but they
were believed to be typical of 1870s school rules.

The reporter told me that she had made a fruitless
attempt to locate the retired teacher who had provided
the rules. Then—like many other writers before her—
she accepted it on faith and just went ahead and published the "Rules for Teachers" in order to show, as she
phrased it, "what life was really like 100 years ago."

In doing so, I believe she was circulating a piece of
modern folklore that tells us more about our view of the
past than about the past itself. (The following item is a
very similar document of equally doubtful origin.)

"Grandma's Washday"—or Was It?

During a visit to the Lakes District Centennial Museum in Arrowtown, New Zealand, recently, I found myself chuckling over a display marked "Grandma's Washday." The display was a collection of old scrub boards, antique irons, and other such gear—and a whimsical list of instructions that told how Grandma used to do the wash:

1. Bild a fire in back yard to heat kettle of rain water.
2. Set tubs so smoke wont blow in eyes if wind is pert.
3. Shave one hole cake of soap in bilin water.
4. Sort, things, make three piles, 1 pile white, 1 pile cullord, 1 pile workbritches and rags.
5. Stir flour in cold water to smooth then thin down with bilin water.
6. Rub dirty spots on board, scrub hard, then bile, rub cullord but dont bile—just rench and starch.
7. Take white things out of kettle with broom stick handle then rench.
8. Blue and starch.
9. Spred tee towels on grass.
10. Hang old rags on fence.
11. Pore rench water in flower bed.
12. Scrub porch with hot soapy water.
13. Turn tubs upside down.
14. Put on cleen dress—smooth hair with side combs— brew tea—set and rest and rock a spell, and count blessins.

Arrowtown, nestled in the scenic Southern Alps, was a gold-mining boom town in the mid-nineteenth century. Today, like many American boom towns, it is booming again as a tourist attraction and ski center. Its picturesque false-fronted main street reminded me of the main streets of Telluride, Colorado, and Park City, Utah. The Centennial Museum in Arrowtown was organized in 1948.

The "Grandma's Washday" display fit right in with the atmosphere of history and remoteness. But I thought there was something awfully familiar about the list in the exhibit, so I asked the museum attendant about it. All she knew was that a local resident had donated a printed copy of the list, assuming it had been culled from from some nineteenth-century document, perhaps a set of instructions for a pioneer girl to follow.

So many visitors had enjoyed the "Grandma's Washday" list, the attendant said, that the museum had printed copies to sell as souvenirs.

I bought one, and I quoted verbatim from it above.

Still, I had to wonder whether the quaint description of demanding handwork, ending with the irony of counting your blessings, was an authentic pioneer document. Like those lists of old-fashioned rules for teachers or office workers, "Grandma's Washday" seemed like a recent composition. And I felt I had seen the same list somewhere else.

When I got back to the States I located another version—also a printed list that lacked any indication of its age. This one was called "Washday Receet" (*sic*) and had been published in 1981 in the *North Carolina Folklore Journal,* which had reprinted it from a 1975 newspaper article, which had quoted an item sent by a reader.

I probably don't need to tell you that the lists are very much alike. The North Carolina list has ten rules, all of them closely matching the rules on the New Zealand one—except for combining items five and six, and dropping items seven, eight, and fourteen (the colorful ending statement). The American version also fails to capitalize sentences, though it improves the punctuation by adding a couple of needed commas and dropping the superfluous one at the beginning of item four.

The folksy spelling of words like "bile," "tee," and "rench" is taken further by the North Carolina grandmother: she uses "heet" instead of "heat" (as in "cleen" and "receet"), "dreen" instead of "drain," and "flour" instead of "flower" in Rule 11. The North Carolina grandma uses "lie soap," and rubs "dirty sheets," not "dirty spots," against a board.

Simply comparing the two lists doesn't enable me to prove which list precedes the other, or whether either, neither, or both are authentic. But the similarities suggest that "Grandma's Washday" has been passed from person to person in written or printed form, undergoing changes as it is transmitted.

In other words, it's an authentic piece of folklore.

If the list was written in recent times using old-fashioned spellings and language, then it's authentic modern folklore. The list shows how we imagine our ancestors living, but not necessarily how they actually lived.

Even if an original text of "Grandma's Washday" is discovered, with a reliable date attached, the anonymous versions with varying wording found in North Carolina and New Zealand (and likely elsewhere as well) may be considered pieces of modern museum folklore.

What curator could resist displaying such an amusing document?

Another copy of "Grandma's Washday" surfaced in response to my column. Dorthe Armstrong of Semmes, Alabama, sent me a typed copy of a thirteen-item list that she says, in a handwritten version, "hung above my mother's wringer washer in a little town in the wheat country of Colorado for as long as I can remember. That was during the forties." Later Mrs. Armstrong hung a copy of the same list above her own laundry appliances in the various places she has lived. But, unfortunately, she adds, "I never thought to ask my mother where *she* got it—and now it's too late."

Mrs. Armstrong's version uses all capital letters, and it continues the tradition of folksy spellings: "het" for "heat," "sope" instead of "soap," "stur" replacing "stir," etc. Rule six begins with the variation "RUB DIRT SPOTS ON BOARD," and Rule 11 is "SCRUP PORCH WITH SOPY WATER." The text concludes in the familiar way with the clean dress, the side combs, the cup of tea, the rocking chair, and the admonition to "COUNT BLESSINGS."

"The Grocery Scam"

When you hear about the outrageous scams some con artists pull—and get away with—it makes you wonder how the victims can be such suckers. And yet who wouldn't fall for the heart-wrenching ruse that's part of the urban legend called "The Grocery Scam":

A young man is shopping in a supermarket, when he notices that an older woman seems to be following him, staring at him in a sorrowful manner. He moves to the next aisle, trying to avoid her, but she follows, still staring.

And when he finishes shopping, he ends up behind her in a long checkout line. Her grocery basket is full to overflowing; his contains just a few items.

She keeps staring at him, sadly, making him feel most uncomfortable.

Finally, she speaks up. "You must pardon my staring," she says, "but you see, you look exactly like my son who died just two weeks ago."

And she begins to sniffle as she repeats her claim that the young man perfectly resembles her late, beloved son. "I mean *exactly* like him," she moans.

Then, as the cashier bags her groceries at the front of the line, the woman whispers, "As a favor to a grief-stricken mother, would you mind saying 'Good-by, Mom' to me as I leave? Somehow it would make me feel so much better."

The young man gulps and agrees to her pathetic request. She gives him a tearful smile, waves, and wheels out her three heavy bags.

"Good-by, Mom," he says, waving back.

All the scene needs to make it perfect melodrama is

violins welling up in the background or maybe a little supermarket Muzak. But before your heart strings are tugged too tightly, listen to how the legend ends:

The young man, reflecting on his good deed, feels such a warm glow of self-satisfaction that he barely notices the cashier ringing up his own purchases. Until, that is, the cashier tells him that the bill comes to $110.

"There must be a mistake," the young man says, pointing at his single small bag.

"Your mother said you'd be paying for hers, too," the cashier says.

I've heard this story from many sources in the United States and Canada and in dozens of different versions. Sometimes the scene is a large discount store. In some, the son is said to have been killed in an auto accident; in others, he was a soldier killed in Vietnam.

Always, though, the woman persuades the young man to call her "Mom," then sticks him with her bill.

Although the storytellers never know the victim of this sentimental scam—it always happened to a friend of a friend—they usually know exactly what was in his shopping basket—"Just a deodorant stick and two cans of motor oil," for instance. And they usually can report the precise amount the scam cost him.

Oddly, no one ever explains why the young man entered the same checkout line that the older woman was in, if she made him so uncomfortable. (See below for one reader's explanation of this detail.)

In a variation of the legend, set in a restaurant, the victim buys a strange woman's story—and dinner for two. She tells him her sad tale, cries a few crocodile tears, then convinces him to stand up and give his "mom" a great big hug.

As the woman goes out, she stops briefly at the cashier's counter, then turns and waves one last good-by.

Not long afterward, the young man gets the bill for his

meal. "Your mother's check was added to yours, sir," the waiter explains, "just as she asked us to do."

HELP FROM AN EXPERT IN UNDERSTANDING THIS STORY

Lest I become too proud of myself as a successful debunker of modern myths, readers sometimes send me letters that bring me down to earth with a bump. They say that in questioning the truth of some stories, I've completely missed the point of them.

Some stories—such as "The Grocery Scam"—contain inconsistencies that render them impossible from the start.

For this legend, Lieutenant Robert E. Wilson of the Baltimore, Maryland, Police Department's Crime Resistance Unit wrote to comment.

I had wondered, when I heard "The Grocery Scam," why the young man would have gone into the same checkout line that the older woman who had been staring at him was already standing in. Wouldn't he have stayed away from her?

"Perhaps he was the other part of the 'team,'" Lieutenant Wilson suggests. "The old lady and the young man could be working a scam against the store. What better way for her to get out and away than to have the young man appear to be a victim?"

It makes sense now that you explain it, Lieutenant Wilson. But it seems like an extremely complicated way to steal a mere bag of groceries. And if you are right, then this is not an urban legend after all, but an actual scam. I'll have to think about that a little more.

AND NOW THE LEGEND BECOMES A JOKE

Are people in Australia and Texas just pulling my leg? I began to wonder when two very similar versions of

"The Grocery Scam" told as a joke came in my mail within a week. Here's the Aussie version, sent on January 3, 1989, by folklorist David S. Hults at the Curtin University of Technology, Perth:

"A young girl was in line at a supermarket checkout counter just behind an elderly woman. The woman stared at the girl, and eventually said, 'Please pardon my staring, but I can't believe it. You're the spitting image of my deceased daughter.'

"The woman then requested, 'I know this sounds strange, but when I leave the store, could you say good-bye to me, and call me "Mom," as a reminder of my daughter?'

"The girl, slightly embarrassed, agreed. And as the woman departed, the girl waved and said, 'Goodbye, Mom.'

"Then the checkout clerk told her that the total bill for her groceries was $67.45, and the girl was stunned, since she was only buying a loaf of bread and some milk. 'But your mother, who just left, said you would pay for her groceries too,' the clerk explained."

So far, so good. Up to this point, this is the straight urban legend. But the Down Under version concluded in a different way:

"The girl ran outside the supermarket to nab the phony mother and force her to explain and to pay for her own groceries. The girl caught up with the woman in the parking lot, just as she was getting into her car to drive off.

"The girl grabbed her leg and tried to pull her from the car. She pulled and she pulled and . . . "

And, at this point the listener to the story usually asks something like, "Good grief, what happened?"

The reply: "Well, she was pulling her leg, just like I am pulling yours now."

Aha! says the folklorist. This is a "catch tale"—one of those stories that leads up to an absurd situation, about which the listener is forced to ask. The storyteller's reply makes a fool of the listener, so he or she is "caught."

Another popular catch tale leads up to someone trying to steal a package that the storyteller says he just got at a butcher's counter. Inside the package, in answer to a listener's question, was "Baloney, just like I'm feeding you."

The most famous catch tale of all was popular during frontier days. The storyteller claims that he was backed into a corner by fierce attackers, perhaps a band of hostile Indians.

"What happened?" ask breathless listeners.

The reply: "They killed me!"

Nobody believes catch tales, so an urban legend modified in this way is no longer a legend, but a joke. What I found remarkable was that I got the same altered "Grocery Scam" story in a letter written just five days later by Charles Wukasch of Austin, Texas.

What I suspect is that this form of the story is becoming popular and that it was simply coincidence that I heard two such far-flung examples a week apart. The only slight difference in the Texas story was that the supermarket clerk herself ran into the parking lot after the con artist. The story concluded the same way as the Australian version: "She was pulling her leg, just like I'm pulling yours."

Wukasch, who heard the story from his brother, knew another version of the straight-scam legend as well. In this one, a soldier asks a high-ranking officer in a restaurant if he will wave back to him in order to impress the soldier's girlfriend. After their meal, as the soldier and his girl leave the restaurant, the soldier waves, and the officer waves back. What the officer doesn't know is that the soldier has told the cashier that the officer is paying for both their meals, and that he will wave back in order to identify himself.

Maybe this is the sort of trick that inspired the military regulation that all personnel must wear name tags.

Back to the Drawing Board
—Some Architectural Legends

Shopping malls, the settings for dozens of urban legends, have lately become the subject of urban folklore themselves. In a series of stories, new malls and office buildings are rumored to be sinking, leaning, or swarming with wild animals.

In early February 1987, Nancy P. Serrell, a reporter for the *Danbury* (Connecticut) *News-Times*, called me to ask if I had heard that the Danbury Fair Mall was sinking. Rumors to that effect circulating in the Connecticut area refused to die, despite her paper's repeated debunkings.

In one article for the paper, Serrell interviewed local people who had heard that the mall was sinking "because it was built on swampland" or because "there's an old reservoir under it . . . or something." Others had heard that design errors would make it necessary for the mall to be demolished and rebuilt eventually.

Serrell guessed that the actual collapse of two other buildings, an office building and a public-housing complex being constructed in nearby Bridgeport, might have helped to perpetuate the rumors. But that didn't explain the bewildering rumor that flooding in the mall's parking lot—a genuine problem—had been planned intentionally by the architects. (But why?)

A year after it first opened, when I checked, the Danbury Fair Mall was still standing. And Serrell tells me that the sinking-mall rumors are finally subsiding.

Meanwhile, in Greensboro, North Carolina, a rumor going around in spring 1987 claimed that the Four Seasons Town Centre mall there was being renovated because its collapse had been foretold by tabloid psychic Jeane Dixon.

Dixon *didn't* predict this, though. And when *Greensboro News & Record* writer Andy Duncan checked the newspaper's files, he found that the same rumor had circulated in the area twelve years before.

These two are just the most current items from my rich collection of shopping-mall rumors. And believe me, there are some crazy ones. Some of them claim that reptiles or vermin are infesting the malls, crawling out of cracks and dark corners or wrapping themselves around patrons' legs during meals in an expensive restaurant. The critters supposedly come from the farmlands, forests, and swamps that were cleared to make way for the mall.

Design flaws of public buildings are another frequent motif, revealing people's distrust of architects and engineers—and maybe of progress in general, too. One good example of this is the rumor about the Oakbrook Terrace Tower, a thirty-one-story office building in a suburb west of Chicago. Architecture critics consider the Tower, designed by Helmut Jahn, a landmark in its postmodernist use of form, space, materials, and decorative accents. But some people simply consider it a doomed structure from the start.

Throughout its construction, the building, which opened in December 1987, was plagued with rumors that construction would be halted because it was leaning four or five feet out of its proper vertical line.

The reasons given for this supposed catastrophe were a faulty concrete mixture, engineering errors, or a failure to anchor the foundation in bedrock. None of these problems existed, but apparently the rumors were fueled by such normal procedures as the removal of a temporary freight elevator, the relocation of worker parking, and a delay in installing windows because of a period of high winds.

When the leaning-tower rumors refused to die, Raymond Chin, structural engineer and the project manager for the building, yielded to public fears. He called in a surveyor to check the vertical alignment for the building. "The tower is perfectly straight and cannot be any straighter," Chin said.

As far as these rumors go, there's no straighter answer than that.

Sometimes a grand, imposing public building just "looks wrong" to the person on the street. Hearing this, the architect might suggest that the public's taste is deficient. But the people themselves often claim that inelegant edifices were the designer's or builder's fault.

People in Glasgow, Scotland, go so far as to say that the Kelvingrove Art Gallery and Museum there was built backward, with the front in back and the back in front. And legend has it that the architect took his own life in despair when he discovered the error.

Glasgow folklorist Gordon McCulloch recently investigated this tradition—"a story," he said, "whose authenticity I saw no reason to question over a period of three or four decades."

He first heard the legend from his father many years ago, then heard it repeated frequently as an adult in Glasgow. It was told as a true story during the television coverage of the 1983 Glasgow Marathon as cameras zeroed in on the gallery while showing an aerial view of the course.

The *Glasgow Herald* opened an article about urban legends published May 14, 1988, with the gallery story. "Every Glaswegian knows," it facetiously began, "that the Art Gallery and Museum at Kelvingrove was built back to front. The architect took it very badly; on the opening day he leapt to his death from the top of his travestied masterpiece, a martyr to the carelessness of the building trade."

The legend seems to fit the building, judging from a picture of it. The back entrance boasts an imposing porch flanked by twin towers, while the main entrance on the opposite side has a less impressive row of three plain arched entries.

But McCulloch's research into the history of the building concluded that not one but two architects prepared the design, which was followed precisely by the builders, and neither architect committed suicide.

The reason for the building's backward look is simple: the gallery, completed in time for the Glasgow Exhibition of 1901, at first had temporary exhibition pavilions mounted behind it. The rear entrance was planned to give access to these structures.

McCulloch collected similar legends of suicidal designers elsewhere in Scotland. The architect of Marischal College at Aberdeen University, for example, is said to have killed himself because his design was mocked by some as "a monster wedding cake in indigestible grey icing."

Fort George, built in the eighteenth century on the coast between Nairn and Inverness, was supposed to be invisible from the sea. But a local tradition claims that when the architect rowed out from shore and saw that a single chimney of the fort showed clearly, "he drew a pistol and blew his brains out."

Such stories aren't unique to Scotland. The Liverpool, England, Town Hall was allegedly built "the wrong way around." And it is said that the French designer of the Taj Mahal Hotel in Bombay killed himself when he found that his design had been rotated 180 degrees in construction. In fact, the hotel was designed by a British architect, and was built according to plan.

There's also a subgroup of legends about suicidal sculptors whose finished statues did not conform to their original intentions—such as the one about the English designer of the ornamental lions on the Chain Bridge in Budapest, Hungary, who is said to have thrown himself into the Danube when he heard that the lions had been cast without tongues.

I had not known about any stories of backward buildings in the United States until I heard from Karen Whorrall of Shoals, Indiana, which is between Loogootee and Paoli on U.S. Highway 150, down around French Lick. (Trust me, I'm not making up these names. As an alum of Indiana University in Bloomington, I know these Hoosier appellations well.)

The backward building that Whorrall heard about is right on the Indiana University campus, though I missed hearing the story when I studied there.

"The Tulip Tree married students' apartment building was supposed to have been curved the other way," Whorral says, "to be more in harmony with the shape of the hill. The architect was very disappointed when he came to Bloomington and saw what they had done."

Whorral's story follows the same pattern as other backward-building legends, lacking only the suicide. But the Indiana variation of the legend is just as spurious as all the other stories, although it is true that the Tulip Tree apartment building is laid out in a long smooth curve along a hilltop.

Rose McIlveen of the Indiana University News Bureau checked the history of the building in the IU Archives for me. The archivist produced the original site plan and blueprints for Tulip Tree, confirming that the building was constructed absolutely according to its design, and that it faces in the direction called for by the architect.

I've also got a pair of backward-statue stories, which

are cousins to the backward-building ones.

The first concerns the statue of Brigham Young that stands on a pedestal at the intersection of South Temple and State streets in downtown Salt Lake City. This figure of Brother Brigham, the nineteenth-century leader of the Mormons, is positioned "with his back to the Temple, and his hand outstretched to Zion's First National Bank."

There is even a folk rhyme about the statue: "There stands Brigham, like a bird on a perch / His hand to the bank, and his back to the church." In Utah, the terms "the Temple" and "the church" always refer to the Latter-day Saints and their headquarters on Temple Square. The implication is that Young was more interested in the church's economic success than in its spirituality, and that he really should have been facing the Temple.

Incidentally, Zion's First National Bank, across the street from Temple Square, is owned by the Mormon Church.

Apparently the legend linked to Young's statue is not just a local, or Mormon, quip—it has at least one parallel elsewhere. I heard a variant in Dunedin, New Zealand. There a statue of Scottish poet Robert Burns stands in "The Octagon"—the plaza in the center of the city. Burns is represented as seated, pen in hand, eyes gazing skyward. But Dunedin residents have noticed that Burns "has his back to St. Paul's Anglican Cathedral and is facing across the Octagon towards the commercial section of the city."

I expect that there are further legends of this kind around, so don't be backward in sending them to me.

Two Trade-related Legends

Urban legends are often told "on the job"—in two senses. For one, lots of legends are first told in the workplace, during breaks from the daily grind. Second, the legends told are frequently about the job itself.

These on-the-job legends often deal with the esoteric details of a particular profession or trade and are best appreciated by co-workers But the legends sometimes get told to outsiders, though they may need to be explained.

Here are two recent job-related legends sent my way by readers. Interestingly, both involve trickery in collecting payment for services.

James E. Hyman, who works for a management consulting firm, sent me a legend that he said is "used to socialize business people to the game of pulling the wool over the bean-counter's eyes."

In other words, it's about the way consultants allegedly hide expenses in the claims they submit to the firm's sharp-eyed accountants.

As told to him recently, Hyman wrote, this incident supposedly occurred "back in the days when my firm's consultants had to wear hats."

One day in the Windy City, one of the firm's consultants lost his hat while rushing to a meeting with a client. He listed the lost hat as a business expense and requested reimbursement. But the firm's accounting department rejected the claim, explaining that a new hat was a personal expense, not a business one. The consultant protested, but his arguments went unheeded. So the next time he filed an expense report, he documented his spending completely, attaching all the receipts for hotels, meals, transportation, and so forth. At the end of the report he added a challenge: "Find the hat." The consultant was giving Accounting notice that somewhere in this perfect expense account he had buried the cost of his lost hat.

Hyman recognized this as an example of "the business sub-species of urban legends," because he'd heard almost an identical story several years ago while working for a large bank in New York City.

He and a colleague were discussing their mutual annoyance with the the bank's accounting department's nit-picking ways. Then the colleague told him about a co-worker who had lost his hat while in Chicago on a sales call and had resorted to the same trick.

Maybe "Find the Hat" belongs to a particular sub-subspecies of the modern folk story: "The Windy City Business Urban Legend."

I heard the second job-related legend from a builder in Youngstown, Ohio, who called a radio talk show on which I was a guest.

The most common bricklaying work, the builder explained, is putting up chimneys, and the hardest part of the job is collecting full payment.

So one bricklayer, he was told, got the idea of laying in a sheet of glass that would completely block the chimney opening about half way up the flue. The chimney would not draw, naturally, and the fireplace would emit choking clouds of smoke as soon as the homeowners lit a fire. But they would probably not notice the sheet of glass when they looked up the chimney for a blockage.

When the homeowners would call the bricklayer to complain, he would come to inspect the chimney. "Yes, I see the problem, and I can fix it," he'd say. "But first you'll have to give me the final payment for the job."

Having collected the full fee, the bricklayer would climb a ladder to and drop a brick down the chimney, smashing the glass and opening the flue.

"The Veterans' Insurance Dividend"

Never try to fool a storyteller with a tall tale. A case in point involves Cindy Guthrie, a professional storyteller in Akron, Ohio.

The story she sent to me begins—on a neatly printed form—"PLEASE PASS THIS ALONG TO YOUR PARENT, OR FRIEND, IF NOT APPLICABLE TO YOURSELF." Guthrie's husband, a clergyman, received several copies of these sheets from his barber so that he could distribute them to veterans in his congregation.

The notice claimed that Congress had passed a recent bill granting World War II veterans a dividend of 65 cents per $10,000 of their insurance for each month of their active duty. The flier warned that "THE DIVIDEND CANNOT BE RECEIVED UNLESS IT IS REQUESTED." (The use of all capital letters is a hallmark of unreliable notices, by the way.)

Suspiciously, a sample dividend figure quoted was off by one dollar, according to the stated rate of the flier, and the mail-in form addressed to the Veterans Administration regional office in Philadelphia began rather unbureaucraticly, "Dear Sir or Madam."

Her storyteller's instincts alerted, Guthrie decided to query me about the matter. Then, she wrote, a few days later the *Akron Beacon-Journal*—as have many newspapers—debunked the veterans' dividend story, headlining its report "VA calls circular a hoax" and tracing it back thirty years. Guthrie went ahead and sent me both the flier and the newspaper clipping to add to my files.

The Veterans Insurance Dividend appeals to human desire, if not human experience. Who wouldn't like to discover a cash benefit that you were eligible for and unaware of? It's a nice dream, even if you have never known anyone who has enjoyed such a windfall.

During the last forty years, thousands of veterans have heard the rumor and applied for their supposed dividends. The story surfaced around 1948, according to VA spokesmen, and different forms of the printed notice pop up regularly, setting off new waves of applications.

Just a few days after I heard from Cindy Guthrie, retired Marine Corps Colonel W. G. Swigert wrote me from California, describing his own embarrassing encounter with the same story in the summer of 1986. Colonel Swigert's son brought home a copy of the flier that his fiancée's mother received from a colleague.

The colonel wrote, "The amount wasn't enough to make me an instant millionaire, but it wasn't insignificant." The next day he mailed his application, and two weeks later, he wrote, the magazine *Parade* ran a story debunking the claim. Colonel Swigert never heard from the VA.

The Veterans Insurance Dividend is more a hoax or rumor than a true legend, because it lacks much narrative content. The closest that most versions come to a story line is when the fliers allude to specific veterans who have supposedly already collected their dividends.

But this hoax does shares a characteristic with bona-fide urban legends—that is variation. For example, one version says that payments of "55 cents to $1000" are possible, figures echoing the more common wording, "65 cents per $10,000." The name of the VA center in Philadelphia also varies, though the P.O. box and zip code stay fairly consistent.

George B. Griffin, a writer for the *Worcester* (Massachusetts) *Evening Gazette* sent me an amusing account of his experiences with the lucky-vets story. He had looked into the claims made by the fliers and written a documented denial of them in 1981.

The *Evening Gazette* reader-response column "Contact" also debunked the dividend myth in 1986. In both instances, spokespersons from the Boston VA office denounced the story as a complete fabrication. Nevertheless, they said, inquiries were still coming in to VA offices across the country at the rate of about a half million per year.

Then, in the winter of 1987, another version of the flyer started circulating in the *Evening Gazette*'s offices, especially through the efforts of an editor who distributed copies to fellow veterans on the staff and posted one on the city-room bulletin board.

Griffin says he had to dig out the previously published debunkings and pass them around in order to convince co-workers that the story was false. But the editor still wasn't convinced until Griffin pointed out that he—that very editor himself—had edited the 1981 story for publication.

People trust this plausible story not simply out of wishful thinking, but because an authoritative-looking printed form cites specific figures and an actual address. There is usually even an index number for the claimed congressional bill, something like the bogus petition number on another anonymous flier that is supposed to refer to a nonexistent petition asking the government to ban religious broadcasting.

Other unverifiable rumors that circulate in printed or photocopied form include warnings against imaginary health and safety threats, and accounts of fictional drug crimes or child-abduction cases.

The government in general and the military in particular—with their complex offices and regulations—are the subjects of several urban legends. These include stories about a verbose government memo setting the price of cabbage, about a mix-up in orders that puts a mathematics teacher in command of a battleship, and about outrageous benefits that welfare recipients have supposedly received within the letter of the law.

But "The Veterans' Insurance Dividend" remains one of the most durable of these stories. On January 4, 1989, the *Madison* (Wisconsin) *Capitol Times* reported that the old rumor was still going strong: "Veterans Being Hoaxed by Phony Insurance Letter," reads the headline. A Veterans Administration spokesman is quoted saying that the "hoax" costs his agency some $5 million to $20 million a year in letters and phone calls to deal with it. The Wisconsin version of the letter specified that payoffs for one, two, or three years of service amount to $264, $316, and $528 respectively. So much cost to debunk such a piddling story!

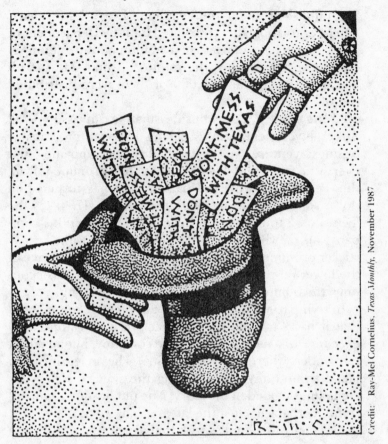

Credit: Ray-Mel Cornelius. *Texas Monthly*, November 1987

"Don't Mess with Texas"

This is just a little legend, but for a big state. Perhaps it reveals the Lone Star State's gift for spawning unbelievable, up-to-the-minute stories.

The story was quoted in the November 1987 issue of *Texas Monthly* magazine. To understand this one, which was published under the headline "Leave Us a Loan," you have to know that the State Highway Department of Texas has issued more than 1 million antilitter bumper stickers printed with the motto "Don't Mess with Texas." As many as 100,000 of them were distributed out-of-state.

In the story, a Texas businessman is canvassing Wall Street investment firms, seeking backers for a major business venture. He visits all the big companies, but every one turns him down. When at one prominent firm, the Texan asks why, the banker who has turned him down shows him where the problem lies. He takes the Texan on a tour of several executive offices in his company, all of which have the "Don't Mess with Texas" sticker prominently displayed. Apparently, in the wake of the lower oil prices that have damaged the Texas economy, the bumper sticker took on a new meaning.

In trying to verify the story, *Texas Monthly* commented that it had "tracked the tale back to a Houston-based executive of a national mortgage company, but he didn't remember where he'd heard it." The magazine also failed to find any proof among the specific New York companies named in the story. The publication's conclusion: "Perhaps it's just the latest urban legend."

I certainly won't mess with that Texas opinion. It sure sounds true to me.

"The Will"

There's a whole lot of storytelling going on all over the world, as my mail continually indicates. Here's a "new" story that was first reported to me in a letter of December 3, 1986, from a Harvard physics professor. He heard it from his sister, who said it happened to a friend's mother's friend. But I came across virtually the same story with just a few variations in details in Cindy Adams's *New York Post* gossip column on January 28, 1987.

A woman is shopping on Madison Avenue in New York City, when she needs to use a restroom. Finding none in any of the stores, she enters a funeral home—the only other public place nearby—and uses the rest room there.

On the way out, she passes a darkened room decorated with flowers. In the center of the room is an open coffin with a dead man's (or woman's) body inside. There are no visitors in sight.

She feels a little guilty about using the facilities on the sly, so she steps into the room and signs the guest book.

Not long afterward she gets a call from the dead man's (or woman's) lawyer (or the state attorney general), who says that the deceased, a person of great wealth, had provided $10,000 in his (or her) will to whoever attended his funeral. The woman had been the only person to show up.

I received three readers' responses to the column containing the above material. One was simply a clipping of my column from a local newspaper with a red-inked correction of the phrase "for whomever attended his funeral." I wrote back explaining that this mistake was the result of an editor's alteration of my original wording, which read as shown above. I do understand the point— that the object of the preposition "for" (or "to") is the whole phrase "whoever attended," though it always surprises me that people read the daily paper so closely as to catch such errors.

The second letter came from a woman in Maryland, who sent me the complete name and address of the woman from New York who had told her "The Will," including exactly to whom the incident had occurred (a friend of her friend), as well as the name of the funeral parlor. The actual amount of money received, she said, was only $1,000. I wrote immediately to the New York woman for further information and got no reply. This proves nothing, by the way.

Letter number 3 about "The Will" came from a woman in Wisconsin who said that she had heard a slightly different version of the story some fifteen years ago while teaching school on a banana plantation in Honduras. (Sometimes I wonder if people make up these things.)

There, she said, an English botanist, whose name she supplied, related an experience of his father, who had been an Anglican priest. He said that after the funeral service for one of his father's parishioners, who was an old and "rather unpleasant man," only one mourner followed the coffin to the gravesite: "He was immediately invited back to the solicitor's office and told that the old man's will stated that whoever came to the grave, other than priest or lawyer, was to receive his entire and considerable estate."

I'm not sure just what to think about this story, except that it encourages me to put in an appearance at any poorly attended funeral, for whoever is dead, of which I may happen to become aware. (If that sentence is wrong, it's my editor's fault.)

"The Homemade Lie Detector"

I read the comic strips faithfully, and every so often I find an urban legend amid the funnies.

Take Hal Foster's "Prince Valiant," for instance, in the Sunday funnies for October 11, 1987. In that strip, Prince Valiant's wife, Queen Aleta of the Misty Isles, drew on folklore to settle a dispute between two men who accused each other of stealing a sheep.

The beautiful and wise queen employed a device I call "The Homemade Lie Detector" and so tricked the thief into revealing his guilt.

She had herself blindfolded—"for justice must be blind"—and then had the sheep in question led into the room. She commanded each man to "grasp the wool on the sheep's back," saying that the sheep itself would identify the thief.

Then the queen removed her blindfold and immediately inspected each man's hands. One man had dirty hands, and the other had perfectly clean ones.

Unbeknownst to them, she had ordered her minions to dust the sheep's back fleece with soot.

The thief, fearing to be unmasked by the queen's odd procedure, had been afraid to touch the sheep, as his soot-free hands proved. Clean hands meant guilt in this case.

The same trick has been attributed to John Napier (1550–1617), the Scottish mathematician who invented logarithms. According to Howard Eves, *An Introduction to the History of Mathematics* (3d ed., 1969), one of many stories "probably unfounded" told about Napier was that he used a "homemade lie detector" to identify a servant who had stolen a rooster from him.

Prince Valiant BY JOHN CULLEN MURPHY

Our Story: ALETA, SUPREME JUDGE OF THE MISTY ISLES, MUST DEAL WITH A GREAT BACKLOG UPON HER RETURN. A SECOND CASE IS BROUGHT BEFORE HER: "YOUR MAJESTY, I AM THE MASTER OF A GREAT NOBLEMAN'S SHEPHERDS, AND MANY OF OUR SHEEP ARE MISSING. THIS MAN HAS TAKEN THEM FOR HIS OWN GAIN."

A SHEPHERD IS BROUGHT IN. "I BEG OF YOU," HE PLEADS, "MY FAMILY NEEDS MEAT AND WOOL, YES, BUT I AM NO THIEF."

THE ACCUSED AND THE ACCUSER DO NOT KNOW THAT ALETA HAD ORDERED THE SHEEP'S WOOL TO BE DUSTED WITH SOOT.

"IT IS JUST AS I THOUGHT," ALETA DECLARES. "YOU, THE ACCUSED THIEF, WITH THE DIRTY HANDS...YOU ARE FREE TO GO. YOU, THE ACCUSER, WHO WAS AFRAID TO TOUCH THE 'SHEEP OF TRUTH'... YOU ARE THE TRUE THIEF. PUT HIM IN IRONS AND BRING ON THE NEXT CASE." NEXT WEEK: The Third Case.

Napier supposedly declared that if each servant placed his hands on the coal-black rooster in a darkened room, the rooster would identify the thief.

Lampblack that had been smeared on the bird's back and rubbed off on the servant's hands was the giveaway this time.

In another version, told in Europe, a cock is placed under a sooty cooking pot, and cock and pot are left in a darkened room. One by one the suspects are brought in.

ALETA COMMANDS, "BRING THE 'SHEEP OF TRUTH' BEFORE US." A FINE SPECIMEN IS LED IN, AND WHEN IT STANDS BEFORE THE COURT THE QUEEN BIDS HERSELF BE BLINDFOLDED. "FOR JUSTICE MUST BE BLIND," SHE SAYS.

"NOW, YOU TWO," ALETA ORDERS, "GRASP THE WOOL ON THE SHEEP'S BACK WITH YOUR HANDS. ARE YOU DONE? GOOD. THEN 'JUSTICE' WILL REMOVE HER BLINDFOLD. AND YOU WILL BOTH RAISE YOUR HANDS."

Supposedly the cock will crow when the thief touches the pot . . . well, you know the rest.

I also have a folder full of international variations of the story. In a Chinese variation sent to me by Professor Nai-Tung Ting of Western Illinois University, a crafty judge places a bell smeared with India ink behind a curtain to detect thieves. Professor Ting believes that the story may go back as far as the Sung dynasty, which lasted from 960 A.D. to 1279 A.D. He also has found a

Tibetan variant in which a learned judge is unable to identify the guilty man, but a clever villager does it via the old smeared-bell trick.

Then there's a Japanese legend about "Ooka the Wise," who sends the suspects to place their hands into the mouth of a stone statue of a god in a roadside shrine. Hands clean of dust from the statue's mouth reveal the thief.

In a Middle Eastern version I found in the May 1963 *Reader's Digest,* a nomad chieftain uses a donkey inside a tent as his lie detector. The animal's tail is dipped in a solution containing mint, and the suspect who fails to pull the tail when he is sent into the tent with the donkey lacks the scent of mint upon his hands when the chieftan sniffs them later.

An Argentine version dispenses with the animals. Two suspects are each given "magic sticks" of equal length to keep overnight. The guilty man's stick is supposed to grow longer while he sleeps.

In the morning, though, the man with the shorter stick is declared guilty. He has cut it himself, believing it would really grow and hoping to remain undetected. This seems similar to Pinocchio's nose growing longer whenever he tells a lie.

The closest I can get to modern legends with this story is some instances of "The Homemade Lie Detector" as American *rural* legends. For example, a version collected in the Ozarks in 1923 but remembered from the 1890s by the storyteller uses a "poppet" (a doll) smeared with walnut juice that stains the hands. A version from Beech Creek, North Carolina, published in 1956 has a preacher use the cock-under-the-pot trick to catch a thief.

The novelist Jack London must have heard this story, too, perhaps in Alaska. In his book *Children of the Frost* (published in 1902), an Indian medicine man, is asked to determine who stole a woman's blanket. So he sets a black raven under a cooking pot—the age-old gimmick that never fails.

Does "The Homemade Lie Detector" have any currency as a truly modern legend? I don't know. Perhaps its appearance in "Prince Valiant" was just the last echo of an old story. I also wonder whether the trick was ever actually used or if it's merely a fictional story told to illustrate somebody's cleverness and somebody else's guilty conscience.

Obviously, I look for a lot more in the comics than your average Sunday-morning reader does. It's tough work, but—no lie—somebody's got to do it.

7

Academic Legends

"The Bird-Foot Exam"

The pressure to do well in school can be intense. But test papers are not the only place where students can display intelligence and wit, as two supposedly true stories show.

One, which I first included in the "Bluebook Legends" section of *The Mexican Pet,* concerns a student in a very large class who disregards the professor's direction that everyone stop writing on the final examination immediately when time is called. He writes another minute or so in his exam bluebook and then steps forward to turn in his work. The professor refuses to accept it.

"What will happen to me?" the student asks.

"You'll fail this class, of course," the professor replies.

Argument is to no avail; the professor stands fast, while the student pleads and argues. Finally the student asks, "Do you know who I am?"

"No," says the professor, "and furthermore, I don't care."

"Good," says the student, and he thrusts his bluebook into the middle of the pile of identical test booklets and stalks out of the classroom. (A student from the University of Maryland told this old legend as a true story on

National Public Radio's "All Things Considered" on May 19, 1987.)

Chalk up one more for the crafty undergraduate in the ongoing battle of wits between faculty and studentry that passes for education in modern folklore. The story of the nameless student is, of course, apocryphal, but it is often told as having happened recently at one particular college campus or another. It's not possible to prove that this is just a legend, but the fact that the same story is told in so many locales suggests that it is not really true. Also, I am told, the "Do you know who I am?" trick has been employed in comedy films and TV series in scenes in which a low-ranking military clerk speaks anonymously to a superior officer on the telephone: "Do you know who I am, General? . . . No? . . . Good! [*click*]."

There is another similar story that also involves a student who is unknown to the professor. This student was taking an ornithology class, for which the final exam counted as half the grade. When the professor handed him his exam, the student was shocked to find that the entire exam was just pictures of birds' legs, with the directions "Identify each species." (In a variation, the professor sets up a row of stuffed birds with bags over their bodies so that only their feet show.) The student was furious and stormed up to the front of the class, ripped his paper into little pieces, handed them to the professor, and said, "This is ridiculous!"

The professor shouted back, "You can't do that!"

And the student returned, "I sure as hell can!"

The professor then screamed, "Then you're going to fail this class. What's your name, anyway?" And he pulled out his grade book to note down the offender's fate.

The student then pulled up his right pants leg to the knee and said, "you tell me, Prof."

"The Unsolvable Math Problem"

The first time I heard this particular college-examination story it was from a reader in Houston, Texas, who heard it from his mother, who got it in a church sermon. The story sounded so unlikely to me that I missed the important clue in that chain of transmission—the church sermon. More about that in a moment.

First, here's the story as I repeated it in my column that was released the week of February 23, 1987:

A young college student was working hard in an upper-level math course, for fear that he would be unable to pass. On the night before the final, he studied so long that he overslept the morning of the test.

When he ran into the classroom several minutes late, he found three equations to solve written on the blackboard. The first two went rather easily, but the third one seemed impossible. He worked frantically on it until—just ten minutes short of the deadline—he found a method that worked, and he finished the problems just as time was called.

The student turned in his test paper and left. That evening he received a phone call from his professor. "Do you realize what you did on the test today?" he shouted at the student.

"Oh no," thought the student. "I must not have gotten the problems right after all.

"You were only supposed to do the first two problems," the professor explained. "That last one was an example of an equation that mathematicians since Einstein have been trying to solve without success. I

discussed it with the class before starting the test. And
you just solved it!"

On June 11, 1987, when the news media carried a story
about an actual event that was similar to this story, I repeated "The Unsolvable Math Problem" in another column (July 27 1987). What happened in the math world
that had made news was that a twenty-three-year-old
University of Chicago physics student named Robert
Garisto had discovered an error in Sir Isaac Newton's
calculations of the laws of motion and gravity in his *Prin-
cipia,* published in 1687. The error had been undetected
for some three hundred years.

When I read about Garisto's feat, I thought at once of
what I considered the apocryphal story concerning the
math student who successfully solved all three problems
that he found written on the chalkboard when he arrived
in class late for an exam. Several readers had noted the
same similarity I did and sent me clippings about
Garisto's achievement. I believed that we were right in
recognizing that this sort of actual incident makes completely fictional urban legends seem plausible.

However, the anecdote about solving the impossible
problem turned out to be based on a well-documented
actual case. Professor C. Hayes of Mobile College, Alabama, called my attention to the experience of famed
Stanford University mathematician George B. Dantzig,
which Dantzig had recounted in an interview published
in the September 1986 issue of the *College Mathematics
Journal.* Dantzig, who the journal described as "a failing
student" in junior-high algebra, has since become re-
nowned as "the father of linear programming." One
early revelation of his genius was his solution of an "unsolvable" problem.

During his first year of graduate study at the University

of California, Berkeley, Dantzig arrived late at a statistics class and saw two problems written on the blackboard. Assuming they were homework, he copied them, and a few days later he turned in his solutions to his instructor. On a Sunday morning six weeks later, the instructor arrived at Dantzig's door, waving a sheaf of papers. It was Dantzig's work written up for publication. It turned out that Dantzig had figured out two statistics problems that had been thought of as impossible to solve. The instructor had merely written them on the board in the classroom as examples in his lecture that day.

This, I conjecture, is the source of the unsolvable-problem legend.

But why has the story changed so much? After all, as subjects go, you couldn't do much better than a world-renowned mathematician showing his stuff while he was a beginning graduate student.

It may be that the new details make the story more dramatic—and, I dare say, more believable. "Homework" in the incident has become an exam in the legend, making the student's lateness more troublesome, his achievement more amazing. The specific subject of statistics has become simply "math" in most versions that are told by nonmathematicians. The number of problems has gone from two to the more folkloric number three, with only one problem being thought of as "unsolvable."

The professor calls the student right away in the reworked story, as befits his excitement. And he invokes the name of Einstein, a universally recognized genius; comparing the student to Einstein sets the student apart as a genuine *Wunderkind.*

One might easily regard this as a typical example of the way the public distorts the truth in the telling. But it turns out that the public has had some help in spreading the story beyond the circle of Dantzig's friends and colleagues, and that's where the church sermon comes into the picture.

While on an airplane flight years after finishing his graduate studies, as Dantzig explains in the published interview, he happened to be seated next to the Reverend Robert H. Schuller, author and host of the "Hour of Power" television worship service at the Crystal Cathedral in Los Angeles. The two men got to talking, and Dantzig told Schuller the "unsolvable problem" experience he had had many years before.

"A few months later," Dantzig says, "I received a letter from him asking permission to include my story in a book." The story, dealing as it does with an "impossible" task that turns out to be possible after all, was an ideal anecdote to illustrate Schuller's philosophy of "possibility thinking."

Dantzig, writing to me, characterized Schuller's retold version as "a bit garbled and exaggerated." Reverend Schuller undoubtedly told the anecdote in one or more of his broadcasts, and he likely included it in one of his numerous books and pamphlets as well. But I assume that the *authorized* Schuller version is the one repeated in his official biography written by Michael and Donna Nason, *Robert Schuller: The Inside Story* (Waco, Texas: Word Books, 1983, pages 168–170).

Reverend Schuller must not have been taking notes on that airplane trip, for he was very imprecise in reproducing the story he heard from the "meek little fellow" seated next to him. As Schuller remembered the story, it concerned a final exam with *ten* problems, out of which George "Danzig"—now a senior student at Stanford—solved eight problems in class and one other, by special permission, later on at home. The tenth problem proved beyond his abilities. The professor arrived at the student's door "the next morning," waving the test paper and exclaiming, "You've made mathematics history!"

282 CURSES! BROILED AGAIN!

The undergraduate, it seems, had come to class late and missed his professor's explanation that the two extra problems were classic unsolvable problems, and "even Einstein was unable to unlock their secrets." (So that's where Einstein came into the story!) Concluding, Schuller mentions the mathematics journal in which Dantzig published his solution (mistaking its title), and he says that "Danzig's" professor gave Dantzig a job as his assistant, and Dantzig has been at Stanford ever since.

Schuller's version—modified in numerous ways—was retold and later reprinted, thus becoming a source drawn on by other ministers for their sermons. People hearing the sermons must have repeated the story, in turn modifying it further. Dantzig himself says that a fellow mathematician at Stanford University heard the story once told during a church service he attended in Indiana, and my readers have sent me other versions they heard in church. Shortly after the Schuller biography was published, the story was repeated in a resource newsletter for pastors called *Parables, etc.* (vol. 3, no. 7, September 1983) with the headline "What You Don't Know Just Might Help You."

The question remains: Should "The Unsolvable Math Problem" still be considered an urban legend? Despite finding its apparent origin, I continue to accept anonymous versions as legendary. Here's why.

An oral story is a story, whatever its origin. As long as a story continues to circulate in different variations, partly by word of mouth, we may regard it as folklore. But probably "The Unsolvable Math Problem" legend should no longer be described as strictly "apocryphal," since we now seem to have found its source, and the deviations from the original incident are easily recognized and are not excessive.

Should you wish to see Dantzig's actual solutions to

the two problems, they are found not only in his Berkeley thesis, but in the following published articles: "On the Non-Existence of Tests of 'Student's' Hypothesis Having Power Functions Independent of Sigma," *Annals of Mathematical Statistics,* 11 (1940), pages 186–192; and in an article co-authored with Abraham Wald (who had independently solved the second problem), "On the Fundamental Lemma of Neyman and Pearson," *Annals of Mathematical Statistics,* 22 (1951), pages 87–93. (Coincidentally, mathematicians had earlier named the first problem "The 'Student' Hypothesis.")

In the first of these highly technical essays, Dantzig barely hinted at the dramatic story behind the solutions, using a conventionally worded footnote: "The author is indebted to Professor J. Neyman for assistance in preparing the present paper." I guess mathematicians stick to the numbers in their publications, saving the good stories for conversations on airplanes.

College Con Artists and How They Operate

The rigors of gaining a college education, especially passing tests and writing term papers, inspire an endless flow of academic urban legends, many concerning cheating or other shady strategies for survival. As a college professor, I thought I had heard all such tales, but readers keep sending me exam and term-paper stories that I haven't encountered.

I especially liked the letter I got from a young man in Palo Alto, California, who neatly printed it on a page of loose-leaf school notebook paper, and began "Hey Jan!" He told a story about his dad's journalism professor in college who had promised that he would never give an unannounced quiz. When a class protested one day that he was giving a test without announcing it, the professor pointed out that he had run an ad in the local newspaper saying "Unit Quiz Today in Mr. McDonald's journalism class at 2 P.M."

"Don't say this isn't true," concluded the letter, "because it is. My dad told me so."

How can I cast doubt on a boy's faith in his dad? I'll accept that the story must be true, although I would very much like to see a copy of the actual newspaper ad. Surely someone in the class must have saved it. At any rate, I think I see a motive in the journalism professor's gimmick. Besides the obvious lesson that students should always be prepared for a test, he may also have been training the future journalists to read the daily newspaper closely, with attention to every detail.

Another wonderful exam story was sent by J.M. of Calgary, Alberta, heard when he was a civil-engineering student at the University of Manitoba in the mid-1970s. It

Credit: Reed McGregor, *Deseret News*.

describes a professor who announces an open-book final examination in which the students "may use anything they could carry into the exam room."

J.M. says that this much of the story is true—several of his professors said exactly that. But he is doubtful about the rest of the story. Supposedly one crafty undergraduate took the professor at his word and carried in a graduate student to write his exam for him.

G.H. of Durham, North Carolina, heard a legend I hadn't been aware of about final-exam papers. He got it from a friend who attended the University of North Carolina. On the day before the final exam, the professor briefly steps out of his office, leaving the door open and the pile of the next day's final examinations on the desk.

A student comes by to ask a question and, when he finds the room empty, steals one exam.

But the professor had counted the exams, and the next morning, he decides to count them once again before going to the classroom. Discovering that one is missing, he cuts exactly one half-inch from the bottom of all the remaining exams. When the exam papers are turned in, the student whose paper is one-half inch longer than the others receives a failing grade.

Several readers have sent me a third classic examination story. This time a philosophy professor supposedly gives his class a one-word final exam: "Why?" The professor gives an A grade only to the student who answered simply, "Why not?"

The way others heard it, the student's answer was "Because." And in a more detailed version, the school is Harvard, and the course is freshman metaphysics. When the students are settled for the final exam, the teacher places a chair on the desk in the front of the room. "Prove that this chair exists," he says. "You have two hours."

As the students begin to chew their pencils and roll their eyes, one student leans back in his seat. He writes, "What chair?" submits his paper and leaves the room, just as the others begin to scribble furiously. As the story goes, this student gets an A, too.

Some years ago C.R. of Azusa, California, sent me a college story that his mother had heard concerning a term paper and a tough prof. This instructor was famous for his low grading scale. After years of giving only D's and F's, one year he finally gave a paper a B minus—his highest grade ever. Word got around campus about the grade. Then the paper itself started to get around. The lucky student sold the term paper to the highest bidder, who then turned it in to the same professor. This time he gave it a B. The paper was re-recycled again the next year, and it received a B plus. Just as the students were beginning to lose respect for the professor, the roving term paper was turned in a fourth time. This time it got an A. The teacher's written comment was, "I've read this paper four times now, and I like it better each time."

The story might be true, I suppose, but I have heard a variation, which suggests that it is merely another college legend. In fact, one of my daughters heard it from a friend who told her it had happened at Harvard: A student in a marine-biology course received an A grade on a term paper in which she included an illustration of a whale. Copied verbatim—whale and all—it was resubmitted by another student the next year and got another A grade. But the third student to turn in the paper accidentally left off the whale picture when copying it over. This time the teacher gave the paper only a B, with the written comment, "I liked it better with the whale."

Here's another campus story on the term paper theme from academe sent to me by a northern California insurance executive who remembered it from his own college days: "At Occidental College in Los Angeles, in the early '60's," he wrote, "we had another legend about termpapers. It had to to with the 'crib' files of old exams and ready-made termpapers kept in each fraternity. It seems that a student dug back about twenty years for a termpaper in the file to put his own name on. But he unwittingly submitted it to the very professor who had written it as an undergraduate and had been a member of that same frat. But the student got an A plus on the paper, with this note on the cover: 'This paper got only a B minus twenty years ago, but I always felt that it was worth more.' "

You know—despite the odds against such a coincidence—I can almost believe that one. Students, I have found, do have amazing recall when it comes to keeping track of how their professors have supposedly deprived them of well-deserved high grades. If only those same students would remember the actual course content as well!

Gordon Hogan of Yakima, Washington, sent me an examination story he heard fifty years ago (1938) when he was a student at the University of Oregon, but it still has the ring of reality about it. Supposedly three graduate assistants in political science are sitting around a large table grading tests for a professor when they disagree about the ranking of a particular answer on one test. They decide to compare the answer given by the student with the answer sheet provided by the professor. But the key has been misplaced on the table, and it takes a while to locate it among the other papers. When they finally do find it, they discover that the key itself had been read and graded as if it were a student paper. It received a grade of C.

Campus legends such as these that help reduce the strains of college life and to spread the reputations of legendary professors. And they keep our hopes alive of someday outfoxing the professors—or the students, depending upon which side you are on.

"The Bible Student's Exam"

I think I must be on to something regarding students of the Bible. They seem to be just as crafty as any other kind of student when it comes to passing their examinations. You might say they know every trick in the good book. Naturally, I have a story in mind to illustrate this—in fact, I have several variations on a theme.

The first example came from Von del Chamberlain in my home base, Salt Lake City. It's about an incident that was supposed to have happened in a history-of-religion class at the University of Utah about 1956, when Chamberlain was a student there. The class became very popular, partly because the final examination question was always the same: "Discuss the journeys of St. Paul." Always, that is, until the year the professor gave a new exam question: "Discuss the Sermon on the Mount." The entire class sat there in dismay, except for one student who began to write vigorously. The others handed in their blank exam books and left the room, then waited outside until the one student came out.

"How could you possibly answer that question?" they asked.

"I couldn't," the student replied. "So I began by writing, 'Who am I to criticize the Master? I would rather discuss the journeys of St. Paul.' After that it was easy!"

Would you believe that in the same bundle of mail virtually the same story arrived from a different reader? In this version, sent by Natalie E. Hampton of Raleigh, North Carolina, the setting is a seminary, the expected question is "Describe the life of the Apostle Paul," and the clever student's exam answer when the topic is switched begins, "Who am I to critique the Sermon on the Mount? I'd rather talk about the Apostle Paul."

Those stories rang a bell for the Reverend Dr. Jeremy H. Knowles, who reads my column in *Foster's Daily Democrat* of Dover, New Hampshire. He wrote: "I heard a similar story while in seminary in Cambridge, Mass., in the 1950's. A certain Old Testament professor always included on his final exam the question 'List the kings of Israel and Judah in parallel columns.' One year, however, he substituted the question 'List the names of the major and minor prophets in parallel columns.' One student alone passed the course when he began his answer by writing, 'Far be it for me to discriminate among such worthy men, but the kings of Israel and Judah in parallel columns are . . .' "

I like the way this version turns to the Old Testament for its plot, and then alters "Who am I?" in the student's answer to "Far be it for me." That seems like folkloristic variation if I ever saw it.

Next I heard from Tom Gentry of Kenosha, Wisconsin, who supplied an earlier published version of the story. He remembered that Bennett Cerf had included it in his humor classic *Try and Stop Me* (New York: Simon & Schuster, 1945). Here, it was more dignified in its language, but easily recognizable. Cerf, citing no source, attributed the incident to "The learned but unworldly head of the department devoted to the study of comparative religions at Harvard." The expected exam question is "Who, in chronological order, were the Kings of Israel?" but the new question is "Who were the major prophets and who were the minor prophets?" The student's tricky response begins, "Far be it from me to distinguish between these revered gentlemen . . ."

Probably Bennett Cerf rewrote an anecdote he had heard told about Harvard. Later tellings of the story— possibly influenced by Cerf's printed version—continued the process of variation.

I have received one more letter, so far, on the subject that shows a shift away from the topic of religion classes. This came from Timothy Hunt, executive director of the Festival at Sandpoint (Idaho) and a former college professor. His version concerns a biology professor who always gives his final examination on the earthworm, until the year when he changes it to "Discuss the elephant." The clever student writes, "The elephant is the largest of all land mammals and is possessed of several distinctive features among which are large floppy ears, enormous paws that are sometimes used as umbrella stands, and a giant worm-like trunk. The earthworm is . . . " The rest of the student's essay, of course, is about the earthworm.

Maybe this is the original elephant joke, but I strongly suspect that it is not the last time I will hear of the students' tricky examination answer.

"The Telltale Report"

Would you believe that missionaries tell urban legends? As a resident of Utah for twenty-odd (sometimes *very* odd!) years, I can assure you that at least the Mormon missionaries do. I learned about this from one of the Mormons' own folklorists.

My good friend William A. Wilson, a former Mormon missionary to Finland, holds a doctorate in folklore and currently chairs the English Department at Brigham Young University in Provo. "Brother Wilson," as a fellow Mormon would call him, has excellent credentials for studying Mormon missionary folklore, which he has been doing avidly for many years.

The swarms of eager young missionaries sent out worldwide by the Church of Jesus Christ of Latter-day Saints (also called "Mormons," or "LDS") are well gromed, earnest in manner, thoroughly disciplined in behavior, and patiently persistent in striving to win converts to the LDS church. You'll surely agree if you have ever been visited by a pair of these dark-suited elders with their white shirts, ties, name tags, polished shoes, good manners, and satchel full of religious tracts.

Restricted as they are to two years of moniltered "clean living," charged with the task of approaching skeptics, and living far from home, it's only natural what their favorite legend is about. The chief subject of LDS missionary folklore is the missionary experience itself.

Professor Wilson tells me that "by far the best known and most popular story" he has collected—and it is a completely fictional one—tells of a pair of enterprising elders who decide to take an unauthorized trip. They grow weary of the daily grind of evangelism, make out their weekly activity reports three months in advance, and leave the reports with their landlady, instructing her to send in one per week to the mission office. Then the missionaries leave on an unearned vacation—to New York, the Riviera, Cairo, Moscow, Easter Island, or the bush country of Australia, depending on where they are said to be stationed. They go surfing or skiing, say, or to Disneyland, or to the World Series or the Olympics. A few weeks before they plan to return, though, the landlady mixes up the reports and sends one out of sequence. And so the two errant elders are caught. Sometimes all the reports are sent in one big batch instead of week by week, as required.

In one variation, the missionaries are discovered when a church authority, watching the World Series (or the Olympics or the Grand Prix) on TV back home, spots them in a shot of the crowd. Another twist on the discovery theme is that they have the bad luck to be the one millionth visitors to Disneyland or the like, and gain unwanted publicity.

Wilson thinks the legend serves as an obvious warning to the missionaries not to break church rules. But, at the same time, the missionaries who tell it often express admiration for their daredevil brothers. Such a dodge is something that most of them wouldn't dare attempt—though the story's popularity suggests that they're tempted to.

Like the notorious trickster figure in Native American and other mythologies, the wayward missionary of the legends provides a tolerated image of deviation from the rules. The stories function as a sort of safety valve for suppressed frustrations.

But as neatly as this legend fits the Mormon missionaries, it has a secular prototype in academic folklore. A similar incident is supposed to have occurred at Harvard University a century ago. It was recounted by historian

Samuel Eliot Morison in his book *Three Centuries of Harvard: 1636–1936* (Cambridge: Harvard University Press, 1936). In 1886, Morison explains, the university adopted a policy of "discretionary supervision." This meant that upperclassmen could either attend or cut classes as they wished. One problem with the policy was revealed when a parent discovered where his son had really been when he was supposed to be attending classes. "The lad had left Cambridge for the more genial climate of Havana, writing a series of post-dated letters, which his chum was supposed to mail to his parents at proper intervals," Morison writes. "Unfortunately, his 'goody' [housekeeper] placed the lot in the mail; the alarmed father came to Cambridge, and no officer of the University had the remotest idea where the son might be. Shortly after, the Overseers offered the Faculty the choice between holding a daily morning roll-call and checking attendance in classes. They chose the latter."

I wonder if the story of "The Telltale Report" was only an urban legend one hundred years ago at Harvard just as it is today among Mormon missionaries.

"The Suicide Rule"

Dear Professor—

I am a sophomore at Southern Methodist University in Dallas, majoring in mechanical engineering. A story that I heard intrigues me, and might be the newest campus urban legend. Everyone in my dormitory repeated this story, and almost everyone took it as fact.

The claim is that if your roommate commits suicide during the school year, you will receive an automatic 4.0 for the semester from the college administration. This is supposed to make up for the emotional shock and trauma that you have gone through.

But a friend at the University of Dallas told me the same rumor was going around there. He thought that it might have originated in New York where, he said, there actually is such a rule.

Many of my friends here said, "If you don't believe me, look it up! It's right there in our student handbook."

I read the entire book backwards and forwards and could not find it. Then my friends said it was a state law. Can you find out something about this story?

> *Ariel Santesteban*
> *Bedford, TX*

Dear Ariel—

While you were reading through your handbook, did you happen to find the rule that specifies how long students are required to wait for a late professor before leaving the classroom? Students keep telling me that this too can be found in their college handbook.

But I think that the rule about roommates of suicide

victims, like the rule about late professors, is just a campus legend. (A 4.0 average, for you non-campus readers, is a perfect straight-A record.)

I first heard about "The Suicide Rule" in a variation several years ago when my daughter Dana was a student at the State University of New York at Potsdam. She came down with bad case of mononucleosis and was hospitalized.

She phoned from the hospital to say she was feeling better, adding that one of her dorm roommates had been to see her. The roommate had joked that if, by chance, Dana suffered a relapse and died before the end of the semester, at least all of her roommates could count on getting A's in all their current courses. There was, she said, a college rule guaranteeing this.

I'd never heard about any such rule anywhere, but when I asked my students at the University of Utah about it, they assured me it was policy at Utah too, but only for suicides.

It turned out that I wasn't the only professor who grew curious about "The Suicide Rule." William S. Fox, a sociologist at Skidmore College in Saratoga Springs, New York, has collected variations of the legend from students.

He says murders and accidental deaths also qualify the victim's roommate for the bonus. So does "any slow drawn-out death, for example, cancer."

The death might have to occur during the last six weeks of the semester, though. And in the case of dormitory suites with several roommates, it's often said that the grade awarded is only a 3.5, presumably to avoid what college administrators call "grade inflation."

The bonus is withheld if one roommate murders another—a wise precaution, it would seem.

Professor Fox's search through college handbooks for these sorts of rules led nowhere, and he has concluded that the legend is false. After all, he points out, "although academic and administrative policies never cease to amaze, it would be quite remarkable indeed if any school granted an automatic 4.0 for any reason."

Students who have known instances of tragic deaths on campus also have written to me to attest that no such rules exist.

One unfortunate student heard the legend, and then in the next year found it put to the test by two tragic deaths—an instance of a student falling out of a window at Harvard, and a stabbing at the University of Chicago.

"I can positively assert that neither Harvard nor U of C has this kind of policy," the student, now studying anthropology at Brandeis, wrote to me.

In both instances, the roommates were offered counseling, and allowed to take "incompletes." But neither was given perfect grades as a reward for enduring such an ordeal.

The suicide-rule legend seems to fit in with other common campus claims about the arbitrary nature of campus grading. There's the rumor about professors throwing exams down the stairs and grading each paper according to which step it lands on. And the one about professors who distribute exams among their family members, giving the youngest child the job of marking all the A papers.

The recent high incidence of suicides among adolescents—including several taking place on college campuses—makes "The Suicide Rule" story especially disturbing to students. A letter published on October 13, 1988, in SMU's newspaper, the Daily Campus, *reflects this, with the writer, a junior majoring in business, urging students to think twice before they spread "such a ridiculous rumor." He was aware of the story circulating on several other campuses "for at least the last two years."*

In February 1989, after a Marquette University sophomore died in a rooming-house fire, the Milwaukee Journal mentioned that the "myth" that an automatic 4.0 grade-point average would be awarded to roommates was "spreading through the downtown campus." The article, however, then quoted Marquette officials, who emphatically denied that any such rule existed.

If there's a college campus in the country that does not have "The Suicide Rule" legend, I've yet to discover it. And if there's one that does have such a rule on the books, I haven't found it yet either.

Let's Give Toll Takers
and Medical Students a Hand

What are the "standard tool-booth gags"?

I came across that phrase in a newspaper article about the "strange tales" told by toll takers who work on the Maurice J. Tobin Memorial Bridge in Boston. The article described toll takers' encounters with topless women drivers, cars stuck in reverse, and tolls paid in clothespins or pennies—but no real "gags" in the sense of pranks or jokes played on toll takers by the public. Most of these gags, I have found, are attributed to medical students.

Maybe the Boston toll takers preferred not to talk about such pranks, fearing that more students would try them again. Or maybe the reason was that, as I suspect, most toll-booth tricks exist only as stories, not as actual pranks.

In the best known of them, medical students remove an arm from a cadaver in the anatomy lab, attach a quarter to the hand, and set out on the highway. At the first toll booth, they extend the arm out the window to the toll taker, who finds himself holding the limb as well as the coin as the car drives off.

I described this gag in an article in *Whole Earth Review,* Fall 1985, asking readers to respond with their own versions.

Some people's recollections were about as skeletal as my teaser. A California reader, for example, heard only that it happened on a bridge in the Bay Area and that the students responsible were expelled from school.

Other versions, however, contained specifics. A student from the Midwest heard that the prank was perpetrated by students from Washington University in St. Louis while crossing the Eads Bridge (then a toll bridge) to Illinois. The students eventually were prosecuted for transporting body parts across state lines.

A writer from Massachusetts set the event on the Tobin Bridge in Boston (this is where I came in!). He had heard that in the late 1960s, medical students from one of the universities in the area painstakingly set up the prank—slipping the stolen limb into a sleeve and sewing a dollar bill between the index finger and thumb—and then staged it successfully. Traced by fingerprints from the disembodied hand, the cadaver was located in the school's lab. The anatomy professor and the police matched the hand to the body, then confronted the students with the incriminating evidence. The pranksters supposedly weren't expelled—but the professor flunked them in anatomy, since they had put a right hand into a left coat sleeve.

A Yale man wrote me saying that he heard the story in his freshman year in the early 1960s, attributed to the Milford toll booth on the Connecticut Thruway. I also heard from a chiropracter in Albuquerque, New Mexico, who remembers hearing the toll-booth story from his junior-high-school science teacher in 1968, then hearing a variation years later when he attended chiropractic school.

But the story is older yet. One writer remembered hearing about it when attending a Naval Supply Corps school in California in 1952.

The most interesting response came from Dr. James S. Miller, a pediatrician in Hemet, California. He recalls an incident from 1939, when his uncle, Dr. Willard Fleming, was dean of the School of Dentistry at the University of California, San Francisco.

Dr. Miller says his family often talked of the time when "Uncle Bill," as acting chancellor of the Medical Center one weekend, was aroused at 3:00 A.M. by a telephone call from the California Highway Patrol, who had detained three students for leaving a hand from a cadaver with a toll taker on the San Francisco Bay Bridge.

Possibly, Dr. Miller suggests, this incident was the source of later medical-student prank stories involving toll booths. He also reports, however, that medical history is scattered through with allusions to "disrespect for the dead" displayed by students or unscrupulous practitioners sometimes removing body parts from cadavers.

Oddly, the wildest toll-booth prank of them all focuses on a toll taker's arm, not a cadaver's, and I heard it not in the United States, but in Auckland, New Zealand.

When the Auckland Harbor Bridge was a toll bridge, the attendant had to put his hand through a hole in the booth to collect tolls. Once, allegedly, two students came by in a car, and one of them put the coin into the attendant's outstretched hand while the second snapped a pair of handcuffs over the attendant's wrist. There was a rope tied to the handcuffs, and it fed out of the car window as they sped away across the bridge. The attendant tried frantically to untie the rope or to break down the wall of the booth, thinking he would be jerked up to the wall and perhaps even lose his arm when the rope pulled taut. But the rope wasn't attached to anything in the car, and the students just tossed the end out the window as they roared away into the distance.

I'm not sure why toll takers become the victims of such gags and stories, nor whether medical students have ever done anything so outrageous. But at least these accounts of toll-booth pranks are a road (or a bridge?) to fame in a boring occupation.

Student Stunts—Kiwi Style

In New Zealand, I learned from my academic counter-parts there, the graduation ceremony is called "capping" and is held in May. I also learned that the New Zealand school year runs from March through November. So naturally I asked, "What has May got to do with gradua-tion?"

Years ago, the Kiwi academics explained, the students' final examinations were sent to England by ship for grad-ing, and the results never arrived back in New Zealand until the following May. So the students wisely post-poned their celebrations.

Nowadays, the local teachers grade their own exams, but the graduation rituals have remained unchanged. The graduates celebrate their liberation by putting on satiric stage shows, publishing humorous magazines, going on "pub crawls," and perpetrating elaborate prac-tical jokes, which have come to be known as "capping stunts."

In one classic capping stunt, students told a crew of road repairmen that if some police tried to stop their work, they should ignore them, since the police were merely students in disguise. Then the students called the police and reported that a group of students posing as road repairmen were tearing up a stretch of highway.

But Moira Smith, a folklorist who was writing her doc-toral dissertation on capping traditions, told me that the prank, although well known, evidently never happened. Everybody seems to have heard about the police, the stu-dents, and the highway workers, but nobody witnessed the prank firsthand.

Sounds like an urban legend to me!

Many of the capping stunts involve spreading a rumor that will cause the public to act in a foolish manner. One year at Victoria University in Wellington, for example, graduates circulated a letter saying that a water supply dam above the city would burst unless every tap and hydrant in the city was opened in order to relieve the pressure. A great many Wellington residents turned the water on.

At another university, students posted notices saying that a shipment of bananas that had recently arrived in New Zealand was contaminated and that people should bring their urine samples to the nearest post office, where a checking station would be set up to test for the presence of disease.

Perhaps the most legendary capping ritual is the students' heavy drinking during capping week. At one time, the pub crawls were so notorious that they became known as "the chunder mile." "Chunder" in Kiwi slang means to vomit—and that's quite enough said about the topic, I think.

The capping shows and parades often feature suggestive material and off-key bagpipe concerts by men wearing women's clothing. The same kind of humor makes up the bulk of capping magazines and has brought on complaints and some restrictions on their distribution.

One former capping tradition that is strictly tabu nowadays is the practice of white students dressing up as Maori warriers and performing mock *hakas,* or ceremonial dances. The Maoris themselves objected to this desecration of their own traditions, and the *pakeha* (white) students have now desisted.

The best capping stunt I heard about involved students from Auckland University. The students drove a hearse down a crowded city street, then pulled over to the roadside, as though the vehicle had gotten a flat tire. After getting out the tools to change the tire, the students—all of them dressed as morticians—removed the coffin from the hearse to get at the jack stored underneath, and changed the tire. Then they drove off, leaving the coffin behind on the pavement, with a chorus of confused Aucklanders shouting after them, "Hold on there—you've forgotten something!"

My informant for this story, however, wasn't quite sure when, or even *if,* the stunt had occurred or what (if anything) was inside the coffin. Could be that it's just another capping-stunt legend.

"Roaming Gnomes"

This is a story about wandering garden ornaments, victims of a plot that may have been perpetrated by students in a prankish mood. Specifically, it's a story about garden gnomes, those plaster figures wearing red stocking caps that some people use as decorations in their yards, as other people do plastic flamingos and concrete birdbaths.

These gnomes have begun to roam, down in Australia, at least. Witness this story from the 1988 issue of *Australian Folklore,* collected by Aussie folklorist Bill Scott in October 1986.

"Some people over on the North Shore [of Sydney] had a gnome in their front garden, one of those holding a fishing rod in the lily pond. One morning they noticed that the gnome was missing. Someone had stolen it! About a week later, they got a postcard from the Gold Coast up in Queensland. The gnome said he was on holiday up there and having a wonderful time—there were more fish there than in the lily pond at North Shore. About a fortnight later the people found the gnome back in their garden. Whoever it was that had pinched him had covered him all over with tan boot polish, to show that he'd been on holiday and had a suntan."

On holiday, indeed.

David S. Hults, co-editor of *Australian Folklore,* has compared roaming-gnome stories from the media and oral tradition, and has found a consistent pattern. First, the gnomes vanish for a few weeks or months. Then the owners receive postcards signed "the Gnome." Eventually, the garden ornament reappears in their yard, sometimes altered in some way by its adventure.

The Australian people whose gnomes have gone walk-about have usually suspected either their co-workers or mischievous students of masterminding the thefts. But in a rash of roaming-gnome stories reported in Perth last year, postcards came in such numbers and from such long distances that reporters wondered whether American sailors may have been responsible for the pranks.

Gnome owners told of their distress on Australian news programs, sometimes referring to their lost gnomes by name ("Gulliver" being a well-publicized example). The press played an active role in elaborating the theft stories, much in the way newspapers and talk shows spread urban legends.

Evidently, the gnomes are getting restless in England, too. In an elaborate gnome prank described in the British men's magazine *Mayfair* in 1986, the perpetrators were said to be oil-rig workers flying out of London's Heathrow airport for duty stints in the Far East. The workers' travels enabled them to send gnome postcards from dozens of exotic foreign places. "Sorry I didn't say anything before, but I have decided I need a holiday," one such gnome wrote home to its owners. "I'll keep in touch." And keep in touch he did—cards streaming in from around the world. The adults in the family didn't know what to make of it, the *Mayfair* article said, but the children "thought it was marvellous and took to running out to see if the postman had another card from the gnome." This family's gnome showed up one morning at its usual place on the front lawn—wearing sunglasses, holding a little suitcase, and sporting a suntan.

(A nabbed gnome in an English town is used as a red-herring clue in Sheila Radley's murder mystery *Fate Worse Than Death,* published by Scribner's in 1986. As the cover blurb of the paperback edition [Bantam, 1987] says, "A treasured garden statue is held for ransom and returned smashed beyond repair." This time it's a plaster gnome named "Willum" who is sitting on a stone toadstool fishing in a lily pond. In a note, the thieves demand a pound of jelly babies for Willum's safe return. But neither his disappearance nor the discovery of his broken bits turn out to have anything to do with the larger crime.)

In Australia, meanwhile, gnomes began to disappear *en masse* from neighborhoods and even whole communities. Months later, some of them were found in a clearing in the bush, gathered around the biggest gnome, apparently holding a meeting.

A recent letter to the editor of the *Kalgoorlie Miner* in Western Australia introduced a new complication: a band of gnome-nappers calling themselves the Gnome Liberation Organization, or GLO. The group threated to hold stolen gnomes for a ransom of $5 each. There was a disclaimer: "The GLO would like to reassure the owners of lions rampant, Grecian statues, birdbaths and the like that these are not at risk. We are specialists dealing in one commodity—gnomes."

Do American garden gnomes roam? If they do, I told my column readers, I'd like to hear about it. Perhaps, I suggested, a postcard would be the appropriate way to send me their roaming-gnome stories.

I heard from several readers who were irate at the nabbers of their own garden gnomes and other lawn decorations. These people seemed happy that I had exposed the whole sordid business.

One reader, however, wrote that she was irate at me for publicizing such a trivial topic and perhaps suggesting copycat gnome-nabbing crimes to an impressionable public.

I got no postcards from roaming gnomes; but, then, I

own no gnomes. My lawn ornaments are living pyracantha topiary animals, guaranteed to scratch anyone who touches them.

Many readers reminded me of the typical, though deplorable, American-student practice of stealing signs and other public material to use in decorating college dormitory rooms, fraternity houses, and apartments. One may say that this practice itself is traditional, the idea passed from person to person with variations in the way that all folklore is.

I also learned about a couple of instances of thievery in which messages were sent to the owners, confirming that the pattern of international gnome-nabbing is found in the United States. While this deduction is not a very significant advance in knowledge, it does show how even trivial elements of tradition may reveal culture contacts. In other words, though we don't know *how* or *when* the gnome-nabbing syndrome passed among Australian, British, and American students, we do know that these cases, both from college towns, are probably not unrelated instances of traditional vandalism with a comic touch.

On to the two reported instances of American student gnome-nabbing—except it was really flamingo-nabbing and fiberglass-entrepreneur-nabbing.

Case No. 1, sent to me by Melanie Pratt of the Ohio Historical Society in Columbus: "This friend lives out on the west side, and had pink, plastic flamingos all over her front lawn. Last October her flamingos began to disappear. Not all at once, but one by one. She called the police, but they couldn't do anything. By the end of October, she had none left. Along about mid-December, she began to get postcards and Christmas cards from her flamingos from all over the southern part of the country. They said they didn't like the cold and flew south for the winter. In early April, one flamingo showed up on her front lawn, and by the end of the month they had all returned."

Case No. 2, sent to me by Heidi Beck of the Stanford University News Service: "This really happened! And though a lifesize fiberglass Col. Sanders isn't exactly your garden variety gnome, I think you'll agree that the perpetrators were inspired (if that's the word) by the same spirit, or perhaps by a similar story."

I certainly agreed when I read the articles from regional newspapers that Ms. Beck enclosed. A five-foot eight-inch fiberglass statue of Colonel Harlan Sanders, founder of Kentucky Fried Chicken, was stolen on Ash Wednesday 1987 from a Palo Alto fried-chicken outlet. Six weeks later on Easter morning, the statue appeared in Stanford University's Rodin sculpture garden. As the *San Jose Mercury News* reported the story on April 21, referring to titles of Rodin statues, "There, in the dewy quiet of Easter morn . . . stood the Gates of Hell, Adam and Eve, a Burgher of Calais—and the Colonel of Chicken." Attached to the wandering statue was a note: "I've seen it all—it's not a pretty picture. Take me home!" And in a postscript to the owners of the Kentucky Fried outlet, "I never meant to worry you, Donna and Paul—I just needed some space. Happy Easter!"

The thefts, the holiday season, the notes, and the returns are details that confirm these two cases as clear instances of the gnome-nabbing practice adapted to different victims.

The irate reader who wrote me also added a postscript to her letter: "P.S. What do you teach your students?"

Why, of course, I tell them not to nab gnomes, flamingos, or innocent statues of any kind. But, if they must indulge themselves in such student rites, then at least they should do the deed in style—the *right* style—which includes sending good-natured notes to the owners and bringing their victims home again.

When Patrick Giblin of Carthage, New York, read my follow-up column on "Roaming Gnomes" published in the *Syracuse Post-Standard,* he sent me the following item from James Ehmann's "Ehmann's People" column of November 29, 1988:

ERRANT BEAR

Two years ago, somebody (probably a Stanford University prankster) kidnapped a 7-foot high stuffed grizzly from the University of California at Berkeley.

Two weeks ago, Berkeley officials got a letter from the bear. It said he had visited Disneyland and Reno, Nev., and had attended the Olympics in Seoul. It also said he might be coming home soon.

One morning last week, the bear was found chained to a fountain in San Francisco's Justin Herman Plaza.

It's now back in its glass case, and the case is outfitted with a new burglar alarm.

"The Trained Professor"

While I'm on the topic of campus folklore, here's a beauty of a story sent to me first by Brenna E. Lorenz of Geneseo, New York. Her father, a professor of physics at the University of the South, originally implied when telling her the story that it was true. (Years later, when she checked again, he said that it had merely been reported as true by the person who told it to him.)

While a student at Syracuse University from 1961 to 1966, Lorenz's father says, a fellow graduate student took a psychology course that included a unit on behaviorism. The friend claimed that his class had decided to put their new knowledge to work by training the professor to lecture while standing on an overturned wastebasket. The students would begin to fidget, yawn, shuffle papers, and the like whenever the prof paced away from a wastebasket in the corner of the classroom. Whenever he moved near the basket during his lectures, they would nod, take copious notes and generally look interested. Continuing this reinforcement of the desired behavior, they gradually got the professor to lecture while standing next to the basket. Then they turned the basket over before class began and rewarded the prof with attentiveness whenever he put one foot, and then both feet, on top of it. Eventually, Lorenz's friend said, the class succeeded in modifying the professor's behavior to the point where each day he would enter the classroom, pick up the basket, carry it to the same spot at the front of the room, turn it over, climb on top of it—and then begin his lecture.

What a wonderful story! But is it true? Probably not, I suspected from the start—but, then, it's my job to distrust such charming anecdotes.

Brenna Lorenz herself trusted the story for years until a friend, a graduate student in mathematics at the State University of New York, Buffalo, told her a variation—that he had heard of a math professor trained by his students to write on only one section of the blackboard.

Readers of my column supplied further variations on "The Trained Professor." Timothy Hunt, executive director of the Festival at Sandpoint (Idaho), had heard the story from Lester J. Hunt (no relation), associate professor of psychology at Northern Arizona University in Flagstaff. A student in Professor Hunt's summer 1968 "Analysis of Behavior" course at NAU set up a conditioning experiment using the rest of the class to try to induce their professor always to lecture from the same side of the classroom. As Professor Hunt recalled the incident to me in a letter written some twenty years later, "The result was that I came to spend 70–90% of the class period on the 'correct' side of the room." However, he also pointed out several flaws in the experiment, and he admitted, "I was aware that I was being trained as early as the first day, but I did not know what behavior I was performing to get the class attention." It sounds to me as if Hunt's class was simply trying out what a reader from San Diego described in a letter as "an ancient legend about the principle of positive reinforcement that has been told for at least twenty years." Right on!

The California letter, by the way, identified the desired behavior as "lecturing with one hand stuck into his coat à la Napoleon Bonaparte, and speaking in terse clipped sentences."

Professor Edward L. Kimball of the Brigham Young University Law School believes that he read about the class conditioning the teacher in an article in *Psychology Today* some ten or fifteen years ago. As Kimball remembers the incident—and as he has repeated it to his own classes—the professor, though naturally right-handed, was trained to shift over and gesture with his left hand. I have not found anything like that in *Psych Today,* and Professor Hunt writes, "I know of no popular literature on the topic of controlling a teacher's behavior through the use of attention."

I think I'll just stick with "ancient legend" as the nature of this beast. It's another true story that's just too good to be true.

"The Small-World Legend"

I have never deliberately made up an urban legend and succeeded in spreading it around, but sometimes I hear about people who do so. They try this as some kind of social experiment—or just out of curiosity, to see what will happen.

One person told me that "The Poodle in the Microwave" legend was invented by a sociologist at an East Coast university who wanted to see how long it would take for the new story to reach California.

The sociologist started telling the cooked-pet legend to everyone he knew, and supposedly it reached the West Coast in three days.

Other people who describe such experiments to me mention a different legend or a joke. But they are usually in agreement that three days after it is planted in the East, the story or joke is going around in the West.

The three-day figure sounds unlikely to me, though, for a couple of reasons. For one, telephones and the mass media make it possible for stories to race from coast to coast in a matter of hours. What's more—and this is what triggered my suspicions—three is the most common folkloric number of all: three little pigs, three blind mice, three on a match—you get the idea.

Several of the people mentioning this experiment have reported hearing about it in a college sociology class. So I mentioned the legend to a sociologist friend of mine, who said it sounded like a generalized description of experiments done by Stanley Milgram at The City University of New York in the mid-1960s.

Milgram summarized his findings in *Psychology Today*,

in an article called "The Small World Problem." Milgram asked here, "Starting with any two people in the world, what is the probability that they will know each other?" He wanted to discover how many intermediate links are needed before *x* and *y* (any two individuals) are connected. In effect, he was testing the idea that "it's a small world," but with the question of number of personal contacts, not number of days.

The experiment was fairly simple. Volunteers in the Midwest were given a "message"—a folder containing instructions for participants in the experiment. They were asked to send the message to a person they knew personally who lived in the direction of the target individual, a resident of Massachusetts.

Eventually, Milgram conjectured, the message would reach someone who knew the target individual personally.

One chain linking a volunteer to the target was only two links long: in other words, the original volunteer knew someone who knew the target individual! On the average though, five people had a hand in sending a folder from the Midwest to its Massachusetts destination.

Milgram and Jeffrey Travers of Harvard University described a larger version of the "Small World" experiment in the journal *Sociometry* in 1969. This time, 296 individuals, some in Nebraska and others in Boston, had mailed messages in the direction of a Boston stockbroker. With the aid of numerous charts, graphs, and formulas, the two experimenters showed that for the 64 "starters" who completed the chain, "the mean number of intermediaries between starters and targets was 5.2."

I'll skip the subtleties of the sociologists' further experiments with the "Small World" problem using dif-

ferent methodologies and social groups. My eyes got
strained looking at all those graphic representations of
networks, chains, pathways, and variables, and the results nearly always averaged about five links anyway.

My own question is this: Is there any link between the
"Small World" experiments and the "Small World"
legend I've heard about? My sociologist friend said that
when he presented Milgram's findings in classes, he lec-
tured from memory, without consulting the published
scholarly work again. He admitted that he probably had
distorted the events somewhat. This is doubtless true
for other teachers as well. Could they have so modified
the experiment until the "messages" were said to be
urban legends? Could the flow of information have
switched from eastward to westward; and then could
"three days," not "five individuals," have become the
standard unit of measurement? And could students
have passed the story along until the legend reached
outsiders like me? If so, then garbled retellings of "The
Small-World Problem," an academic inquiry, have crys-
tallized into "The Small-World Legend," a piece of
modern academic folklore.

One further piece of evidence that supports this hypothesis is another story that seems apocryphal. A student once told me that his sociology professor in a Midwestern university had described "The Small-World
Problem" in a class, adding an anecdote that "proved"
it. He had heard about the experiments spreading oral
stories being discussed at an academic gathering, when a
member of the audience—another professor—stood up
and said, "Wait a minute. Do you mean to say that there
are going to be only three people between me and, say,
Haile Selassie?"

A murmur went around the room as the speaker
groped for a reply, until another professor spoke up.

"Well, I happen to know Haile Selassie, and I know professor so-and-so here. So there's your connection in only two links."

It's a small world!

INDEX